W9-DAD-947

KOMÁROV

A Czech Farming Village

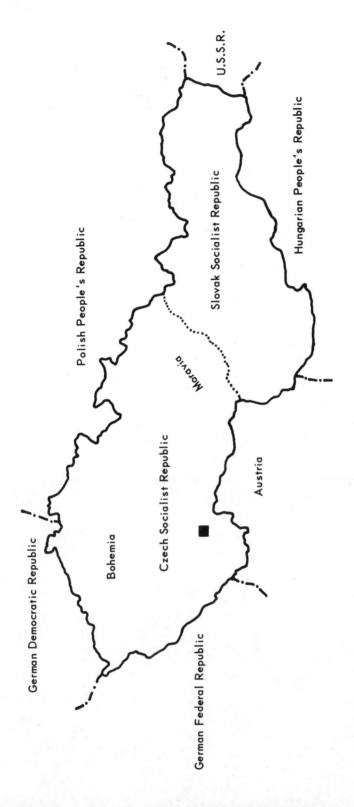

Czechoslovak Socialist Republic and its neighbors; the region of the Blata is indicated by a small black square.

KOMÁROV
A Czech Farming Village

By

ZDENEK SALZMANN

University of Massachusetts at Amherst

and

VLADIMÍR SCHEUFLER

WAVELAND

PRESS, INC.

Prospect Heights, Illinois

For information about this book, write or call:
Waveland Press, Inc.
P.O. Box 400
Prospect Heights, Illinois 60070
(708) 634-0081

Foreword

ABOUT THE AUTHORS

A native of Czechoslovakia, Zdenek Salzmann came to the United States in 1947. Having interrupted his studies at Caroline University in Prague, he went on to receive his Ph.D. from Indiana University. His original interest was in American Indian linguistics and folklore, a field in which he has published numerous articles.

Intensely concerned with the contribution anthropology could make to secondary education, he authored the first general anthropology text for high school students, published in 1969 by Harcourt Brace Jovanovich, with a second edition appearing in 1973.

Since 1968 Salzmann has taught at the University of Massachusetts at Amherst, where he is professor of anthropology and adjunct professor of Slavic languages and literatures. His most recent professional work includes both the study of Central Europe and assistance to the Arapaho Indians of the Wind River Reservation in Wyoming in their efforts to preserve the Arapaho language.

In 1983 Salzmann was visiting professor of anthropology at Yale University. He has published many articles and several books, among them *Humanity and Culture; Introduction to Anthropology* (1978; with Oriol Pi-Sunyer), *Three Contributions to the Study of Socialist Czechoslovakia* (1983), and *Dictionary of Contemporary Arapaho Usage* (1983).

Vladimír Scheufler received his Ph.D. from Caroline University in Prague, specializing in ethnomusicology, ethnography, and archaeology. His subsequent professional interests extended to research concerning Bohemian folk pottery, early folk drama, folk dance, primitive water transport, and urban anthropology.

In addition to fieldwork in various parts of his native country, Scheufler studied the Czech-speaking minorities in Romania and Yugoslavia. As a foremost expert on pottery, he has frequently acted as consultant to various museums. He is author of numerous articles and several books, the most recent concerning Bohemian folk pottery.

Before his retirement, Scheufler was a senior member of the research staff at the Institute for Ethnography and Folklore of the Czechoslovak Academy of Sciences in Prague, and for a time acted as deputy director of the Institute. Until 1972 he was chief editor of *Český lid*, the journal published by the Institute. Scheufler is a member of several Czechoslovak as well as foreign scientific societies and serves as scientific consultant to the Institute for Ethnography and Folklore.

ABOUT THE BOOK

East Central Europe is not well known ethnographically even to most professional anthropologists and is virtually unknown to most students. Ethnographic literature in English for the whole of this area is quite scarce and it is virtually nonexistent for Czechoslovakia. This case study will therefore be of interest to colleagues as a contribution to the literature, as well as of use to students as an instructional unit in general anthropology courses and in the proliferating courses in European ethnography.

Quite appropriately for a case study in a country whose written tradition stretches a thousand years into the past, the authors have explored the existence of Komárov through its long and interesting history. The study starts with an historical overview of the changing situation of the Czech peasant and continues with constant attention throughout to the time dimension. Much of what is described, of course, is part of a traditional pattern that has been greatly changed since World War II and the subsequent collectivization of lands and agricultural production. The authors give us a sense of these changes by constantly moving back and forth among the present, the immediate past, and the more distant past, as well as providing one chapter on the socialist cooperative.

The collectivization of Komárov's agricultural production will be of particular interest to Americans. Traditional methods of agriculture are on the wane everywhere in the world, and the process is far advanced in the industrialized nations. Family-based agriculture, requiring many hands to work relatively small pieces of land, functioned adequately in Europe, as in America, until the rural exodus began. Labor became scarce, and machinery was substituted for human and animal power. With these changes some form of collectivized or corporate management of agricultural production has become imperative. The transformation from the family farm to the industrialized and rationalized agricultural enterprise in capitalist countries has been no less traumatic for the people involved than the collectivization of formerly peasant farmers in socialist countries. Both have attempted to further agricultural production through rationalization, mechanization, and professionalization, and incentives are being offered in an attempt to slow down or stabilize the rural exodus. It is interesting that this attempt in the context of Czechoslovakian collectivization is apparently not much more successful than parallel incentives such as subsidies or increased wages in capitalist countries. The rural exodus continues. Young people are not interested in farm labor or usually even in agricultural management, and they are not willing to give up the life-style of the city or suburb. The problems connected with agricultural production as faced by both the socialist and capitalist countries appear to be fundamentally the same. The solutions, of course, differ, but even here there are many parallels.

The authors leave no doubt that we are witnessing the Czech peasant's ultimate passing from the scene. The disappearance of peasants seems inevitable in virtually all of Europe in the very near future, if indeed it has not occurred already in most of it. The authors make the observation that "The centuries-old view of land and weather, of crops and livestock, all as part of an indissoluble whole, is rapidly giving way to the industrial worker's or bureaucrat's fragmentary and compartmentalized conception of production or employment." The processes leading to this fundamental change in one Czech community are the basic materials of this case study.

George and Louise Spindler
Portola Valley, Ca.

Preface

The village that serves as the subject of this book is a small farming community in southern Bohemia, and Komárov is its real name. With the publication of this study, information on the changing life-style and work conditions of a Czech village, from its earliest beginnings up through the present, will become available for the first time to readers of English.

Preparation of the book gave both authors a sense of great satisfaction. For the senior author (Scheufler), it was an expression of affection for the region and the village of his maternal roots. For me, it was a welcome opportunity to revisit both in thought and in actuality the country of my birth and student years. There were a number of reasons why we did not think it practical or particularly desirable to present Komárov and its people in the highly personal manner of some of the other case studies in this series. Instead, we endeavored to explore the life of the community through its long and interesting history. For this we offer no apology: it would be inexcusable to do otherwise when focusing on a country whose written tradition reaches back a full one thousand years.

It would be a long list were we to attempt to acknowledge the many colleagues of Scheufler's in Prague and of mine in this country who were helpful to us in the course of our work. We are indebted to them all. It is also my pleasant duty to thank the International Research and Exchanges Board (IREX), the American Philosophical Society, and the Wenner-Gren Foundation for Anthropological Research for the grants that enabled me to visit Czechoslovakia to do research in the field. While there on several occasions during the 1970s, I deeply appreciated the helpfulness of the Komárov villagers. The hospitality that they extended to me was in the very best Czech tradition. The one person who must not remain unmentioned, however, is Joy Salzmann, my wife, whose steady editorial help has been most enlightening and painstaking. Since for the final English version of this book I am entirely responsible, all shortcomings must be charged to me alone.

Although the cooperative effort of authors separated by the Atlantic, as well as trained in two different traditions of anthropological research, would seem likely to present a number of special obstacles, our collaboration has proved to be so rewarding that we recommend that others follow our example. The personal gains to be derived from such an experience are great.

Finally, it is only fitting that we dedicate the book to the memory of Josefa Krutinová Scheuflerová (1883–1967), Scheufler's mother, and to the memory of my mother, Ludmila Chržová Salzmannová (1900–1974), both of whom would have much enjoyed reading it.

Zdenek Salzmann
Amherst, Massachusetts
January 1986

Terminological note

A terminological note is in order with respect to the proper adjective "Czech" used in the title of this book. In English, this term is used almost interchangeably with the term "Bohemian," although it overlaps with it only in part. Strictly speaking, the adjective "Czech" denotes the institutions and the ethnic or linguistic specificity of the Czechs—as when referring to Czech settlers (Czech-speaking settlers) or Czech dialects. By contrast, the adjective "Bohemian" has reference to a historicogeographic entity known for centuries as the Bohemian Kingdom or to Bohemia—as when speaking of the Bohemian Forest, Bohemian Massif, Bohemian Germans, or Bohemian kings. In some contexts it seems crucial to distinguish between the two terms: for example, not all of the Bohemian nobility can properly be referred to as "Czech nobility" because a great many nobles holding land or residing in Bohemia, particularly after the Thirty Years' War (1618–1648), were of foreign—especially German—origin. Discriminating English usage thus parallels the difference between the German *böhmisch*, "Bohemian," and *tschechisch*, "Czech." Interestingly enough, this rather subtle (and frequently confusing) terminological distinction does not obtain in Czech, which employs the single adjective *český* in both senses, "Czech" and "Bohemian."

The reference in Chapter 1 is to Czech-speaking peasants, who had been living in their historical homeland, the so-called Czech Lands, for over a thousand years. If one were to speak of "Bohemian peasants," one would refer in a narrow sense to all peasants settled in Bohemia or, more broadly, in the Bohemian Kingdom as a whole, which included Moravia and Silesia. One would imply the inclusion of German-speaking peasants, who for centuries had lived in the area in substantial numbers until the end of World War II.

Contents

Foreword   v

Preface   viii

Terminological Note   ix

1. Czech Peasantry: An Historical Overview   1
2. Natural Setting and Historical Background   16
3. Farm Buildings and Living Quarters   26
4. Making a Living: The Traditional Pattern   36
5. Making a Living: The Socialist Cooperative   50
6. The Village as a Community   63
7. Family and Friends   70
8. Nonfarming Villagers and Outside Visitors   78
9. Contact with the Outside World   84
10. The Wedding   88
11. Birth and Death   98
12. Traditional Observances and Beliefs   103
13. The Church and the State   116
14. Arts and Crafts in the Blata   124
15. Folk Music and Dances of the Blata   134
16. Epilog: From Local Cooperative to Regional Consolidation   144

Chronology of Major Events   159

Pronunciation Guide   160

Glossary of Czech Terms   161

References   165

1 / Czech peasantry:
an historical overview

Until recent times, the life of a small rural community in much of Europe was one of relative isolation from the measured busyness of the regional market town and of complete separation from the pomp and circumstance of the capital. And yet the fundamental aspects of village life were determined in great part by the political fortunes of the larger world, which the peasant sustained with his labors but over which he had little or no control.

The small village of Komárov was no exception, engulfed as it was by the eventful history of the Bohemian Kingdom. Studying such a village, the anthropologist cannot avoid becoming a culture historian as he strives to see the particular group, however small its size, in the larger context of time and space. And so the study of Komárov, a minute detail on the tapestry of Central Europe, should properly begin with a glance at the tapestry as a whole—an historical overview of the Czech peasantry and its changing socioeconomic status over the past thousand-odd years.

There is general agreement among archeologists and historians that the first waves of Slavs must have entered the territory that came to be referred to as the historic Czech Lands no later than the fifth century of the Christian era. Like the populations that had preceded them, the incoming Slavs practiced agriculture and animal husbandry. Employing in all likelihood the two-field system of crop rotation, they raised hemp, flax, and all of the common cereals, and tilled their fields with both wooden and iron plowshares. They used rotary mills for grinding grain and manufactured a modest variety of ceramic ware for domestic use. Although initially members of each settlement group probably held both cattle and cultivated land in common, archeological evidence suggests that the institution of the extended family, characteristic of other Slavs, rapidly yielded in this new home to an arrangement of clustered dwellings, each housing a nuclear family. It thus appears that a very early shift had occurred from collectivities based on descent to settlement groups bound together by ties of common territorial and economic interest—a process that was fully completed by the beginning of historical times.

During the next several centuries a slow but steady change marked the social and economic conditions of these western Slavs. Finds from the ninth century attest to the employment of an asymmetrical plowshare in light and fertile soil, and it is conceivable that the three-field system was at least in partial use. Still

1

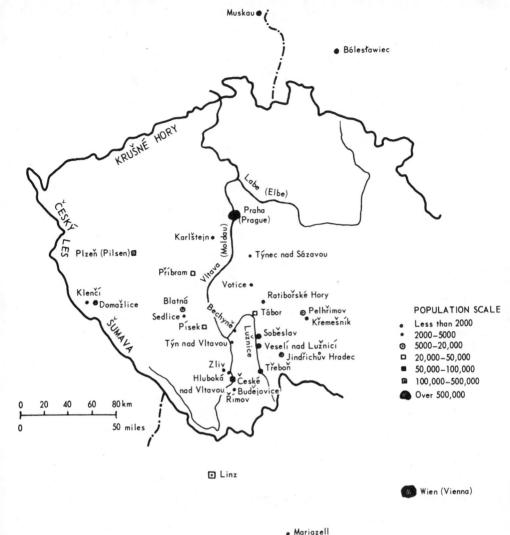

Figure 1. Map of Bohemia with special reference to geographic features referred to in the text.

more significant was the noticeable tendency toward social and economic differentiation among these Slavs. Tribal and regional chieftains, making use of their growing political power, acquired control of substantial tracts of productive land and began to exact from the peasants within their domain contributions in kind in return for protection and goodwill. By the time the Great Moravian Empire fell to the invading Magyars around 900, the foundations of a feudal system had been laid.

By the end of the twelfth century, feudalism had been fully established throughout the western portion of what had been the Great Moravian Empire and was about to become the hereditary Bohemian Kingdom. Except for a relatively small number of peasants who managed to retain full rights to their holdings, most had been forced into tenancy on the land. The territorial princes initially gave the land itself in temporary fief to the most deserving members of their retinues, and later in patrimony to the growing number of nobles. In return for the right of occupancy, the peasants were obligated to pay tribute to their lords. They made their payments customarily in grain, eggs, meat, and cheese as well as in compulsory labor service (*robota*) whenever their manpower was needed. Beginning in the twelfth century, payments were made sporadically in cash. Sizable portions of the land also came to be owned by the Church, especially by the monasteries, which the ruling princes richly endowed in order to strengthen their own political power.

The thirteenth century was characterized by rapid growth of the Bohemian Kingdom. With the three-field system in general use, crop yields improved, and the new practice of cultivating fodder plants helped increase cattle holdings. More and more soil was being reclaimed at the expense of a large supply of forestland. These developments in turn were closely associated with the rapid growth of specialized crafts, the chartering of numerous cities by the crown, and the rise of busy markets. Once or twice a week the peasants brought whatever they could spare to the nearest marketplace, where it was exchanged for products manufactured by the craft specialists.

When the drive to expand the land under cultivation met with a shortage of local manpower, large numbers of colonists from the surrounding German-speaking territories were brought in at the invitation of the king, the Church, or the nobles. In order to promote this large-scale undertaking, the newcomers were granted significant reliefs. The feudal lord and landowner contracted with an entrepreneur (the *locator*) for the division of a designated area into fields, and arranged for dwellings to be built for the use of the German colonists. The rights and obligations of the new settlers were set down by the lord of the domain in a written document. It was customary to exempt the new settlers from all taxes for a period of several years (commonly eight to twelve), after which their regular payments in cash were due twice a year as initially stipulated. Moreover, under the so-called emphyteutic, or German, law applied to these new settlements, the colonists were given hereditary rights to their property, subject, of course, to their continued cultivation and proper management. Emphyteusis was a distinct improvement over the domestic right, under which the land of a peasant was subject to escheat, that is, reversion to the lord upon the death of the original grantee. After the middle of the fourteenth century, payments made by the peasant tenants were generally in the form of money rent, and the right to inherit cultivated land, though not to dispose of it, was extended to the majority of the domestic peasantry as well.

Whether or not the transition to payments in cash provided relief for the peasants is subject to some disagreement among historians. However, it seems doubtful that the conditions of the peasantry could have improved appreciably even during the "golden age" of the reign of Charles IV, the Bohemian king who became the Holy Roman Emperor (died 1378). The Church increased and consolidated its holdings with the result that more than one third of all agricultural land was owned by parish priests, monasteries, prelates, or the archbishop. In addition to their regular payments, the peasants continued to be subject to some labor obligation or, in lieu of it, to extraordinary payments, some of which were

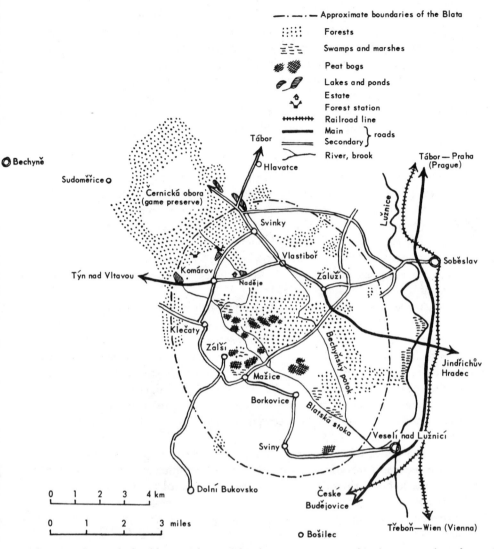

Figure 2. Map of the Blata with special reference to geographic features referred to in the text.

collected for the royal treasury. Still another obligation was the parish tithe, collected from the peasants as well as from their feudal lords. It was commonly paid not only from crops (*decima grani*) but also from livestock (*decima animalium*). Those who were landless paid with labor.

With the appearance of markets and a money economy, the socioeconomic differences among the peasants significantly widened. Not infrequently, children of small peasants were forced by circumstances to enter the service of those with larger holdings which yielded greater surpluses and sizable sums of money. Any advantages that the peasants gained during the first half of the fifteenth century, when they actively contributed to the victories of the Hussite armies (mobilized as part of the Bohemian religious and nationalistic movement originating with the reformer Jan Hus) over mercenaries recruited from lands as distant as Spain and Sweden, were offset by the ravages of war wrought upon the land. By the end of that century, the economic burden felt by the peasant serfs and the restrictions placed on their personal freedom became severe enough to spark the first series of regional rebellions, all of which were brutally suppressed.

Economic developments during the sixteenth century were marked by the concentration of agricultural lands in fewer hands and the increasing tendency of the nobles to add land to their domains and to cultivate grain crops for income. Thus, in 1600, eleven of the foremost noble families owned one half of the agricultural land in Bohemia. In these circumstances the treatment of the serfs further deteriorated: on many an estate, not only were the serfs subject to both rent and the labor obligation, but they were not allowed to marry, seek employment outside, or send their children to study without the permission of the lord. Once again, the peasants rose in revolt in several localities, only to be effectively put down.

With the loss of Czech independence in 1620, following the battle of White Mountain, conditions further worsened, both during the Thirty Years' War and after. As a result of an extended period of wartime conditions, the wholesale flight from the country of the persecuted non-Catholic nobility and bourgeoisie, and epidemics of plague and other diseases, the population of Bohemia was reduced by about one half, and that of Moravia by about one fourth. Despite a number of peasant uprisings during the Thirty Years' War, the labor obligation, which in the past had amounted on most estates to several days per year, had been increased by some of the landlords to several days per week. In Czech historiography, the ensuing period is referred to as the "second serfdom." Exploitation reached such an extent that in 1654 the provincial diet saw fit to issue an ordinance whose aim was to restrain the landowning nobility and their officials from the excessive insistence that the peasants render labor obligation on Sundays and holidays. Such demands by the landowners were viewed as encroachments on the Church's requirements concerning days of obligation. Special permissions for serfs' sons to learn a trade or to study were granted only upon payment of a high fee, and thus were accessible only to the richest of the peasants. Taxing took all of the three possible forms: exacted labor, payments in cash, and payments in kind. Moreover, grinding of grain was permitted only in designated mills under the landlord's control, and beer and other products had to be purchased from sources owned by the lords themselves—a practice established earlier. And as if all this were not enough, the peasants had become subject to a state tax on the land they cultivated, while the lands of the nobles were exempt. The unbearable oppression once again sparked several minor rebellions and, in 1680, a major one, coupled with petitions from the serfs to Emperor Leopold I. His official answer, given in a patent issued on March 22, 1680, did little but legalize the conditions against which the peasants were protesting and included a warning that military sanctions would be imposed if there were any further disobedience. Continued pressure, however, brought about the issuance of a second patent on June 28 of the same year setting forth the most important duties the serfs owed their lords. The patent limited the regular labor obligation to no more than three days in any given week except during emergencies, such as harvest. Sending (except at harvesttime) serfs to lands other than those to which they were bound was discouraged as was also physical punishment that could cause injury to health. Among still other provisions of this patent was a request addressed to the landlords not to expropriate farmsteads in those cases in which there were surviving children. This first serious attempt on the part of the emperor to regulate the relations between the feudal lords and their serfs thus eliminated only the very worst excesses, and sanctioned legally the heavy burdens that in the course of time had fallen upon the shoulders of the peasants.

There were some notable exceptions to the condition of general servitude exacted from the Bohemian peasantry. The most important was the special status accorded to the inhabitants of eleven villages in the Chodsko region near the city of Domažlice. Situated in the heavily forested frontier of southwestern Bohemia, these villagers—known as the *Chodové*—were assigned to guard the means of approach to the kingdom, in particular the two important trails from Bavaria and the Palatinate. For these valuable services, dating back to the end of the twelfth or the beginning of the thirteenth century, they enjoyed special privileges reaffirmed in no less than twenty-four royal charters between 1325 and 1612. Directly subject to the king, they were obligated to pay a fixed tax to the royal treasury, but in every other respect they were free. They enjoyed considerable administrative autonomy and could move away from their villages, sell or bequeath their landholdings as they saw fit, and claim various other rights long since denied the rest of the peasantry. Most important of all, they were excused from all compulsory labor service.

In the course of the fifteenth century, however, the fortunes of the Chodsko peasants began to decline. With their importance as frontier guards progressively waning, their villages repeatedly came to serve as security given to noble families or to the city of Domažlice by Bohemian kings for debts they had incurred. Despite desperate legal efforts and valiant physical struggles to preserve their age-old rights, which suffered still more erosion during the Thirty Years' War, the peasants of Chodsko eventually lost their privileged status completely. The end of their freedom came in the final years of the seventeenth century, when they were forced to submit to military strength and their courageous leader was publicly hanged.

The continuing struggle of the peasantry against their landlords forced the imperial government again to consider conditions in Bohemia and Moravia, and in 1717 Emperor Charles VI issued a patent that on the whole confirmed the provisions of the document of 1680. In no way did the patent lighten the burdens resting on the serfs. Instead, it specified, for example, that they were due to begin their labor obligation on the land of their lords "early, that is, immediately after sunup, and to work conscientiously, according to the needs of the lord's land, until the proper time, that is, sundown, and not earlier, with two hours off for meals and rest."

A subsequent patent was issued by Charles VI for the Bohemian crownlands in 1738 to quell the ever-increasing unrest among the peasant serfs. In effect it reaffirmed once again the legal advantages that the landlords already possessed. Its various provisions were weakened by many qualifications: for example, the length of a working day for a peasant using a draft animal during long spring and summer days was to be "at the most ten hours every day," but a statement was appended that "during the relatively short season of haymaking and harvesting the usual ten hours cannot be strictly observed."

Precipitated by extraordinary circumstances, the first serious blow to the feudal order was finally dealt in 1775. Catastrophic rains ruined the crops of 1770 and the succeeding year, and about a quarter of a million people, or one tenth of the population of Bohemia, died as a result of starvation and diseases that followed in its wake. The desperate situation brought the agrarian problem sharply into focus and resulted in the imperial government's beginning to press for a fundamental revision of serf–seigneur relations. The noble landholders, jealously guarding their privileges, were anything but cooperative in this effort and managed to frustrate whatever constructive moves the government initiated. After several years of obstinacy on the part of the landlords and of indecision on the part of the state, the serfs had had enough. Refusing to wait for a large-scale organized uprising planned for May of 1775, during which Prague was to be seized and the authorities forced to heed the demands of the long-exploited peasantry, the serfs rose spontaneously in January in several regions of Bohemia, attacking the residences of the lords and settling accounts with their hated officials. By April, the rebellion was militarily suppressed but, significantly enough, Maria Theresa promised a "general pardon" for all of the rebels, and during the summer of that year issued a patent setting down the extent of the peasants' obligations toward their lords.

According to the amount of land tax they paid, serfs were classified into two large classes: those whose compulsory labor service included the use of their draft animals and those who worked manually. The former classification was divided into four categories, the lowest requiring labor performed with one draft animal three days per week, the highest labor performed with two pairs of animals three days a week with an additional three man-days of manual labor a week during the period between Saint John the Baptist's Day (June 24) and Saint Wenceslaus's Day (September 28). The second classification consisted of seven categories, in which obligations ranged from thirteen days per year (for landless serfs) to three days per week. These assessments were designed as the upper limits of compulsory labor service, and the serfs were given the option of continuing with their previous quotas of obligation if these were thought to be more advantageous. The merit of the patent was in setting forth a precise assessment of the amount of *robota* required of the different classes of serfs according to their property, but the lords were determined to evade its provisions in every possible way.

Of greater significance than the patent itself was a reform begun with Maria Theresa's enthusiastic support in 1776 and administered by Franz Anton von Raab, after whom it came to be known. The aim of the reform was the abolition of *robota* and the distribution of manorial land to the peasant, who was to become a hereditary leaseholder of the land without having to pay for his lease. He was to have full possession of the land, his chief obligation being the payment of a fixed rental fee to the lord. Even though it was argued by the proponents of abolition that the arrangement would enhance agricultural productivity and ultimately benefit the lords, the opposition of the landowners was such that the Raab system could be carried out only on estates under state control. But even though the benefits of this reform were thus limited to a small portion of the Bohemian peasantry, the seeds of destruction of the old system of personal servitude had been sown. Under the circumstances, the first radical step toward the emancipation of the largest social class in Bohemia was not long in coming.

In the historic patent of November 1, 1781, Emperor Joseph II restored to the peasants certain essential freedoms: the right to move from one estate to another or to settle wherever they pleased (subject to having satisfied their debts), to marry according to their own choice, and to pursue higher forms of education —all without the express permission of the lord. The patent further abolished the compulsory service due the lord by orphans and the children of peasants. However, it emphasized that compulsory labor service must still be rendered by the peasants unless money payments were substituted.

Welcome as the relief was, its benefits proved to be short-lived. While the large landowners began to increase their yields during the second half of the eighteenth century by introducing more rational methods of agricultural production, the peasants were put at an ever greater disadvantage by the conservative character of their operations. The clock was set back once again in 1821, when Emperor Francis I stopped all substitution of money payments in place of actual labor.

With the downfall of absolutism in March of 1848, the peasant question once again assumed a prominent place on the public agenda. In fact, the threat of an open revolt became real enough for a group of Bohemian nobles to petition the emperor to abolish, for due compensation to the landowners, the obligations of the peasantry. With telling promptness, an imperial decree was issued on March 28, which provided for the cessation of all compulsory labor service not later than March 31, 1849, the extent of compensation to be determined later. Similar legislation, with an even earlier deadline, was enacted in Moravia. After a fierce debate in the Imperial Parliament in Vienna as to whether or not the peasants should be required to pay compensation, a vote on August 31 decided the issue in the affirmative. Finally, the bill providing for the abolition of serfdom was approved on September 7 and promulgated into law by an imperial decree of the same date.

Thus the year 1848 held historic significance for the Bohemian peasant: after centuries of servitude, he became a full-fledged owner of his land, eligible to exercise the franchise and to be represented in a legislative assembly of the law. Ironically, no sooner did the newly landed peasants receive the right to vote than they became fearful of being outvoted by the numerous landless elements of the rural population—the cottagers and agricultural workers. In the end, the bulk of the rural population did become enfranchised—all those paying a "direct tax," which included the landed peasants as well as many cottagers, but no farm laborers or domestics.

The problem of compensation was settled in the course of the next five years. Ultimately, just under a million peasants in the Czech Lands fell within the scope of the compensation law, and the number of estates to which compensation was due amounted to 1912. The share to come from the peasantry was to be paid over a period of twenty- years. In most cases, the average sum owed by an individual peasant was below 10 guldens annually, an amount that did not impose an undue hardship. Yet the compensation provided the landowner with capital permitting him to introduce further improvements, which put the newly liberated peasant at an even more distinct disadvantage. Then, too, the fragmented and scattered fields, characteristic of peasant landholdings under feudalism, continued into the present century and prevented any substantial growth of agricultural production. However, in the worst situation of all was the landless peasant, whose hunger for land remained completely unsatisfied. His opportunity did not come until the birth of the Czechoslovak Republic at the end of World War I.

One of the most ambitious tasks confronting the First Republic immediately after the war was the redistribution of agricultural land—*pozemková reforma* (land reform). Although according to official statistics, agriculture in 1921 was a means of livelihood for nearly 40 percent of the population of the country as a whole, a disproportionately large share of land was in the hands of landholding families from among the prewar nobility. The primary motivation for land reform, to be sure, was to improve the lot of those with very little or no land of their own at a time when large-scale dissatisfaction with governmental policies could have easily brought the young republic to the brink of social turmoil. However, the redistribution of land was also seen as an historic act of justice long overdue: many of the large landed estates belonged to foreign noble families, whose landholdings dated back to the tragic battle of White Mountain in 1620, after which they had received property confiscated from domestic nobility as a reward for helping to crush Czech independence. The economic position of these large landowning families was indeed formidable. Prior to the land reform, the 150 largest estates totaled nearly a million and a half hectares of land (some 3,700,000 acres), or over one tenth of the republic's area. The Schwarzenberg family was the largest landowner in Bohemia with 248,000 hectares; then came the Liechtenstein family in Moravia, with 173,000 hectares.

The initial move toward the introduction of land reform was the Act of November 9, 1918, suspending the disposition of large estates in the historic Czech Lands without prior consent of the authorities. On April 16, 1919, an act was passed that provided for the expropriation of agricultural land (fields, meadowland, gardens, vineyards, and hop fields) in excess of 150 hectares (370 acres) or of land in general in excess of 250 hectares. The land subject to expropriation was to be allotted to smallholders, farming cottagers, small craftsmen, workers in agriculture and forestry, landless persons, and others for the purpose of establishing new independent agricultural holdings that would serve as an adequate source of subsistence for the owner and his family. To prevent speculation with or misuse of these allotments, restrictions were placed on their sale, leasing, or mortgaging. Compensation to the former landowners was to be based on the average prices paid on the open market during the years 1913–1915 for estates in excess of 100 hectares (247 acres), with subsequent improvements made on the land to be paid for in full and agricultural equipment taken over at the market price.

Although the Czechoslovak land reform was at that time the most extensive to be attempted in Central Europe, it fell far short of its intended target. The number of estate owners affected came to 1913, and the total extent of land available for redistribution, both arable and wooded, amounted to 4,068,370 hectares, or 29 percent of the entire republic. Yet for various reasons—among them a number of exemptions written into the law, which the former landowners were quick to claim—as of January 1, 1938, only 13 percent of the entire area had changed owners: 1,800,782 hectares, or 44.3 percent of eligible land had been alloted to new owners (of which 868,601 hectares were in arable land), with 45 percent of the land left to the original holders and 10.7 percent remaining subject to transfer. Table 1 details the distribution of agricultural land before and after the land reform, according to size of holding.

TABLE 1.   DISTRIBUTION OF AGRICULTURAL LAND ACCORDING TO SIZE OF HOLDING, BEFORE AND AFTER LAND REFORM

Size of Holding	Before the Land Reform	After the Land Reform
	(in percent of agricultural land)	
Less than 2 hectares	7.8	7.6
2–5 hectares	14.3	18.8
5–20 hectares	44.1	46.5
20–100 hectares	17.8	17.1
Over 100 hectares	16.0	10.0
	100.0	100.0

Since the expropriated lands were not evenly distributed throughout the republic, only about 8000 communities out of a total of some 17,000 were able to benefit directly by the reform. Worst of all, about 30 percent of those landless farm workers and smallholders who applied for an allotment were left empty-handed. The shortcomings of the land reform were to be corrected in a new bill prepared in 1937, but the political events of the subsequent years prevented its consideration.

Immediately after World War II, patterns of land tenure were profoundly affected by the transfer of Germans and Hungarians from the territory of postwar Czechoslovakia. For the purposes of a new land reform, a presidential decree of June 21, 1945, provided for immediate confiscation, without compensation, of the agricultural land owned by three categories of persons: those of German or Hungarian nationality regardless of their current citizenship, of traitors and enemies of the republic, and of corporations whose managements had knowingly and deliberately aided the conduct of the war by the Third Reich.

The first stage of the land reform in the Czech Lands concentrated on the liberated border regions, in which about 1,955,000 hectares were confiscated, about 67 percent of which was agricultural land. Of this total, some 157,500 applicants received over 937,000 hectares.

The second stage of postwar land reform was directed against those estates that remained in the hands of landowners, large farmers, and the Roman Catholic Church. The draft of the proposed bill dealing with this redistribution generated heated discussions both in the villages and in the country's parliament. On July

11, 1947, despite the strong opposition of several political parties, it was passed. The fundamental provision of the law, which was originally designed as a revision of the prewar land reform but which became a hotly political issue in the context of the postwar power struggle, was to limit the extent of privately owned land to 150 hectares and in certain special cases to 50 hectares of agricultural land.

The third stage of the postwar redistribution of land, the so-called new land reform, was enacted on March 21, 1948, a month after the government crisis from which the Communist party emerged in complete control of the government. The act laid down the main principle that land serving agricultural purposes belonged only to those who tilled it. Furthermore, it stipulated that 50 hectares was the maximum amount of land, including forestland, which might be owned by a farmer's family, and that inventory, including livestock, was to be expropriated in the same proportion as land.

The implementation of this last stage of the postwar series of land reforms was still not complete when collectivization of agriculture was set into motion in 1949. The instrument of collectivization was the Unified Agricultural Cooperatives Act of February 23. Article I of this law gave little indication of the course that Czechoslovak agriculture was to take in future years:

> In order to ensure wholesome development of the agricultural cooperative movement and eradicate the fragmentation of cooperative farming operations inherited from the past, unified agricultural cooperatives shall be established on a voluntary basis in order to consolidate the various existing agricultural cooperatives and to bring about significant benefits for the working farmers. . . .

Among the main stated objectives of this program were the consolidation of the many scattered individual plots of cultivated land, the mechanization of agricultural work, and the rationalization of other aspects of agriculture in order to increase the lagging productivity of the country's farms. The designation of the collective farms as "unified agricultural cooperatives" was to appeal to the very extensive voluntary cooperative tradition prior to World War II, of which the postwar program was supposed to be a more progressive stage.

On the whole, the opposition to the program was such that the transition from private to collective ownership was to be accomplished in several phases, roughly corresponding to the four basic types of unified agricultural cooperatives:

Phase I: Ownership of land remains in private hands, as does also crop and animal production; large capital investments are made jointly; common use is made of draft animals, implements, vehicles, and machinery, and certain basic farming operations are undertaken on a collective basis.

Phase II: Crops are cultivated collectively on tracts of land created by the ploughing up of field boundaries and the amalgamation of fields; animal husbandry remains under private ownership and care; crops raised on collectively cultivated fields belong to individual members according to the acreage of land contributed to the cooperative.

Phase III: Collective management includes both crop and animal production; some unearned income exists in the form of cash compensation for the use of the land brought by members into the cooperative; the major source of income is labor, and compensation is on the basis of work units.

Phase IV: Collective management includes both crop and animal production, and the only source of income is labor contributed and compensated for according to work units.

The subsequent period was one of continued pressure upon the peasants to collectivize and of persistent harassment of the "village rich," with occasional easing of pressure and financial incentives to enlist the villagers' cooperation and trust. Despite the continuing growth of the socialized sector, crop production remained perilously close to prewar levels until about 1960, when collectivization was brought to its practical conclusion. The highest number of cooperatives (12,560) was reached in 1959. Since that time their total has been steadily declining as a result of consolidations (to 5871 in 1971, with 876,245 members). At present, the organization of cooperative agriculture is fairly well stabilized. Both living conditions and earnings of the villagers have decidedly improved over the past decade. It is significant that not a single unified agricultural cooperative dissolved during the fluid conditions of 1968.

Besides the collective farms, which constitute the major form of agricultural organization, there were 326 state farms in Czechoslovakia in 1971, accounting for 20.3 percent of both agricultural and arable land and employing 146,736 permanent nontechnical full-time personnel. The state agricultural sector also includes machine and tractor stations, which numbered 100 as of the end of 1971.

The private agricultural sector is of little consequence. The great majority of full-time private farmers are in the mountainous and submountainous regions of Slovakia, and their number has been steadily declining. More than three fourths of their holdings amount to less than half a hectare (1.24 acres) of agricultural land.

In terms of land area, as of the end of 1971 unified agricultural cooperatives in Czechoslovakia controlled some 4,241,000 hectares of agricultural land, of which 3,226,000 hectares were arable land. Private plots of members of cooperatives amounted to about 287,000 and 204,000 hectares of the larger totals, respectively. The state sector accounted for some 2,083,000 additional hectares of agricultural land, making the share of the socialist sector 90.1 percent of the country's total agricultural land.

With the broad historical background given above in mind, we can now turn to the peasant's changing status in the social and economic life of the Czech Lands. As we have already seen, the earliest Slavic inhabitants of this area were subsistence-oriented peasants, occupied with the raising of crops and secondarily with the raising of cattle. Detailed information is lacking concerning their progressive differentiation into a landholding class and a dependent farming population. Occasional crop failures or other local or regional catastrophes no doubt brought some into indebtedness to or dependence on those more fortunate. Various other factors must have furthered the establishment of an elite and aided the rise of numerous warlords, who exercised power from their strongholds. Offering protection to the farming folk in their own locality, they raided neighboring regions with the help of their retainers, many of whom had been drawn from among the peasants. One of the common methods of social and economic advancement was clearly the use of naked force applied by the strong to the weak.

Instances are also on record of some freemen becoming dependent by "purchase" or "voluntary submission," undoubtedly under the threat of economic or physical force.

The maintenance of a life-style characterized by warring and wining, which encouraged consumption rather than production, quite obviously required an increased expenditure of labor from some portion of the society, and it was exacted from the dependent peasantry. A significant factor, too, was the growing influence of the Church, whose interests closely coincided with the emerging centers of secular political and economic power. Two distinct sociocultural orders—a dependent peasantry on the one hand and a class of landholding lords on the other—had thus crystallized by the end of the twelfth century. To be sure, there were the remnants of farming freemen, who fit neither category, but in the absence of any historical record of their active opposition to the rapid feudalization of Bohemia, one is justified in surmising that their influence by this time had greatly waned.

The official view of society, then, distinguished originally between two major classes of people—the lords and the serfs. By the beginning of the thirteenth century, however, when the Church had achieved economic and political power comparable to that of the secular aristocracy, a third class was added—the clergy. The popular adage of the time, *Tu ora, tu protege tuque labora* ("You [clergy], pray; you [lord], protect; and you [serf], work!"), well expressed the prevailing theory of the appropriate functions of these classes. By the fifteenth century the burghers, or city dwellers, had been added.

Agricultural productivity made rapid strides during the early feudal period, reaching a level by the fifteenth century which was not significantly surpassed until nearly 500 years later. This development greatly facilitated the division of labor between agriculture and craft specialization, as well as the transition from payments in kind toward money rent and toward a money economy in general. Under these circumstances, the Czech Lands began to witness the rapid development of cities and the rise of the burghers. The peasant culture of the dependent villagers had become established in all its major features as it was to exist for another half a millennium.

The peasants, burghers, and aristocrats had little or nothing in common socially and culturally save their religion and language (excluding, of course, German colonists and the German-speaking members of the privileged classes). Except for their periodic visits to the nearest market town, the peasants paid little heed to the changing ways of the city and were almost totally uninfluenced by it as a source of innovation for the village. Besides, tied as they were to their fields and their obligations, their network for wider sociocultural sharing was limited and ineffectual. What few innovations did reach them were channeled through the representatives of their landlords, to whom they were bound in the mutually complementary relationship of the exploiters and the exploited. And since the manorial influences were rather uniform throughout the Czech Lands, a surprising unity of peasant customs developed, despite the social and cultural isolation of the individual peasant villages.

The differences between the city dwellers and the villagers had become clearly established during the course of the thirteenth century. Physically, the cities contrasted with the village in their fortifications; legally, they differed by virtue of the privileges accorded them by the lordships, and in larger cities chartered by the crown, by virtue of the personal freedom their citizens enjoyed; and economically, cities were dominant as a result of the concentration of trade and commerce. The well-to-do burghers, merchants in particular, took unashamed advantage of the peasants, cheating them and looking down upon them with scorn. Those practicing trades or handicrafts—bakers, butchers, brewers, smiths, and others—behaved no better, as many rhymed satires from the fourteenth century vividly portray. On the other hand, they were aware of their partial dependence on the villagers both as customers and as the source of cheap labor.

Disinterested outsiders looked upon the villagers as peasant serfs regardless of the size of the holdings they cultivated. But while there were no *class* differences among the medieval villagers—the rich peasant as well as the poor one was irrevocably subject to the lord to whom he paid feudal rent—manorial records indicate that noticeable *socioeconomic* differences did exist, as did also the awareness of them among the villagers themselves. Aside from village priests, occasional rent-free landholders, village judges who represented the lord and exercised local legal authority, millers, and innkeepers, several other categories had become established by the fourteenth century. At the top were the well-to-do peasants, who were relatively few in number. An occasional peasant held a parcel of land sufficiently large to be able to lease some of it to fellow villagers for a consideration. In 1349, for example, it was recorded that poor peasants from a village near Prague complained that the rich ones were eager to rule them, and there is other such evidence. However, the bulk of the villagers were the peasants with middle-sized holdings. Below them were those who farmed tiny plots of land. Others, who were landless, worked exclusively for the lord and ranked between the landed farmers and the farmhands and domestics.

For the fifteenth through eighteenth centuries, the best approximation of the social makeup of an average Czech village may be represented in percentage as follows in Table 2.

TABLE 2.   MAKEUP OF AVERAGE CZECH VILLAGE, FIFTEENTH THROUGH EIGHTEENTH CENTURIES (FEMALES GIVEN PARENTHETICALLY)

	Villagers of Productive Age			
Peasants	Those with Farmhouses and Tiny Plots	Farmhands	Domestics	Others
9% (9%)	4% (4%)	3% (3%)	9% (11%)	2 % (2%)

	Unproductive Persons		
Children	Retired Farmers	Superannuated and Village Poor	Beggars, Invalids, and Young Orphans
16% (18%)	2% (3%)	.5% (.5%)	2% (2%)

From about the middle of the nineteenth century, when serfdom was abolished, until World War II, anyone who worked on or derived income from agricultural land in the Czech Lands held one of the socioeconomic statuses differentiated as follows:

Czech Term	English Equivalent	Definition
podruh	farmhand	One who was landless and boarded with the farmer for whom he worked.
domkář	cottager	One who owned a modest cottage with little or no adjacent land.
chalupník	farming cottager	One who owned a very small farmstead, generally no larger than approximately 3 acres.
malý sedlák or čtvrtláník	small farmer	One who owned approximately 10 acres of land.
střední sedlák or půlláník	middle farmer	One who owned approximately 20 acres of land.
velký sedlák or celoláník	large farmer	One whose land amounted to 40 acres on the average.
statkář	landowner	One who owned a large tract of land.
velkostatkář	large landowner	One whose landholdings were unusually large.

Prior to World War II, agriculture was the second largest sector of the economy, after industry. The typical unit of agricultural production was the privately owned "family" farm. Its owner, customarily the head of the household, managed the land entirely on his own with the help of his family, employing hired labor seasonally only if the size of his operation required it. Most of these farms were too small to yield sufficient income without supplementary activity of some kind. The disadvantages of the small-sized holdings and the meager incomes they provided were partly offset by a network of voluntary credit, processing, and marketing cooperatives; these had been organized by the small- and medium-sized farmers themselves and were among the best developed in Europe. Even though a steady rural exodus had been taking place for a century or so, it was largely the surplus population that was being drawn off. Thus the village was able to retain its autonomy despite the ever-increasing forces of industrialization and commercialization.

The Czech peasant could be characterized as educated, politically conscious, and genuinely religious, despite his materialistic inclinations. His land was far more than just a source of income to him: it was the cornerstone of his existence, a family heritage forged through the many centuries of servitude. The village in which he lived was economically and socially self-sufficient, or nearly so, and its members maintained tight-knit relationships. It was from this recognition of village collectivity that the peasant derived his own sense of identity.

2 / Natural setting and historical background

Komárov belongs to a group of villages that lie in one of the boggy regions of southern Bohemia. Because of its natural character, the area is commonly referred to as the Bogland, or the *Blata*. More specifically, the local people speak of it as the Bogland of Veselí (*veselská Blata*) or the Bogland of Soběslav (*soběslavská Blata*), the two towns to which the villagers particularly relate. In recognition of its fertile soil, which favors the cultivation of cereals, the region has also long been called the Bogland of Plenty (*bohatá Blata*) or the Wheat Bogland (*pšeničná Blata*).

The Blata proper is far from extensive. It includes nine villages: Komárov; Vlastiboř; Svinky and Záluží, both of which today are administratively joined to Vlastiboř; Zálší; Klečaty and Mažice, both of which now belong administratively to Zálší; Borkovice; and Sviny. The area is shaped roughly like an ellipse, the longer axis oriented north to south and extending a little more than seven miles (about twelve kilometers), the shorter about five miles (eight kilometers). The entire Blata covers only about thirty square miles (seventy-five square kilometers), unless one also includes some eight or nine villages lying along the periphery, as has been done on occasion.

The area lies in the northern part of the Třeboň Basin, whose origin dates back to the Tertiary period, during which the Alps and Carpathians were formed. The mountain-making movements profoundly affected the Bohemian Massif, shattering it by faults and lifting some portions while depressing others. In time, the floors of the depressions leveled out and began to fill with deposits. During the Miocene, a recent epoch of the Tertiary, the floor of the Třeboň Basin became a freshwater lake, whose remains were in evidence until early historic times.

No doubt the character of the land has been responsible for the relatively sparse settlement of the Třeboň Basin. Compared to Bohemia as a whole, the population density of the basin continues to be low, even though it has been slowly increasing since the beginning of historic times. Noticeable growth occurred during the Middle Ages, when some of the densely forested areas were cleared and brought under cultivation, and much of the unproductive wetland was converted to fishponds. The setting of lakes and the development of fish-farming, concentrated in the Třeboň area, became exceptionally advanced as early as the sixteenth century.

The Blata itself is a gently undulating plain lying at an average altitude of

1300 feet (400 m) above sea level, with the highest elevation at about 1570 feet (475 m). Komárov lies a little over 1400 feet (430 m) above sea level. Because of the slowly declining watercourse of the Lužnice River, which drains the entire basin, the rather humid climate, and the largely impermeable surface soil, fairly extensive peat bogs and swamps remain in the region to the present day. Peat bogs developed in those depressions of the prehistoric lake which were floored with a layer of impermeable clay. Decayed vegetation, consisting primarily of pine, mosses, lichens, and whortleberry shrubs, sank slowly beneath the surface and eventually changed into peat. Taken together, the peat bogs cover an area of nearly three and a half square miles (about 900 hectares), with an estimated volume of 27 million cubic yards (21 million cubic meters) and a maximum thickness of twenty-seven feet (8.25 meters).

Since the end of the Middle Ages, the appearance of the Blata has changed somewhat. As the population of the region increased and farming techniques became more efficient, it became necessary to clear more and more of the woodlands for cultivation, thereby reducing the extent of the forests. The portion of the Blata covered with swamps and peat bogs remained fairly extensive until 1906, when draining of the region was undertaken, and unprofitable or exhausted peat bogs were brought under cultivation. A second large conversion of bogland to farmland was accomplished in the mid-1920s, but enough of it remained for each of the Blata villages to continue to have one particular peat bog on which to draw. The largest of these were located near Klečaty and Borkovice. Since the 1950s, extraction of peat has assumed an industrial character. This is evident on the face of the countryside, where there are extensive areas from which the soil overlying the peat deposits has been stripped. Periodically the surface soil is restored and the land readied for subsequent cultivation.

What remains of the bogland today is overgrown with plants, some of which are rare enough to have been protected by law for years: Siberian iris (*Iris sibirica*); grass-of-parnassus (*Parnassia palustris*); round-leaved, or common, sundew (*Drosera rotundifolia*); European cranberry (*Vaccinium oxycoccos*); marsh tea (*Ledum palustre*); bog rosemary, or moorwort (*Andromeda polifolia*); and two species of pine (*Pinus uncinata* and *Pinus ulginosa*). This unusual plant cover has helped to preserve some rare varieties of butterflies, dragonflies, and locusts, and also some varieties of amphibians and reptiles.

The only mineral resource of the area is a whitish clay, almost pure kaolin, found in certain places of the bogland. During the last century, it was used by ceramic works in the nearby town of Bechyně and also in Prague.

The Blata is drained by Bechyně Brook (*Bechyňský potok*) and its tributary, which is referred to by various local names, and by the Blata Canal (*Blatská stoka*), begun in 1906 and completed in 1925. The only bodies of water of any size are near Komárov. Nearly half of the region is still covered with woods.

Because the sediments deposited in southern Bohemia during the Tertiary period are low in lime content, the soil of the Blata does not especially favor the cultivation of certain commercial crops; as a result, legumes, potatoes, and fruit trees are not found to any great extent. However, the soil is suitable for the cultivation of grain crops, and these have been rather profitable.

The Blata was not recognized as a culturally distinct region until the beginning of the nineteenth century, but its character must have taken shape over a period of several hundred years. While the existence of most of the Blata settlements has been established by documentary evidence found in Latin records for the middle of the fourteenth century (1354), that of Komárov is not attested until a century later (1462). The subsequent reference to the village, this time in Czech, is for 1543. However, there is no reason to conclude that Komárov was the last of the Blata villages to be founded. The relatively late documentation merely indicates that prior to 1462 Komárov had not been involved in any legal proceedings significant enough to merit recording.

There are two possible sources of origin for the word *Komárov*. One is the old possessive form (*Komáróv*) of a descriptive name, *Komár*, which could have belonged to the founder or an early settler. The other possible derivation is from *komár*, meaning "mosquito"; the suffix *-ov*, derived from the possessive, was used to designate a geographical locality. Considering the swampy nature of the area, the second explanation is as plausible as the first. The name itself is common, as there are over a dozen Komárovs in Czechoslovakia.

The lands belonging to Komárov cover an area of about 2120 acres (860 hectares). They form an irregular elongated polygon oriented from north–northwest to south–southeast, with dwellings concentrated near the southwestern corner. For the most part, the northern portion of the village lands is covered with woods, which form a southerly extension of the forest complex stretching northward toward the Lužnice River. Except for villages in sparsely populated mountain regions, the village acreage is well above average for Bohemia. According to the land survey (cadastre) compiled around the middle of the eighteenth century during the rule of Queen Maria Theresa, the area under peasant cultivation amounted to approximately 34 percent of the total. Specifically,. this amounted to the following:

Fields	22.5%
Meadows	2.0%
Pasturelands	6.1%
Wooded areas	1.9%
Unused lands or peat bogs	1.3%

Included in the figures above were communal lands consisting of pastureland (4.3%) and woods (all of the 1.9%). The quality of the soil was judged to be 4, which, according to the criteria of the cadastre, meant that the yield of the fields amounted to four-and-one-half times the weight of the seeds sown. For Bohemia this was better than average, and Komárov was clearly a prosperous village. The remaining area of the village lands, some 66 percent of the total acreage, was taken up by farm buildings, roads and paths, or water surface, and particularly by the fields, meadows, pastureland, and forests of the lord's estate.

The overall utilization of land during the past centuries presents roughly the following picture: over one-half of the village area was under cultivation either as fields or as meadows, about one third was covered with forests, and the remainder consisted of farmsteads, roads, pasturelands, useless land, and several large ponds. The general trend during this period was to bring pastures and unused land under cultivation as fields and meadows, with the result that arable land was expanded at the expense of pastureland.

Once rational methods of forest management were introduced during the eighteenth century, the timberlands began to receive considerable attention. The care and protection of the Komárov forests have been the responsibility of several foresters; in all probability the two forest stations that house them today have been standing in their present locations for several hundred years. About half a mile east of the Komárov settlement lies the former estate Hope (*Naděje*), which belonged to a noble family and was first mentioned at the beginning of the sixteenth century. Its designation suggests a late Renaissance origin, since at that period it was the custom to name estates or residences for virtues or other abstract traits. During the eighteenth century the estate had become the property of the family of the Counts of Paar and was leased periodically to well-to-do individuals from nearby towns. Finally, in 1923, it was parceled out to local farmers as a result of the post-World War I land reform.

The peasant fields, very long and narrow strips, belonged to three naturally defined sections that almost completely encircled the settlement. The fields belonging to the estate, on the other hand, were irregular and much larger, their width frequently approximating their length. The arrangment of the peasant fields, characteristic of land allotment under the so-called German, or emphyteutic, law places the founding of Komárov sometime between the second half of the thirteenth century and the end of the fourteenth. According to this legal innovation, introduced to attract German settlers to Bohemia during the period, the use of agricultural land was granted to peasants on a long-term basis or in perpetuity, subject to certain conditions, such as the payment of rent, but with the right to the full and unrestricted use of the soil. Originally, in order to help identify the location of peasant fields, the several naturally bounded tracts of village lands were referred to by such descriptive names as "The Hanged (Man)," "The White (Land)," and the like; the significance of these terms was lessened following the trigonometric land survey during the first half of the last century, and completely lost with the transition to joint farming in socialist cooperatives in the mid-1950s. Today, these ancient designations are rapidly becoming forgotten.

The village plan of Komárov also conformed in general to that followed for settlements under the old emphyteutic law. Individual farmsteads surrounded a rectangular village common. Located on the common were a pond, a chapel, a smithy, a cottage for the village pasturer, and several small farmhouses. Placing new farmhouses on commons land began in the eighteenth century, when government decrees of 1753, 1771, and 1786 limited the subdividing of farms in Bohemia whenever there were multiple heirs in order to prevent fragmentation and economic weakening of the peasantry. As a consequence, communal lands and the village common began to be utilized for the setting up of new units. The cluster of buildings located in the southern part of Komárov near what at one time was the second village pond undoubtedly came about as a result of these

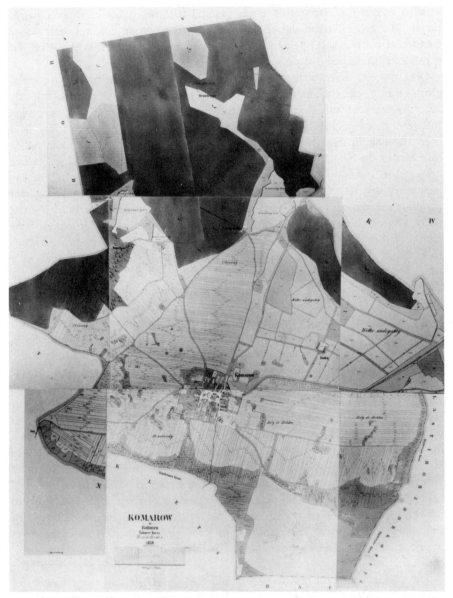

Komárov and its lands shown in a cadastral map dating from the first half of the nineteenth century. (Composite made from photographs in the archives of the Institute for Ethnography and Folklore of the Czechoslovak Academy of Sciences.)

measures. In general, the historical development of Komárov was of a type common in Bohemia. The estate Hope, with its buildings forming three sides of a rectangle, was likewise typical.

The ponds on the common and on the village periphery go back at least to the time of the rule of Maria Theresa and Joseph II when every larger settlement

Same map in greater detail. (Composite made from photographs in the archives of the Institute for Ethnography and Folklore of the Czechoslovak Academy of Sciences.)

was required to arrange for a ready supply of water as a means of protection against fires. The evidence of archeological excavations and medieval iconography points to the widespread presence of water reservoirs in rural settlements. Whether their construction was the result of measures taken as early as the fourteenth century by Charles IV to check the spread of frequent fires or whether they served simply as millponds cannot be determined with certainty.

Komárov has long been accessible from all directions by roads connecting it with neighboring villages. Today, the road running through the village from east to west is undergoing substantial improvement in order to serve as the main highway between Jindřichův Hradec and Písek. A second road, passing through Komárov from north to south and connecting it with Tábor and Veselí on the Lužnice River, retains its secondary status. Other historical roads, recorded in surveys and on maps of the last hundred years, were discontinued when individual fields were joined together and brought under the present cooperative management.

The two towns to which the people of Komárov have always related are Soběslav and Veselí, both lying in an easterly direction, one about seven miles by road, the other eight. Before the cooperative system eliminated the balks (unplowed dividing ridges) between the fields, the towns were separated by a comfortable distance which could easily be covered by foot in two hours if one took a shortcut through the fields. Besides their proximity to Komárov, both were located on the road that has served since prehistoric times as an important trade route between central Bohemia and northern Austria and connects Prague with Linz (at present, it is highway E 14). Since 1872 both Soběslav and Veselí have also been stations along the railroad line between Prague and Vienna, formerly called "Emperor Franz Joseph's Line," with a branch to České Budějovice and points further south. Of more immediate cultural importance was the establishment in Soběslav of a teachers college in 1870, replaced in the mid-1950s by a secondary school designed to prepare students for the university by stressing the classics, history, mathematics, and modern languages.

The towns west of the region—Bechyně in particular—were never of any particular significance for the Blata villages despite the fact that for a long time Bechyně was the seat of an administrative district as well as the residence of the landowning nobility under whose control Komárov belonged. For one thing, Bechyně was separated from Komárov by a game preserve (*Černická obora*), which until 1848 was closed to traffic. Soběslav, on the other hand, was easily accessible, and furthermore was conveniently located along an important commercial route. Another decisive factor was undoubtedly the pull exerted by some of the other Blata communities (Vlastiboř, Záluží, and in part Svinky), which were under the control of Soběslav, one of the towns belonging to the extensive patrimonial domain of the noble family of the Schwarzenbergs. The preference of the Blata villagers for Soběslav and Veselí as their natural "metropolitan" centers was largely responsible for their cultural homogeneity.

Until 1751 the Blata villages belonged administratively to the district of Bechyně with its regional seat in České Budějovice. When the administrative boundaries of the region were revised in 1751, the villages of the northern Blata, Komárov included, came under the jurisdiction of Tábor; those to the south came under the jurisdiction of České Budějovice. Komárov lay just north of the regional boundary. When the traditional division was replaced in 1862 by more numerous smaller administrative units, the Blata villages were apportioned among three different political and judicial districts. Not until 1949, when Soběslav became a district seat, were the Blata villages brought together as one administrative unit. This situation had not changed in 1960, when small administrative districts were abolished in favor of larger ones, with the result that all of the Blata villages came under the jurisdiction of a district with its seat in the city of Tábor.

One of the rewarding aspects of the study of European villages is the depth of available historical documentation. In this respect Komárov is no exception. Historically it belonged to the patrimonial domain of Bechyně, which passed from the ownership of the Bishop of Prague to a succession of noble families: the Šternberks (ca. 1340–1397), to Jošt, the Margrave of Moravia (1397–ca. 1405), the family of Kunštát and Poděbrady (ca. 1405–ca. 1414), Bechyně of Lažany (1414–1477), the family of the Šternberks (1477–1528), the Švamberks (1528–1569), the family of the Rožmberks (1569–1596), once again the Šternberks (1596–1715), and finally into the family of the Counts of Paar through marriage to the last local Šternberk heiress (1715–1848). During the 1520s, a part of Komárov belonged to the Rožmberks when Anne of Hradec, married to one of the Rožmberks, owned and administered one half of the Bechyně lands.

Ecclesiastically Komárov was assigned to the parish of Saint Andrew in Hlavatce to the north, which in turn belonged under the jurisdiction of the dean of Soběslav and the vicar of Týn on the Vltava. When the keeping of all the parish registers was turned over to local civil authorities in 1945, Komárov remained under the jurisdiction of Hlavatce for several more years until it was transferred to the registry office of Soběslav.

The statistics for Komárov show a peak population around 1900. Table 3 provides a summary of the last three centuries.

TABLE 3.   POPULATION TRENDS IN KOMÁROV, SEVENTEENTH
TO TWENTIETH CENTURIES

Year	Number of Farmsteads	Number of Inhabitants
1657	13 (plus 4 cottages)	about 70
1757	21	about 100
1842	37	266
1899	40	291
1921	41	242
1930	41	239
1972	50 (of which 45 are occupied by families)	193

The very sharp population increase during the second half of the eighteenth century and especially the first half of the nineteenth was not peculiar to the region but was typical of Bohemia and Central Europe in general. It was made possible by governmental measures guarding against the incidence of famine, improvements in sanitary conditions, and advances made in preventive medicine; in the Blata it was sustained by the conversion of pastureland into fields. The marked slowdown in population increase during the second half of the past century had its roots in the ecconomic situation of the region. During the first half of the past century, Soběslav and its environs—like all of southern Bohemia —were a typically agricultural area, specializing in cereal crops. Not possessing conditions favorable to industrial growth, which was rapidly progressing elsewhere, the area became economically stagnant. Even in agriculture, the three-field system persisted here and there in the Blata well into the second half of the past century.

The reduction of population during the subsequent period, especially from the 1880s onward, was a specifically South Bohemian problem. Possibilities of employment did exist in Soběslav and Veselí, but they were greatly limited. A number of Komárov villagers sought industrial employment as laborers in Tábor and České Budějovice, or even further away in Pilsen (Plzeň). Some of the young women had to leave home in order to find employment as maids or children's nurses in well-to-do-urban families. A great many people from the region were forced to go abroad, especially to Austria, and some even as far as the United States. These were primarily single males for whom there was neither place in the family farmsteads nor opportunity to serve as hired agricultural laborers.

The front of a Komárov farmhouse and granary built in 1888. (Photograph taken in 1956. From the archives of the Institute for Ethnography and Folklore of the Czechoslovak Academy of Sciences.)

A letter received in the Blata from the United States toward the end of the century includes the following:

. . . I must inform you that our journey lasted an entire month, and we were on the water twenty-one days. Then [I] arrived at John and Katie's,

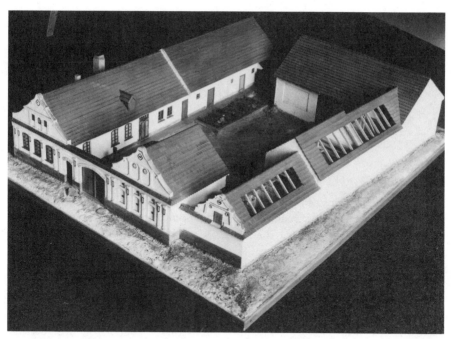

A model of the large Komárov farmstead shown in the foregoing photograph.

who received me like their own brother. I am still with them, because they are well supplied with everything. They still live in harmony and contentment. . . . I couldn't help being completely amazed when I arrived—they have their own meat all year long, and the rest of their livelihood is extremely good because things are extremely cheap here and yet the pay is high. But don't you think for a minute that—as they say in Bohemia—whoever lives well retains little. Here one saves a pretty penny. John has managed very well in a short time—what he has here now would be worth at least two thousand in Bohemia. He has quite a bit of money [saved] already and works the year round. He takes in daily one dollar and a quarter—that amounts to three guldens and ten kreuzers of our money. I also have a job, working in a brickyard and making just as much—one dollar and a quarter [per day]. . . . Life is good here in America, if only one wants to work. . . .

Since the end of the last war, the number of Komárov farmhouses has remained constant at fifty, but five of these are not occupied by families. As a result of the continuing rural exodus over the past several decades, the official number of inhabitants has declined to just below 200 with only about 180 actually in residence.

Despite the somewhat unusual character of the Blata landscape and the economic pressures to which southern Bohemia was subject in recent history, Komárov is a fair representative of those villages in the Bohemian lowlands which have been oriented primarily toward agricultural production. Furthermore it serves as a good example of the more prosperous villages in Bohemia in general.

3 / Farm buildings and living quarters

The Blata farmstead, consisting of the farmhouse and the adjacent utility buildings and service areas, could scarcely have been better suited to the needs of individual farming. It provided the farmer with an adequate dwelling place for his family and help, if any, as well as with all the required work and storage facilities. In its appearance, it underwent two major changes—the first around the middle of the nineteenth century and the second after World War II.

For the medieval period there is no descriptive account or pictorial record of the layout and appearance of a Komárov farmhouse. Most probably it was not unlike the thatch-covered log house that could still be seen in the area during the 1860s. In its simplest form, such a farmhouse consisted of three rooms. As a rule the entrance hall was subdivided in order to provide a separate area for the so-called black kitchen, deriving its name from its walls, which were darkened with smoke and soot from an open hearth. The living room, located to the left of the hallway, was sometimes divided into two separate areas. On the opposite side of the entrance hall was a space that originally was used for storage but later was commonly converted into quarters for the retired farmer after he had made over the farmstead to his heir. When necessary, this room too was divided into two separate chambers to accommodate the farmer's grown children or, in larger farmsteads, the help. Along the same axis as the dwelling unit were the stables; across from and parallel with them was the granary, which was usually constructed of stone. Opposite the stables, adjacent to the granary, larger farmsteads had their pigsties and roofed enclosures for poultry. The rear of the farmstead was closed in by a barn and a shed, the front by a wall with a small gate for people and a large one for farm equipment and livestock. In the middle of the farmyard and next to the stables was the manure pile. Behind the barn was a garden, customarily fenced in, but sometimes leading directly to the fields.

The largest farms of the Blata—those with the full original farmland allotment, which for the purpose of taxation used to be based on the quality of the soil rather than on size—averaged about 75 acres (30 hectares). The corresponding farmsteads were about 100 feet wide and 200 feet long. The dimensions of the smaller ones were more or less half that size. The entire farmstead complex, including the farmyard, occupied an area ranging approximately from one-eighth to one-half of an acre (a little over 20,000 square feet for the largest farmsteads). Only on the farms of farming cottagers were the buildings arranged in the shape

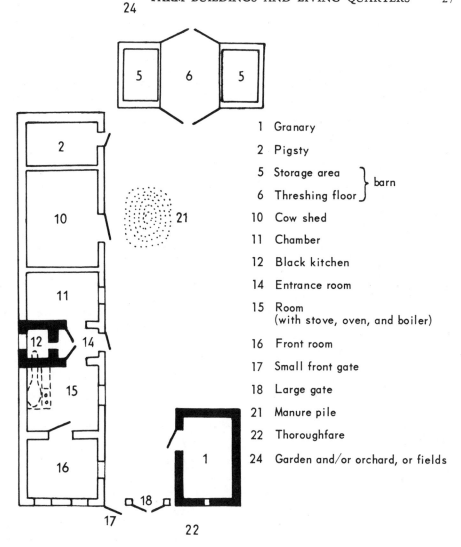

1 Granary

2 Pigsty

5 Storage area ⎫
                ⎬ barn
6 Threshing floor ⎭

10 Cow shed

11 Chamber

12 Black kitchen

14 Entrance room

15 Room
    (with stove, oven, and boiler)

16 Front room

17 Small front gate

18 Large gate

21 Manure pile

22 Thoroughfare

24 Garden and/or orchard, or fields

Log wall with window

Masonry wall with window

Figure 3. Reconstruction of an old log house (from about 1800–1850) with a black kitchen. (According to an old informant from the 1930s.)

of the letter L, with the barn forming the rear end of the farmyard. Their living quarters and utility buildings were correspondingly limited in size and number.

Economic conditions following the Austrian state bankruptcy of 1811 favored producers and ushered in prosperity not only among the Blata farmers but elsewhere as well. The value of land rose sharply, as did also the price of agricultural products. Prices of other commodities and wages, however, registered only slight increases. The location of Komárov near the main connecting routes between

Prague and Vienna made for good marketing opportunities, and the surpluses that the farmers were able to sell brought in more cash than had ever before been the case. The villagers flourished in this situation, using their cash earnings for improvements and rebuilding that extended into the second half of the century.

Another factor indirectly contributing to the changing outlook of the Blata villages was the construction activity in the Austrian capital, which by the middle of the nineteenth century had become quite intensive. The shortage of qualified labor in Vienna attracted many masons, both masters and journeymen, from southern Bohemia for seasonal work from about March to November. In Vienna they learned current techniques of construction and became acquainted with new styles and forms of ornamentation. The experience which these men gained was subsequently applied, according to their individual conceptions and abilities, to the peasant dwellings of southern Bohemia, particularly in such prosperous regions as the Blata. The influence of contemporary urban architecture was especially noticeable in the ornamentations of the Blata farmsteads. For the most part, these decorations were attributable to master masons František Šoch of Zálší (died 1874) and Martin Paták of Vlastiboř (died 1889); it was Šoch who worked in Komárov.

Finally there was the growing sense of pride on the part of the peasant. Having been released from serfdom by the patent of 1781 and freed completely in 1848, he was becoming ever more conscious of his important role in keeping the population of the land supplied with the basic sources of sustenance. This tendency toward self-assurance among the peasantry received its initial impulse from the physiocratic policies of Joseph II, which stressed a sound agricultural economy through governmental nonintervention with natural economic laws as the indispensable foundation of the state.

Thus by the 1860s the physical character of the Blata villages had been completely transformed. Wooden structures gave way to masonry buildings. The gable walls of dwelling units and of granaries faced the village thoroughfare and, together with the connecting wall, were richly stuccoed in rusticized Empire style and the so-called second rococo. The colorful ornamentation contrasted vividly with the whitewashed walls.

The basic plan of the dwelling unit continued to be tripartite, with each of the three parts further subdivided. One entered the entrance hall of the farmhouse from the yard. To the left of the hallway was an area that served as the winter kitchen and as a workroom. In large farmsteads, this room tended to be partitioned lengthwise to provide for a storage area. From here one entered the large front room, which housed the farmer and his wife, its windows facing the village common or thoroughfare. In large farmsteads this room too was subdivided lengthwise, in which case the smaller area became the bedroom for grown daughters or other adults related to the farmer. To the right of the entrance hall were the quarters of the retired farmer. If he or his wife were no longer living, the room was used as sleeping quarters for the help or the farmer's grown children, or as storage space. Like the rest of the rooms, it was divided when the occupants of the farmstead became too numerous. Construction of the black kitchen was discontinued in the 1860s when the space came to be used for cooking during the warm months of the year only.

The utility buildings of the farmstead followed the traditional arrangement.

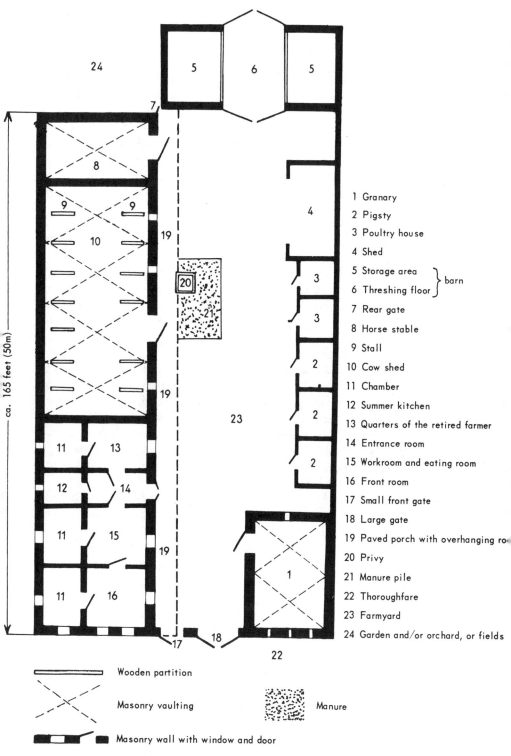

1 Granary
2 Pigsty
3 Poultry house
4 Shed
5 Storage area ⎱
6 Threshing floor ⎰ barn
7 Rear gate
8 Horse stable
9 Stall
10 Cow shed
11 Chamber
12 Summer kitchen
13 Quarters of the retired farmer
14 Entrance room
15 Workroom and eating room
16 Front room
17 Small front gate
18 Large gate
19 Paved porch with overhanging ro
20 Privy
21 Manure pile
22 Thoroughfare
23 Farmyard
24 Garden and/or orchard, or fields

Wooden partition

Masonry vaulting

Manure

Masonry wall with window and door

Figure 4. Typical ground plan, on the same scale, of the buildings and adjacent service areas of a large farm.

The stables were of vaulted brick masonry to make them resistant to fire and space was provided under the roof for the storage of hay. The barn was separated from adjacent buildings by fire-resistant brick walls. Its central portion served as the threshing floor, with a large area on either side providing for storage of straw or unthreshed cereals. Quite often the granary, an independent structure that by this time had grown substantially in size, was decorated more elaborately than even the front of the dwelling unit. It had two or even three floor levels, and because it held the threshed grain as well as other foodstuffs and valuables (money, legal documents, dress clothes, and the like), it was constructed with utmost care and thoroughness. Grain was kept on the upper floor, the remaining supplies and property on the ground floor. In cases of fire, only the roof and its timbers were destroyed, the vaulted spaces of the granary remaining undamaged. The remainder of the front side of the farmstead was enclosed by a wall with the customary two gates. Thus the entire complex was basically three-sided. Four-sided farmsteads were also found occasionally. These were partially open, with the side of the granary fronting the thoroughfare and hiding much of the farmyard from full public view.

On the whole, then, the Blata farmstead was a highly functional unit and, for its time, one of the most efficient peasant establishments to be found anywhere. From an architectural point of view the Blata villages, after the rebuilding around the middle of the past century, were unsurpassed in all of Bohemia and considered among the most attractive in Europe.

Some of the fundamental changes in housing standards also go back a century or more. One important innovation was the so-called Italian flue to replace the black kitchen. Ranges took the place of ovens, and heating stoves furnished with flues became widespread. Both were produced and installed during 1855 to 1911 from the workshop of Josef Lenner of Bechyně, who became so well known throughout southern Bohemia that his stoves and ranges came to bear his name (lenerovky). Ceramic works in Bechyně and Zliv also contributed to the improvement of cooking and heating units in the Blata.

As late as the 1860s, some villagers still obtained light by burning a pinewood torch placed on a special stand in the middle of the room. Subsequently, tallow candles were used, supported by a holder with snuffers attached. Although oil and kerosene lamps provided with glass cylinders and reflecting mirrors began appearing in the Blata villages during the first half of the past century, they did not become standard equipment until the seventies. Such lamps were placed on a table or hung from the ceiling.

An improvement in the housing of the few families of farmhands in Komárov and the nearby estate Hope was effected by a governmental decree of 1906 prohibiting the occupation of one room by more than a single family. Innovations in the interiors of peasant houses were no doubt promoted through the influence of members of the family who became teachers, officials, and the like, or who married into the middle class. But there were also those among the Blata farmers who were becoming aware of the historical value of the traditional furnishings and made every effort to preserve them, if only by donating them to museums. During the 1920s, every family had at least one piece of traditional furniture, usually a wardrobe or a chest, and the main room of about every seventh household was still furnished according to the taste of the past.

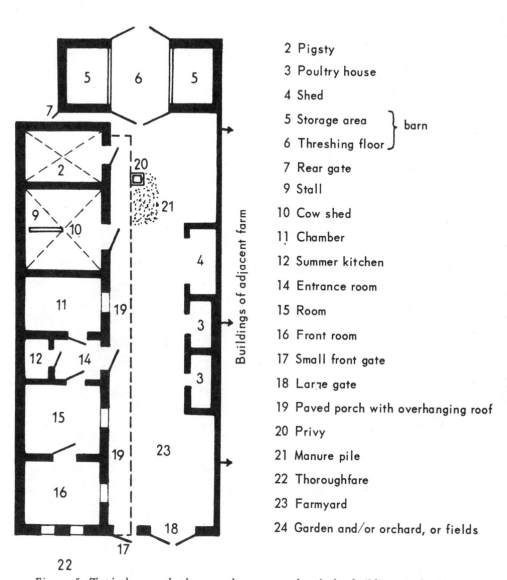

2 Pigsty
3 Poultry house
4 Shed
5 Storage area } barn
6 Threshing floor
7 Rear gate
9 Stall
10 Cow shed
11 Chamber
12 Summer kitchen
14 Entrance room
15 Room
16 Front room
17 Small front gate
18 Large gate
19 Paved porch with overhanging roof
20 Privy
21 Manure pile
22 Thoroughfare
23 Farmyard
24 Garden and/or orchard, or fields

Figure 5. Typical ground plan, on the same scale, of the buildings and adjacent service areas of a small farm.

A traditional arrangement of furniture was the rule through most of the 1920s. In the corner of the main room next to the door and away from the window were the oven and range, and across from them a table with chairs and a corner wall bench. A crucifix customarily hung on the wall near the table. In a third corner a bed made up with a thick layer of bedding served the head of the household and his wife. If there was an infant in the family, it was kept in a cradle beside the bed. Along the wall between the oven and the bed stood a wooden wardrobe for clothes and a painted chest for linens and bedding. Along the oppo-

The front of a newly rebuilt family house in Komárov. (Photograph taken in 1972.)

site wall were a cupboard, a shelf, a weight-driven clock, and a small corner case or other minor pieces of furniture. The remaining members of the family slept in small chambers, the retired farmer and his wife in the room reserved for their use, and the help in the chamber serving as the farmhands' quarters or in the stable (male help) and the loft (female help).

Once the majority of the Blata villages became electrified and provided with telephone connections during 1923, modernization made rapid strides. Laundry rooms, bathrooms, and other installations improving hygiene were built. Old ranges were replaced by electric or gas ranges, and in some houses even central heating made its appearance.

Until the recent introduction of cooperative farming, the efficiency of the Blata farmstead had never come into question. Since then, the farm buildings have been put to only partial use and, as a result, some show visible signs of deterioration. Initially, granaries were used by the cooperative for storage of grains. Since the construction of large new storage facilities, the granaries have been kept largely empty. The utility of the rest of the service buildings is limited to the maintenance and storage of minor equipment and to the housing of the few animals and the keeping of the produce from the small personal plots that are permitted the families of members of cooperatives. Several barns and stables are used by the cooperative, which in lieu of compensation pays the insurance charges on the owners' buildings. As for the remaining barns, today they frequently serve as garages for privately owned cars.

Conspicuous changes in the standard of living began to take place in the 1950s, paralleling the villagers' growing tendency to approximate the city in life-style. These changes reflect postwar technological advances, measured by increasing mechanization. Much of the work of the agricultural cooperative is done in shifts, and consequently the workers have gained more time during the day to spend in their homes than was earlier the case. They have used their increasing prosperity to rebuild and equip the living quarters more comfortably than when their use was limited largely to meals and sleep. The rooms once set aside for retired farmers have been refurbished, and portions of the stable areas have frequently been converted to living quarters, with the result that on the average families now have two more rooms than they had forty years ago. Some farmhouses have in fact been completely rebuilt inside and out.

Another trend was introduced toward the end of the fifties by the spread of television. What used to serve primarily as a kitchen and farmer's bedroom has become a combination kitchen and living room, or simply a living room. The preparation of meals has shifted to one of the small chambers or to the former black kitchen area, adapted to modern standards. Kitchen activities are being made easier with the use of electrical appliances and food storage facilities. The young contemporary housewife in Komárov is no less aided by laborsaving devices than is her metropolitan counterpart in Prague.

One of the chambers now usually serves as private quarters for the head of the family and his wife, as master bedrooms have become popular. The rest of the house is furnished according to family needs and financial means. Among young couples who are starting out, or old couples whose requirements tend to be limited, only the kitchen and living room may be fully set up, the rest of the

Two views of a Komárov farmyard. (Photographs taken in 1972.)

house remaining unfurnished. Modern furniture and decorative complements have completely replaced the traditional setting, which is preserved only among a few old-timers, and not so much out of conservatism as for show.

The overall budget of a household has also undergone substantial changes since the transition to cooperative management. Before 1955, the largest items were expenditures for agricultural machinery and tools, and their maintenance and repair; work done on the farm buildings; commercial fertilizers; additional or new seeds; and items of daily use, clothes and shoes in particular. Among the food supplies, most of the money went for salt, sugar, coffee, and coffee substitute (chicory), spices, and beer. Soap was also purchased in large quantities, but some households were able to boil their own. The farm itself provided the basic foodstuffs. Since 1955, however, expenses for equipment, fertilizers, and other supplies have been eliminated, but repairs and improvements on privately owned family houses are costly. Among the new sources of expenditure are household furnishings and modern appliances, which are also quite expensive. More money is spent for items of personal apparel, care, and adornment, and recreation. This is the inevitable consequence of the ever rising expectations and standard of living of those living in the village.

The prestige of a family today is measured differently than it was prior to the last war. Then it was determined by quality and quantity of livestock, yield of the fields, and the overall equipment of the farmstead and standards of the farming operation, and not by the household itself. Today the criteria are the size and furnishings of living quarters and, of prime importance, the ownership of an automobile, particularly a car of foreign make. Among the furnishings, certain items are considered especially desirable: a refrigerator, television set, modern sectional furniture (whether or not it is put to appropriate use or is suitable in given circumstances), rugs, and armchairs. The condition of the house itself and the appearance of its immediate surroundings are of much less consequence.

Today Komárov, as one of the best preserved regional villages, is the object of ethnohistorical interest for the frequent visitors, who wish to see what the traditional Blata peasant farmhouse was like. For the few remaining old folk of Komárov, some of whom have never quite brought themselves to fully accept the idea of socialist farming cooperatives, the maintenance of the external symbols of the "good old peasant ways" is the only means of personal gratification left to them.

4 / Making a living:
the traditional pattern

Three distinct phases marked the efforts of the Komárov villagers to raise crops and livestock during the last several centuries:

1. the three-field system, from the Middle Ages until about the middle of the past century;
2. crop rotation, or intensive farming, from the middle of the past century until the mid-1950s;
3. socialist cooperative farming, from 1955 onward.

The three-field system, which came into general use early during the feudal period, was geared to an essentially subsistence-oriented production; whatever meager surpluses existed were taken to market in the nearby towns. The fragmented nature of the peasant-cultivated fields did not further the development of sizable marketing centers and as a result the villages remained in relative economic isolation. Fundamentally each farm was a separate production unit where small quantities of a variety of crops were grown, making the farming operation barely economical while requiring a great expenditure of labor. For the most part this situation persisted into the first half of the nineteenth century, although large landowners in the nobility began to adopt more progressive methods of production as they converted their enterprises to intensive farming.

However, some changes began to take place in the peasant villages after the lessening of the labor obligation toward the end of the eighteenth century and also in response to the growing demand for food resulting from the Napoleonic Wars at the beginning of the nineteenth. During this incipient transformation of the Bohemian farming village, crop specialization (mainly rye and wheat in the Blata) and the employment of seasonal hired help, drawn largely from among the farming families with small landholdings, helped to strengthen the economic position of the larger peasants.

What meager information there is concerning the three-field system of land cultivation has to be gleaned from written sources. Under the system the lands of individual farmers and of the community as a whole were divided into three sections—one to be sown in the spring, one in autumn (the winter crop), and one to be left fallow. To the fallow section all of the livestock owned by the local farmers were brought for pasturing. The basic idea underlying the three-field system was to rotate the three sections on an annual basis in order to permit the soil to replenish its resources each third year.

On the sections to be planted, both the spring crop and the winter crop con-sisted of cereal grasses. The farmlands set aside for the winter crop customarily were sown in full with wheat and rye to insure the farmers a means of subsistence. The spring crop was frequently divided among barley, oats, and other plants— peas, flax, beets, hemp, and others—depending on the use made of the fallow or on the prevailing demand for oats or barley. In later times, probably from the seventeenth century onward, a sizable portion of the fallow was sown with secondary crops—peas, vetch (a soil-building plant valuable for fodder), hemp, flax, buckwheat, cabbage, and the like. These secondary crops helped restore the soil by loosening it, stifling the weeds, and enriching it with green manure (an herbaceous crop plowed under while green to enrich the soil). Peas were con-sidered particularly useful for this purpose. It was necessary, however, to take care not to unduly restrict the grazing cattle, whose dung helped fertilize the ground. Portable fences were frequently used to prevent the cattle from trampling the sown portions.

If the three-field system was to work, it is obvious that each individual farmer had to be willing to give up his right to decide what and where to sow on his own land. Complete cooperation was an absolute necessity. The division into three sections was approximate. The primary criterion was the full exploitation of the total land area within the limits of specific local conditions.

An important innovation during this phase was the introduction of the potato for consumption. Even though potatoes did not enter common use until after the starvation suffered during the Seven Years' War (1756–1763), they quickly became a basic component of the diet not only among the peasants but among the city dwellers as well. Besides that, they served as important feed for pigs and poultry and as raw material for distilleries.

The joint grazing of cattle, pigs, and sheep was a necessity and required the full-time services of one or several village employees. Livestock were in pasture from early spring until the first snow. During the early spring they grazed in the young meadows, later on the fallow ground, village pastureland, or cleared hayfields, and after harvest on the stubble. Grazing was also permitted in the woods, but the damage to underwood and forest clearings was considerable. The result was that the use of forests for pasture was progressively restricted by law, and in the middle of the eighteenth century prohibited altogether except for the forest owner and the foresters in his employ, who were partially exempt. Further-more, regulations came to require fences to be constructed or mended each year before Saint George's Day (April 24) to prevent destruction of growing young plants.

Prior to the second half of the nineteenth century, meadowing was not very highly developed. Cattle grazed from spring until the first snow and required little or no additional fodder. Only after the introduction of intensive farming was it necessary to feed cattle until the first hay was available. In order to fatten the cattle and increase the yield of milk, feed was supplemented with chaff, the rakings from the threshing floor, straw, dried pea plants, bran, pollard, and certain kinds of grain—oats, barley, and rye of inferior quality. Because of their value, however, grains were used only when other food was in very short supply.

Sheep were a particularly important part of the three-field system. They required less fodder than the cattle, managed well on the most modest pastureland until wintertime, and yielded more rapid returns to their owner. Furthermore, extensive farming depended heavily on the sheep's manuring of the ground. But even for sheep there had to be winter fodder—dried pea and lentil leaves, barley straw, wheat chaff, and especially hay. After milking of sheep was discontinued during the eighteenth century, the main product of sheep raising was wool. Shearing was done twice a year: in the spring at the time the moon was waxing, as it was believed that the wool would then grow rapidly; and in the autumn, when the moon was waning, so that the wool would grow slowly. Stud rams were permitted to cover the females one or two weeks before Saint Michael's Day (September 29) in order for the lambs to be sufficiently strong for spring pasture. Young rams were generally gelded at Easter by a shepherd, but many farmers knew how to geld as well.

The transition to intensive farming during the second half of the past century was an inevitable consequence of technological advancement, more particularly the introduction of commercial fertilizers and more efficient farm implements, which facilitated a far greater utilization of the soil. Agricultural production, in Komárov and elsewhere, became oriented toward the sale of surpluses in a growing number of urban markets. Livestock, which formerly had been kept by the peasants largely for their own consumption and as a source of power, also became a market commodity. For example, at the beginning of the present century, the supply of pigs for the Soběslav market came primarily from Komárov farmers, some of whom kept as many as seven sows for breeding purposes.

For the Blata, the introduction of intensive farming constituted an innovation that profoundly affected the whole structure of its economy and was responsible for a great many changes in the traditional ways of the villages. The raising of livestock shifted from the outdoors to the stables, necessitating the construction of large stable areas to insure increased standards of cleanliness. The extent of the new enterprise called for more adequate storage of winter fodder and its protection from dampness and spoilage as well as from spontaneous ignition. It was further necessary to arrange the storage areas in such a way as to facilitate convenient unloading of fodder in the fall and the withdrawing of it during the winter.

The management of meadows and pastures likewise required a great many new techniques. Meadows had to be drained by ditches and pipes or, alternately, irrigated. During the spring and fall they needed regular clearing of molehills, rocks, and pieces of thick sod and had to be strewn with additional manure when necessary. Old meadows had to be periodically replowed and resown, acid and mossy ones brought under cultivation, and much pastureland converted into meadowland.

The feed base used during summertime was referred to as "artificial," a term subsuming clover, alfalfa, and sainfoin (a forage herb). These plants were known as early as the first half of the eighteenth century, but did not enter into general use until a century later. They were fed to the livestock fresh, or they were dried for winter use. Preserving of feed with salt in casks was done among some of the farmers who had attended the agricultural school in Tábor. The increasing use of clover brought about intensive production of clover seed, which was in great demand commercially.

With the fallow discontinued, the fields required intensive manuring. Since commercial fertilizers were not available in the Blata during much of the nineteenth century (and the local peasants were a long time in overcoming their suspicions of them even after such fertilizers became available), both solid and liquid manure had to be carefully preserved. The only fertilizer in the Blata region other than that generated in the farmyard or the green-manure crops was peat, which had been used during the three-field system. Intensive farming considerably increased the farmers' yields and consequently called for the construction of more spacious barns and granaries. The raising of sheep came to a stop as a result of the disappearance of the fallow and pastureland and also, beginning in the second half of the nineteenth century, due to the competition from foreign producers of wool, especially Australian wool, which was both cheap and of good quality.

The division of labor among the farmer, his wife, their children, and the farmhands became even more sharply drawn. During the period when farming was characterized by intensive rotation of crops, specific kinds of work were distributed to each member of the farm.

The farmer was responsible for the overall organization of work for the farm as a whole, with the exception of those activities under the authority of the farmwife. More specifically, his duties included:

1. all the basic tasks associated with the cultivation of the fields: preparing the soil (plowing, harrowing, fertilizing, plowing under), sowing, reaping, plowing under stubble, bringing crops home from the fields, and threshing (manually and later by means of machine);
2. the basic tasks associated with cultivating meadows and growing fodder plants: preparing the soil, fertilizing, sowing, haymaking, and harvesting of fodder plants;
3. the basic tasks associated with the tending of livestock: cleaning of stables and cowsheds, including the removal of dung, as well as the treatment of animals for diseases and injuries;
4. the maintenance and repair of farm implements and the manufacture of some of the simple tools or their parts: for example, the care of handles, scythe cradles, and swiples, the resewing of leather bindings on flails, and the like, unless the work required was too specialized;
5. the repair of utility buildings and living quarters and their furnishings, unless the services of specialized craftsmen were required.

The farmer's subsidiary activities, often reflecting his personal inclinations, included:

1. beekeeping, rabbit raising, pigeon breeding, fish-farming and maintenance of ponds;
2. work in the woods if the farmer's land included a forested area or if he purchased standing timber;
3. cutting of peat (only by small farmers and farming cottagers), and tending of fruit trees;
4. assistance with the upkeep of the household: large purchases, whitewashing of structural surfaces, and painting of woodwork;
5. hauling of loads for neighbors without horses or for the forest management;

6. representation in civil or private transactions (for example, sales or purchases), public and official village functions, and cultural, religious, and social activities except for those considered exclusively the domain of the farmwife.

The farmwife's responsibilities were designated with equal specificity. They included:

1. the preparation of meals and the upkeep of the household, including cleaning and shopping, and the care of the children;
2. the basic tasks associated with the care of livestock: the milking of cows as well as helping with the cleaning of stables, the tending of poultry and pigs, and the handling of milk and the production of dairy items;
3. the manufacture and repair of clothes, linens, and textile furnishings by sewing, crotcheting, knitting, and the like, and their decoration with embroidery or appliqué; until the 1880s, the spinning of vegetable and animal fibers (flax, hemp, and wool) and the basic activities associated with the cultivation of flax and hemp;
4. the tending of the vegetable and flower gardens; the plucking of geese and ducks and the stripping of feathers; and assistance with assorted tasks around the farmstead;
5. auxiliary tasks, and occasionally even some of the basic ones connected with the cultivation of the fields and meadows: spreading of manure and later the application of commercial fertilizers, sheaving and shocking, helping with the loading, hauling, and unloading of the harvest, threshing by hand and later by machine; and turning and drying of hay and fodder plants and helping to carry them to the farmyard;
6. organization and supervision of the work done by the female help in the domains under her supervision;
7. representation in community social, cultural, and religious activities analogous to those involving the farmer, particularly in legal proceedings such as inheritance matters and the like.

Grown offspring, similarly, had their areas of responsibility. Adult daughters helped with all tasks normally assumed by the farmwife, as well as with care of younger siblings. Adult sons living at home were responsible for all tasks normally assumed by the farmer whenever he was unable to attend to any of the duties or activities expected of him, provided the jurisdiction of the farmwife was not encroached upon. If adult sons were away from home for study, they assisted during vacations or holidays with whatever activities were called for at the time, particularly at harvest.

Children were expected to assist with household and field chores and the care of livestock, orchard, and garden, depending on age and sex. Specifically, boys helped with cultivating the soil, producing crops, raising livestock, running errands, and managing the farm; girls were kept busy with housekeeping activities and the various other duties and responsibilities expected of them as future farmwives.

Retired farmers who had made over their land to their heirs, but still reserved some portion for their own use, were expected to lend help during periods of peak activity, subject, of course, to their physical ability. At the least, they and their wives were expected at harvesttime to watch over small children, prepare meals, and keep an eye on the farmstead in general while all other members of the farmstead capable of such work were harvesting in the fields. At other times, an old farmer kept busy with beekeeping, caring for the vegetable garden and fruit trees, and looking after goslings, turkey chicks, and the like. His wife spent much of her time sewing or embroidering (and also spinning during the last century), stripping feathers, and helping with light tasks that would otherwise have kept the farmwife from more important or more difficult duties.

Male farmhands rendered assistance with all the tasks of the farmer. Whenever there were two farmhands, the older—the so-called plowman (*oráč*)—assumed the more responsible tasks while the younger hand, primarily a stableboy (*pacholek, pohůnek*), performed auxiliary tasks according to his ability and experience.

Female farmhands assisted the farmwife. Here, too, whenever two maidservants were present, the senior of the two (*staršinka*) was charged with more responsibility than was the junior (*mladšinka*).

Among the farming cottagers, who could ill afford hired help, the duties of the husband and wife were not as strictly divided as they were among the larger farmers. And in times of emergency or illness, their children were expected to assume an added measure of responsibility.

In addition to permanent farm workers, there were often others who were hired for peak periods during the summer months or for short-term nonroutine jobs. Itinerant handicraftsmen—tinkers, castraters, peatmen, and others—were engaged whenever their appearance in Komárov coincided with the need for their specialized services.

Running chores included daily care of all livestock. Cattle had to be fed three times each day, looked after, and milked; horses curried; sheep taken to pasture (true only for the 1860s to 1880s) or turned over to the care of a shepherd; the hogs looked after and fed three times a day; hens fed with grain or other feed twice a day, and so on. Also among the running chores were the preparation of meals and the daily upkeep of living quarters, as well as all personal care and grooming.

Besides the running chores, the work of the year consisted of peak, preparatory, auxiliary, and exceptional activities, and of a period of relative inactivity.

Peak activities included:

1. in springtime, field chores during March and April, and even through early May after a particularly long winter: for example, the preparation of fields for cultivation, the actual sowing and planting, clearing of meadows, and the like;
2. in June, haymaking: cutting, curing by drying, hauling to the barn, and storing there;
3. during the second half of July and all of August, harvesting: mowing, drying, hauling, storing, and—after the introduction of threshing machines —threshing (a steam-driven threshing machine made its appearance in Komárov in 1911);
4. in August and September, harvesting of aftergrass and potatoes;
5. in September until as late as the end of October, autumn chores: clearing and preparation of fields for the winter crop and for grain sown in the spring, cultivation of meadows, and the like.

The busiest and most important peak period came at harvest, and large farmers regularly arranged for additional help then. Farming cottagers were willing to assist at harvest in exchange for services rendered them during the year by their richer neighbors (such as plowing their fields), and farmhands were engaged for board, room, and meager compensation. In Komárov itself, only the three largest farmers employed hired help, though not on a permanent basis.

Preparatory tasks included readying tools for the peak period, making binders from straw or cord for tying sheaves, selecting seed for sowing and potato sets for planting, and the like.

Considered among the auxiliary chores were all activities associated with the orchard, vegetable and flower garden, the cutting of peat, the sale or purchase of livestock, and the purchase of necessary tools. In addition, during late summer some members of the farm family went to gather mushrooms or other forest produce for their own use or for sale. Until 1928, merchant middlemen came periodically to Komárov to buy mushrooms. Whortleberries are being bought to the present day. Family members of the farming cottagers also collected cones and brushwood for fuel. All of these tasks were carried out during periods of less intensive work or when there was little else to do.

Among the exceptional chores were helping with the foaling of mares and the farrowing of sows, preparing feasts in connection with the butchering of a pig, and, more importantly, arranging for such occasions in the life cycles of community members as weddings, christenings, and funerals, all of which required extraordinary efforts. Whenever possible these were planned in advance so as not to fall in the peak season; nevertheless, a sudden death or severe illness could disrupt the steady course of farm activities and more frequently than not caused an inordinate work load. Because of the established division of labor and the skills which members of the farmstead acquired, each individual knew exactly what to do and how to proceed in any and all situations. If an emergency arose, as a rule no special instructions were necessary to bring matters under complete control.

The period of relative inactivity fell during winter. At that time, all of the auxiliary chores that could not be accomplished during the rest of the year were completed. Many of the cultural, social, legal, and other activities commonly occurred during the winter. Among them were carnival festivities, meetings of village organizations and of the community council, business deals, and weddings —the latter by far the most ambitious undertaking in an individual's life. The farmer spent a good deal of time repairing tools or manufacturing new ones, and the farmwife gave special attention to the condition of her family's wardrobe, repairing it or adding to it as necessary.

Among the regular days of relative inactivity were Sundays and holidays. The great majority of the Komárov population were earnestly practicing Roman Catholics and, with few exceptions, days set aside by the Church for special worship were strictly observed. Members of farmsteads worked on Sundays or holidays only under the most extraordinary circumstances—before an approaching storm or threat of hail, or in the event of a sudden clear day after a series of rainy days that had prevented urgent work in the fields. These practices did not change substantially even after World War I, although religious observances relaxed noticeably.

The daily schedule varied somewhat according to the season. During the peak agricultural period, members of the household rose about four in the morning and were in bed by ten in the evening. The men had their breakfast and, after gathering the necessary tools, left for the fields, where they remained all day. Quite commonly they first helped with tending the livestock before going out to the fields and again after returning in the evening, chores customarily handled by the male farmhands. The female members tended the livestock and milked the cows three times daily. The farmwife, sometimes with the assistance of a maid or an older daughter, prepared a simple midday meal and later a light evening meal. The noon meal was delivered to the fields unless the men were working close to the farmhouse; in that case, they returned home for the short time needed to eat. Snacks were eaten both at midmorning and midafternoon. These were either taken along to the fields by the men, or an older child or maid was sent from the field to get them.

A typical day during the period of auxiliary chores and relative inactivity was somewhat more leisurely. Household members got up about five during the summer and about six during the winter. By ten at night everyone was in bed unless some special social activity was taking place—for example, feather stripping in one of the households or a dance in the inn, either of which was likely to last until midnight. The menfolk helped with tending the livestock three times a day and otherwise worked at the tasks they knew best, according to the disposition of the farmer. The farmer himself frequently devoted the afternoon to affairs not directly connected with the farm such as meetings with other farmers in the village inn to discuss matters of mutual concern or to plan special activities. The female members observed a similar schedule. When necessary, farmhands had an afternoon free to take care of pressing personal needs. Saturday afternoon was free from work.

On Sundays and holidays the household was stirring by six during the summer, and at least by seven during the winter. Bedtime depended on the day's activity, but was usually later than on weekdays. Everyone helped with the livestock, the work being done faster and more superficially than on other days, partly because a thorough cleaning of stables and cow sheds occurred every Saturday. The women did the milking. The farmer and his wife customarily attended the early morning mass at eight, while the children and the farmhands attended the sung mass with a sermon at nine thirty or ten o'clock. In the afternoon it was the custom for everyone to attend vespers. Except for attendance at these two services, the day was free, and household members entertained themselves according to age, sex, or individual interest.

The typical meals of the Komárov villagers at the beginning of the century were simple: soup thickened with browned flour or milk soup for breakfast; soup and dumplings with cabbage, sauerkraut, or apples, or a local variety of scones or pancakes for lunch; and cabbage soup and potatoes for dinner. A snack in the fields consisted of beer and bread with butter and honey. On Sundays there was coffee with milk and bread or fluffy buns with sweet filling in the morning, and for the main meal poultry in summer and occasionally meat from a butchered pig during winter. By comparison, meals today are a great deal richer and more varied, with meats playing a much larger part. Pork roast with dumplings and sauerkraut is a favorite, as are also goose and duck. Other common meals are sauerbraten, beef roast or stew, and goulash. Older people prefer soups and poultry or veal.

Until the 1870s, farming activities were performed manually with simple implements—plows, harrows, rollers, scythes, sickles, rakes, forks, and flails. The villages of the Blata were among those that used a simple regional type of plow. The furrow it made was shallow—two or three inches at the most. About the middle of the past century this simple plow began to be replaced by a more efficient type invented in eastern Bohemia in 1827. Provided with a curved iron mouldboard, it not only turned over the soil but mixed it as well. The older regional plow, however, was retained into the present century for specific purposes, particularly the cultivating of potatoes.

The original wooden harrow disappeared in Komárov apparently as early as the middle of the nineteenth century and was replaced by an iron one, which was used until recently. The iron harrow consisted of four bars to a section, with two or three sections joined together. As far back as people can remember, mowing was done with scythes. The older type of scythe was one with a cradle consisting of five rods, joined with a spring. The grain harvested in this manner was left lying in swathes on the ground for two or three days before it was bound in sheaves and set up individually. The disadvantage of the method was that it was necessary to turn the swathes over during rainy weather, and the sheaves had to be rebound. During the fifties and sixties of the past century, wooden forks were replaced by iron ones, and cradle scythes by ordinary scythes. The sheaves came to be made up into shocks of six to eight sheaves each, and cattle were put into a collar yoke instead of the earlier yoke attached to the animal's forehead.

The mechanization of farming began in the 1870s with threshing machines, first driven manually by two strong men and later propelled by one of the draft animals. Mowing and sowing machines and cultivators came into use in the 1880s and 1890s. As a rule several farmers joined together to purchase a threshing machine, which would be moved from one farmyard to another. Use of the machine was decided according to prior agreement or the amount of individual investment. All grain was threshed at one time and stored in the granary. (In earlier times it had been the custom to thresh portion by portion during the entire winter.) Until about the 1950s there were no further technical advances of basic importance, although small improvements continued to be made; as a result the farmer's work load was progressively lightened. For the villages of the Blata region, the main suppliers of farming machinery were factories located in Tábor and Pelhřimov. After World War I, horses or oxen as sources of mechanical power for farm machines were replaced by engines powered by gasoline or diesel fuel, and from 1923 onward electricity provided yet another source of energy.

Cows were not used as draft animals in the Blata region. To draw loads, farmers used teams of horses, while farming cottagers used yokes of oxen. Because it

A roller, called a "hedgehog" (ježek), *used until World War II to crush clods in the fields.*

was not economically sound for smaller farmers to maintain a team, it was usually arranged for their fields to be plowed by a farmer who had horses. To compensate the owner of horses for plowing and also for hauling their harvest home from the fields, small farmers gave assistance during the peak season.

Farming in the Blata was of a high standard. Undoubtedly this was the legacy of some of the South Bohemian landowning nobility like the Paars, who managed their holdings wisely, seeing to it that they prospered and that tenants kept abreast of agricultural developments. Village heads, who in feudal times represented the lords, were kept informed through meetings held at the castle, and priests were urged to call new farming methods to their parishioners' attention. The farmers were generally receptive to new ideas.

In 1870 an agricultural school was opened in Tábor, with provision made for a winter course of study. In the villages of the Blata the majority of farmers' sons finished at least this winter course. While it was true that some farmers sent their sons to agricultural school as a matter of prestige rather than out of concern for agricultural progress, and that the sons, who were well aware of their fathers' purposes, did not always apply themselves to their studies with any great seriousness, the school nevertheless left its mark on them. Again because of the desire for prestige, less progressive farmers made it a point to keep up with those who were sincerely interested in improving farming practices. Finally, there was the financial incentive: it was easy to see that investments in mechanized equipment (threshing and mowing machines and generators), livestock of high quality,

Figure 6. Regional type of plow commonly used in the Blata until the middle of the past century. (From Československá vlastivěda, Vol. III, p. 31.)

and better varieties of grain and other crops soon paid for themselves many times over.

Although it is impossible to arrive at the actual profits realized by individual farmers, a reconstruction based on the recollection of old-timers and available farming surveys may be of interest. The profits of a Komárov farm came from three sources: field crops (in particular, rye, wheat, barley, clover seed, and potatoes, and to a lesser degree fodder and oats); animal production (cattle, hogs, poultry, eggs, geese, and ducks); and dairy products (milk, cream, butter, and cottage cheese). Other income, from such sources as honey, skins, goose down, and pigeons, was negligible. The farmwife kept the proceeds from the dairy products, eggs, poultry, geese, and ducks; income from all other sources was the farmer's. The earnings of the farmwife amounted to about 20 percent of the total gross income from the farm.

Table 4 shows income of Bohemian farmers for the last 120 years to be as follows: after the middle of the nineteenth century, profits rose steeply as a consequence of the transition to intensive farming employing crop rotation. The trend reached its peak in the 1880s. In 1882 the importation into Europe of large surpluses of grain from the United States and Canada brought about a

TABLE 4. BOHEMIAN FARMERS' APPROXIMATE NET PROFIT PER HECTARE
(2.47 ACRES) FROM 1860 TO 1940.

Year	Profit
1860–1870	30–40 K (Austrian *kronen*)[1]
1880	200–240 K
1900	200 K
1914	210 K
1920	2000–2200 Kč (Czechoslovak *koruny*, pl., approximately equal to 210 K)
1930	2500 Kč
1935	1000–1500 Kč
1940[2]	2000 K (Czech *koruny*)

[1] Approximate value equivalents, based on the cost of food and clothing, are as follows: 1 Austrian K = ca. 10 Kč of the First (Czechoslovak) Republic (1918–1938) = ca. 15 K of the Protectorate currency = ca. U.S. $1.00.
[2] This was at the time of the German occupation during the Protectorate of Bohemia and Moravia.

considerable decline in prices of agricultural products, and as a result profits diminished and stagnation set in, which lasted until the beginning of the present century. From that time on there was once again an upswing until the economic crisis of 1929–1935. During both world wars, when the agricultural labor force was substantially reduced, it was necessary to deliver the required quotas at low prices; at the same time it was impossible to make repairs properly, and many raw materials were unavailable, commercial fertilizers in particular. However, high prices on the black market offset the otherwise unfavorable situation for the farmer, who sold to people in the cities, where agricultural products were in very scarce supply. As a result, many farms at last became free of oppressive debts and mortgages.

Other than farming, the only source of production carried on in the Blata region was the cutting of peat, either in peat bogs privately owned or in bogs that belonged to the large landowners and were leased to individual farmers. Assignments were made for a small fee on a "first come, first served" basis (and occasionally for a small bribe given to the official in charge of the assignments). Until the end of the 1940s peat cutting was done manually, usually by the farmhands and the older children of the farmer or, among the farming cottagers, by the man himself or his wife. Convenient times for working in the bogs were between the spring activities and May haymaking, and between haymaking and harvest, beginning during the first half of July. Professional peat-cutters worked for the large landowners and on occasion for the very large farmers. The cutters, for the most part single young farmhands, used a narrow spade to cut the peat into narrow blocks, which they threw out from the peat bank. The work is still remembered as having been exceptionally strenuous. Others, primarily girls, placed the blocks of peat on the ground in long rows. When they had dried a bit they were stacked into conical heaps and allowed to dry completely. Peat

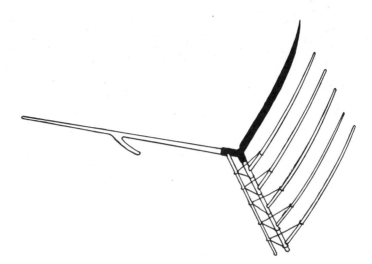

Figure 7. Reconstruction of a cradle scythe of the type used in the Blata region until a century ago. Materials were iron, wood, and hemp twine or bast cord.

Blocks cut from the peat banks are placed in long rows to dry. (Photograph taken in 1956.)

was then used at fuel for the household or as litter, fertilizer, or insulating material, and sometimes for therapeutic purposes. On occasion it was sold to industrial plants.

Today peat bogs are nationalized, and peat is obtained solely on an industrial basis for balneological purposes (baths for medical therapy in Třeboň) and in gardening. About five adults from Komárov now have permanent jobs in the industrial mining of peat.

The traditional pattern of earning a livelihood in Komárov was by no means an easy one. However, the farmers derived satisfaction from knowing through their own experience that the land was generous, the climate benevolent, and that hard work brought good results. A great many changes have occurred during the last two decades under the socialist cooperative management. Yet, except for the several difficult years marking the transition to a system that was without precedent, the villagers have accepted the break with their economic past as inevitable, and Komárov continues to enjoy its usual measure of prosperity.

5 / Making a living:
the socialist cooperative

In Komárov the changeover to cooperative farming took place in 1955, six years after the adoption in Czechoslovakia of the Unified Agricultural Co-operatives Act on February 23, 1949. Initially the farming villagers joined a "Phase I" cooperative—that is, they began to organize the main work in the fields on a collective basis and to pool vehicles and machinery, but they did not plough up field boundaries or consolidate the farmland and livestock they owned. Then, in 1960, the organization of the cooperative was changed to "Phase III." At this point private tenure of agricultural land was virtually abolished and joint pro-duction of crops and of livestock instituted.

Collectivization marked the beginning of Komárov's integration into the agroindustrial complex of the state-run national economy. The conversion from individual private ownership to the unified agricultural cooperative (*jednotné zemědělské družstvo*, or *JZD*) system of management brought about a distinct change in the life-style of the Komárov villagers as well as in the structure of the community as a whole. The transformation was not accomplished without some sharp pains.

Seventeen years later, as of the beginning of 1973, the Komárov Unified Agricultural Cooperative and the cooperatives of some dozen other communities to the east and northeast were joined together to become the new, large Unified Agricultural Cooperative "Victorious February," commemorating February 1948, when the Communist party emerged from a governmental crisis in complete control of Czechoslovakia. The new consolidated cooperative, which also includes the Blata villages of Svinky and Záluží, is administered from nearby Vlastiboř. In the official view, greater efficiency is expected to result from this new arrangement, which will eliminate some duplication and promote partial specialization of individual villages.

Komárov, for instance, is to concentrate on the keeping of brood sows, while other villages will devote themselves to cows, poultry, and so on. Komárov's crop production, on the other hand, will continue essentially as before. A valid assess-ment of the advantages and/or disadvantages of the consolidated cooperative to its Komárov members cannot be made at the time of this writing, since the period of adjustment has so recently begun. The description that follows, there-fore, applies primarily to the operation of the Komárov Unified Agricultural Cooperative (1955–1972).

In line with the countrywide pattern, the establishment of the local unified agricultural cooperative required that the farmers bring in with them all of their land and livestock, and also their farm machinery, implements, and utility buildings if the cooperative needed them. Records of individual transactions were kept for future compensation, this to be based on the original assessment, or for use if a farmer later decided to leave the cooperative or was expelled from it (neither has ever occurred in Komárov). By 1975, 80 percent of the assessed value of livestock and machinery, subject to the financial ability of the cooperative, is to be repaid to those farmers whose original landholdings were below 10 hectares (ca. 25 acres). Strictly speaking, the land owned by the farmers has remained their property, but all decisions concerning its use are made by the cooperative. Forestland belonging to the village came under the state forest administration. Living quarters remained in the personal possession of those who owned and occupied them, as did utility buildings for which the cooperative had no urgent use.

At the very beginning of the transition to cooperative management the three largest Komárov farmers were evicted from their farmsteads without compensation and branded as kulaks—members of the rural bourgeoisie bent on exploiting the landless or the small farmers. Prosperous though these peasants were, the rest of the villagers had never considered them anything but wealthier members of the community, and the official wrath directed against them was largely due to their reluctance to cooperate with the efforts to collectivize. All three farmers, together with their families, were moved from the village, resettled, and then given menial agricultural work assignments. Their Komárov farmsteads have remained uninhabited but are utilized by the cooperative. One farm houses a clubroom for the government-sponsored cultural youth organization in a portion of the former living quarters, and about thirty head of cattle are kept in the utility buildings. The second farmstead has been converted into offices for the cooperative, with the service area used as a pig-feeding station, and the third has served as a place for keeping brood sows and storing their feed.

The consequences of standing in the way of collectivization were not lost upon the other villagers, and only two farming cottagers, each with about 2 hectares (5 acres) of land, waited until the early 1960s to join. All in all, the Komárov Unified Agricultural Cooperative was set up with no special difficulties, but with even less enthusiasm on the part of the peasants. The economic prospects for the villagers under the new agricultural regime appeared to be bleak.

An organizational chart of a typical unified agricultural cooperative is given below. In large cooperatives some of the highly specialized professional functions are further differentiated, while in small cooperatives, such as the Komárov enterprise through 1972, some of the supervisory positions are often combined. In all cases prime responsibility rests on the chairman, who directs the day-to-day activities of the entire cooperative, subject to the general guidelines decided upon in the periodic meetings of the membership. Between these gatherings the chairman works with the management committee, which acts as the executive arm of the membership.

The board of auditors, management committee, and the chairman of a unified agricultural cooperative are elected by the membership to serve a term of at least two years. Other positions of responsibility are filled by appointment. Membership in the Communist party, or at least a strong commitment to collectivism,

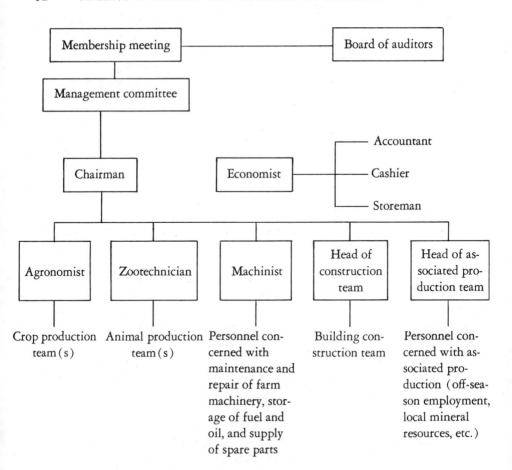

ORGANIZATIONAL CHART OF A TYPICAL UNIFIED
AGRICULTURAL COOPERATIVE.

has been the necessary prerequisite for holding a responsible function, particularly in the initial period of socialist cooperative management.

The work of a cooperative proceeds according to a production schedule and financial plan drawn up in advance for a period of one calendar year, and is coordinated with the overall state economic plan. The seasonal character of crop production and the potential effects of unpreventable forces of nature upon it require continued periodic monitoring of how well the goals are being attained.

The system of remuneration has undergone considerable evolution over the years and can be presented here only in its most basic outline. Underlying it is the principle that the members of a cooperative must have a collective stake in the overall results of their activities and thus an incentive to hard work. Consequently, compensation for the same work is not necessarily identical in individual cooperatives but, in general, is proportionate to annual productivity. The basis for remuneration is a production or output norm, which is measured by the "work unit" (*pracovní jednotka*). An output norm stipulates the quantity (in hectares, quintals, pieces, and so on) to be achieved in a given time, usually one shift, or the amount of time necessary for the accomplishment of a specific task by an individual worker or team. All jobs are described and categorized uniformly for all cooperatives according to the complexity, responsibility, and physical effort involved. In general, work assignments in crop production are classified within the job category range of 2 through 5, those in animal production 3 through 5, and those filled by tractorists and other specialized workers within categories 4 through 6. Monetary compensation equals the product of the work units earned, the tariff coefficient of the corresponding job category, and the basic rate of pay per unit in crowns (Kčs).

For example, the loading of approximately one long ton (ten quintals) of hay onto a wagon was rated in the Komárov Unified Agricultural Cooperative at 0.6 work units per load. An additional worker—usually a woman—who was situated on top of the wagon to arrange the loaded hay, earned the same amount. The worker who did the loading also drove the wagon of hay from the field to the village, and for this he was credited with 0.1 work units per trip. In the scale of job categories, all of these efforts were assigned to the fourth category, with a tariff coefficient of 1.25. For five times the amount of work described above, the worker who did both the loading and the hauling was credited with (0.6 + 0.1) × 5 × 1.25, or 4.375 work units. If each work unit was compensated at, say, 10 Kčs, his remuneration for the job amounted to 43.75 Kčs.

During the 1960s, the original scale of seven job categories was replaced in most cases by a six-step scale. Below are the tariff coefficients for this new scale:

Job category	1	2	3	4	5	6
Tariff coefficient	1.00	1.10	1.25	1.45	1.70	2.00

For example, the sowing of cereal grains with a team of horses is classified on the six-step scale as being in the third job category. The output norm is set at 5 hectares, and the compensation amounts to 1.25 work units (one work unit times the tariff coefficient). Accordingly the rate per hectare amounts to $1.25 \div 5 = 0.25$ work units.

The system of remuneration takes a number of different forms, the choice being guided by the specific circumstances of individual cooperatives and the need to provide an incentive toward greater output on the part of the workers. Among the forms of remuneration the basic and most important is one designed to reflect the results achieved—that is, both the quantity and quality of the work performed. But there are situations in which workers must be paid according to the time they spend on the job. In such cases provisions for an efficiency bonus are frequently built in, and these tend to offset the intrinsic drawbacks of timework.

How much a member of a cooperative is actually paid for each work unit, limited of course by the overall schedules set by the state, depends on the economic results achieved by a cooperative during a particular year. In the Komárov cooperative, the basic monetary compensation in 1955 amounted to 4 Kčs per unit, fluctuating in subsequent years to the following amounts:

1956: 8 Kčs
1957: 10 Kčs
1958: 11 Kčs
1959: 8 Kčs

Each member of the cooperative had to pay about 2 percent of his gross wages toward his health insurance and retirement plan, and an average of about 10 percent in wage tax, according to the number of dependents and amount of earnings.

In 1960 all social premiums were assumed by the cooperative, but even so the monetary value of the work unit in Komárov continued to increase:

1960: 13 Kčs
1961: 14 Kčs
1962: 15 Kčs
1963: 18 Kčs
1964: 19 Kčs
1966: 20 Kčs
1967: 21 Kčs
1968: 23 Kčs
1969: 25 Kčs
1970: 26 Kčs
1971: 33 Kčs
1972: 28 Kčs

In fact, for the year 1971 Komárov ranked among the highest-paying (30 Kčs or more per work unit) 16 percent of unified agricultural cooperatives in the Czech Socialist Republic. The drop in 1972 was due to administrative and organizational complications that came about as the Komárov enterprise began anticipating its inclusion in the consolidated cooperative.

One reason for the upward climb during the past fifteen or so years was the need to offset the rising cost of living resulting from increased prices for services, clothing, and selected industrial products. Despite the official figures, based on countrywide statistics, indicating that the consumer price index rose by only a little more than 10 percent for members of cooperatives, there is reason to believe that the actual differential was somewhat higher. However, it was probably quite a bit less than the subjectively felt 50 percent claimed by some consumers.

Among other factors contributing to the upward trend of the value of the work unit were increased productivity, the substitution of cash payments for compensation in kind, the partial liberalization of marketing that occurred in the latter part of the 1960s, and the effort to stem a continuing sharp decline in the agricultural population. On the whole the later wage schedules were clearly an improvement over those of the initial years, and the attitude of the Komárov villagers toward the cooperative system changed markedly.

Because compensation was determined by the yearly production figures of the cooperative and its overall financial plan, members drew a monthly advance of about 50 percent of the expected value of their work units, receiving the balance only when the yearly accounting was completed (by February of the following year). This method of payment had both advantages and disadvantages. While drawing advances, farmers were short on cash. However, when the balance was paid out to them in lump sums, they had substantial amounts of cash to spend on major items, which workers in other sectors of the economy could scarcely manage to save up enough money to buy. In the early years of the Komárov cooperative, the happy occasion of the yearly payment was celebrated by a joint feast for which one or two hogs were slaughtered. But there were arguments as to how much each member should contribute to the feast, and eventually supplies were arranged by the cooperative. Invariably plenty of beer as well as a variety of food was consumed, the party lasting until the next morning. Later the members of the cooperative came to be paid just as industrial workers are—once a month, in full.

The Komárov Unified Agricultural Cooperative, which was relatively small, had two basic components—one concerned with animal production, the other with crop production. Workers in animal production on the average received much better compensation, but care of animals requires both interest and responsibility. Jobs in crop production paid substantially less, except for those involving the operation and maintenance of farm machinery.

The cooperative holdings of livestock in early 1972 included 104 cows, 322 young beefs, 120 brood sows, and 240 hogs for fattening. Work continues throughout the year in livestock production, and animals must be fed and cared for seven days a week and sometimes at night as well. The best-paid assignment in the Komárov cooperative was (and no doubt continues to be under the new arrangement) the care of brood sows, which was handled in two separate locations. In 1972, three members of a family in one of the areas were responsible for a total of some 70 sows, although by mutual agreement only two family members did the bulk of the work. Of the sows, 23 had not yet farrowed. The care of each of these was compensated for by a flat 28 Kčs per month. For the remaining sows, remuneration was geared to the production of suckling pigs. Compensation for their care was put at 56 Kčs for each pig per month up to a weight of 15 kilograms (33 pounds). Added compensation for each 100 kilograms (220 pounds) of additional weight increase was 115 Kčs. Determination of the increase was made at the time of the sale of the pigs to a large meat-packing plant, Gigant, in Třeboň, with which the Komárov cooperative had a contract.

In addition to these amounts, there were overtime premiums of 50 percent for each Sunday and every other Saturday spent on duty. (Workers regularly worked on alternate Saturdays.) During June of 1972, which was no better than an average month for that year, each of these three employees earned 3238 Kčs plus 328 Kčs in premiums (the amounts were equal because the members of the family requested an even split of the remuneration due them), or 10,698 Kčs of take-home pay for the three together. Although the overall plan called for 19 piglets per sow annually, in this case the actual production was over 20, bringing an additional one-shot premium to be paid at the end of the year. These earnings of about 3700 Kčs for each of the three workers during the month of June compared very favorably with earnings received in other sectors of the national economy. Using preliminary figures for 1971 for the Czech Socialist Republic, their wages appear quite impressive next to the following average monthly earnings: 2330 Kčs in transportation, 2306 Kčs in building construction, 2058 Kčs in industry, 1903 Kčs in education, and 1700 Kčs in retail business and public food services.

In general, averages are somewhat higher in the large cities, such as Prague, and lower elsewhere.[1]

The achievement of such earnings, however, requires a work schedule that most workers simply are not eager to maintain. The farrowing of a sow, in two litters per year, occasionally lasts throughout an entire night. Care must be taken to separate each piglet immediately after its first nursing lest it become acci-

---

[1] To the extent that it is possible to deal in a brief note with such a very complex matter as how the Czechs typically spend their earnings, the following data may serve as illustrations of the economic midrange. All three examples below are from my field notes and refer to residents of Prague. It should be noted that for the urban population the cost of food and services is very high in comparison with the cost of renting an apartment. The bonuses mentioned below are received only by employees in those sectors of the economy that are financially self-sustaining and yield profit; administrative officials, clerks, and others like them are not entitled to bonuses.

1. A single woman with sixteen years of education, including an engineering degree from a technical university, earns about 2400 Kčs per month. Of this total, wage tax deductions amount to about 500 Kčs; rent to ca. 170 Kčs; gas and electricity to ca. 45 Kčs; telephone to ca. 20 Kčs; food, personal upkeep, and minor repairs to about 900 Kčs. Clothes and major purchases are likely to come, in part, from her yearly bonus, which amounts on the average to about 3000 Kčs.

2. A married man with a wife and two children, educated as in the example above but with twenty years of experience, may earn about 3500 Kčs per month. Of this total, wage tax deductions amount to about 700 Kčs, but supplemental allowances for his children add 430 Kčs (300 Kčs until the end of 1972). Expenses include the apartment, according to size and style, ca. 200–500 Kčs; food ca. 2000 Kčs; electricity, gas, and telephone ca. 150 Kčs; and upkeep and minor purchases ca. 200 Kčs. The amount of the yearly bonus and the use made of it would be much the same as in the previous example.

3. A manual worker with specialized training (carpenter, lathe operator, and the like) may very likely earn the same amount as in the example above. Moreover, he has an opportunity to earn additional money on the side despite the fact that side income is officially frowned upon.

As of April 30, 1973, the exchange rate, according to nominal New York closing quotations for interbank payments provided by the Foreign Exchange Trading Division of the Chase Manhattan Bank, was 1 Kčs at $0.171 (i.e., 5.85 Kčs to $1.00). Several other exchange rates exist for different transactions, such as tourist exchanges and official purchases of hard currencies.

The purchasing power of the Czechoslovak crown may be roughly derived from the current (1973) prices of selected items given below. The prices listed are the official ones at which commodities are actually sold.

1 kilogram (2.2 pounds) of bread	1.95–3.40 Kčs (according to quality)
1 kilogram of potatoes in season	0.70–0.90 Kčs (new potatoes up to 10.00 Kčs)
1 liter (1.057 quarts) of whole milk	3.10 Kčs (skim milk 1.90 Kčs)
1 kilogram of wheat flour	3.80 Kčs (best quality)
1 kilogram of sugar	7.60–8.00 Kčs
1 kilogram of pork cutlets	30.00 Kčs (average)
1 liter of beer (10°)	3.70 Kčs
cigarette (one piece)	0.16–1.00 Kčs (American brands at 1.00 Kčs per piece)
restaurant meal (third price category)	14.00 Kčs (average for soup, meat with vegetable, dessert, and small beer, without tip)
warm midday meal, adequate but simple, subsidized by place of employment	4.00 Kčs (average cost to the employee)
pair of men's leather shoes	150.00 Kčs (average)
men's shirt, cotton, long sleeves	70.00 Kčs (and up)
ticket to a movie theater	5.00 Kčs (average)

dentally smothered or crushed by the sow. Any loss would be felt in the pocket of the employee on payday. The breeding of the cooperative's five stud boars with the sows, with at least two couplings to insure settling, is also included among the duties of these workers.

By comparison, caring for calves brings much lower wages. One Komárov woman who has charge of some twenty-five to thirty calves earned only about 750 Kčs in an average month during 1972. Weight increment is relatively slow after the first ten days, at which time the calves are weaned and fed with dried milk. Because the Komárov sheds are inadequate in size, the calves have to be moved out of the village at an early age. Were more spacious facilities available in Komárov—as is the case in Vlastiboř—permitting the feeding to extend over a longer period, the take-home pay would rise significantly. However, as long as the calf feeder is able to do her work well and responsibly, she may supplement her income with another assignment—in crop production, for example—although at considerable expenditure of additional time and effort.

The main crop of the Komárov Unified Agricultural Cooperative during 1972 was wheat, amounting to roughly 33 percent of the total crop production. Other crops, in descending order of production, were rye (17%), oats (12%), red clover (12%), barley for malt (8%), potatoes (8%), flax (5%), and rape for oil, corn for silage, and feed cabbage (together 5%). About 15 percent of agricultural land was maintained as pastureland and hayfields.

The highest-paid jobs in crop production during the same year were those held by the seven men operating heavy farm machinery. A tractorist manning a heavy five-furrow gangplow, who managed to cultivate four to five hectares in eight hours at 19 Kčs per hectare (2.47 acres), could make about 80 to 90 Kčs a day, or about 400 Kčs a week without overtime. Collecting hay or straw from the fields was even more profitable. At .64 Kčs per quintal (220 pounds), plus a small additional payment for hauling over a distance of more than one kilometer (0.62 miles), a skillful tractorist with a well-maintained machine, moving as much as thirty tons per day, could earn a total of about 190 Kčs (before overtime at 50 percent extra).

Eight people in 1972 were employed in medium-paid manual jobs. Low-paid work was performed for the most part by a handful of retired women, who received 4.40 Kčs an hour for such minor chores as clearing fields of rocks, sweeping storage areas, and the like. Heavier work, such as cocking hay or unloading straw brought in from the fields, paid correspondingly better—as much as 50 Kčs for half a day and over 100 Kčs for a full day. But this work is strictly seasonal, lasting no more than about a month during the entire year.

To offset the disadvantages of the seasonal nature of employment in crop production, the Komárov cooperative provided for off-season work by arrangement with various regional enterprises. During the fall the cooperative would place its tractorists in industrial jobs in Soběslav or with highway maintenance crews. The men were paid by their substitute employers according to the jobs they held, with payment channeled through the cooperative. Those who worked in the lumber mill of the nearby forest were paid a larger amount than they received for the crop production assignments, but the work was heavily taxing.

Transportation for commuters is provided by public buses or private automobiles.

Buses travel to and from Soběslav three times daily, to Tábor twice. In owner-ship of private automobiles, Komárov is above average for the country as a whole: as of May, 1973, there were twenty-four automobiles for the 181 Komárov inhabitants, three of the cars in one particular household.

To avoid the necessity of commuting, a special arrangement was made for women needing off-season employment. For example, the cooperative contracted with Fruta, a produce plant in Veselí, to bring into the village several wagon-loads of onions for the women to peel. Depending on the volume handled, each could earn as much as 60 Kčs per day. At other times supplies were brought into the village for putting together paper boxes used for cheese and other dairy products. These were assembled in empty premises belonging to the cooperative.

Because the rural exodus has been creating a chronic shortage of agricultural manpower, especially among young people, members of cooperatives have been receiving preferential treatment in recent years. Their wages are not subject to deductions as is the case in other sectors of the economy—an exemption that extends also to those who hold substitute jobs during the off-season period. Fur-thermore, retired workers may hold full-time employment in agriculture without incurring a reduction in their retirement benefits. However, the one decided advantage that accrues to members of most cooperatives—and to all those of Komárov—are the private plots (záhumenek, sing.) to which they are entitled for their personal use.

The private plot customarily lies behind the family farmstead. Its maximum size is determined by the membership meeting of each cooperative, but must not exceed the limits set by law for the country as a whole. As a rule, the first two members of a family who are members of the cooperative are each entitled to twenty-five ares (one-quarter of a hectare, or approximately 0.62 acres), the maximum thus being half a hectare (1.24 acres) per family, including garden or orchard.

In addition, they as well as other family members who have joined the co-operative qualify for special benefits in kind—for example, permission to pur-chase certain amounts of the commodities produced by the cooperative at a lower than usual price. Until the end of 1972, such allowances were quite gen-erous; currently they are commensurate with the number of work units earned up to a ceiling of 400 units. In cases where three or four members of one family are members of the cooperative, the savings effected may be considerable. Villagers who are not members of the cooperative are able to benefit from the special prices only to the extent that they have worked for the cooperative during the year.

What a family may raise on its private holding is limited by law. Certain crops—for example, grapes, vegetables, strawberries—are restricted to an area no larger than one-tenth of a hectare. The keeping of animals is likewise restricted, the limit being one cow and two hogs at any one time, ten beehives, and a reasonable number of other small animals and poultry. Work required for the private plot must in no way encroach upon the duties a member owes his co-operative. A family may choose to substitute for part of its private plot a corre-sponding piece of a cooperative field. In this case, the family receives its due share when the yield of the field is prorated after the harvest. For example, if a hectare of a wheat field yields thirty quintals of grain and a family shares ten ares of it, it is entitled to three quintals (ca. 660 pounds) of the grain. Since it supplies food for a very small cash outlay, the private plot helps greatly with food costs, which in Czechoslovakia take up roughly twice as much of spendable earnings as is the case in the United States. The private plot invariably receives great care. Not only does it provide a most welcome addition to the family's earnings, but it is the last remaining link to the time when the land was the villager's to do with as he chose.

Finally, besides the private plot and the various benefits, every member of the Komárov cooperative contributing full-time service during the entire year had a right to the so-called green portion (*zelený dílek*), consisting of a certain amount of green fodder for his cow. The fodder came from the cooperative field, and in 1971 it amounted to clover from about fifteen ares (ca. 0.37 acres). With everyone contributing a share of work, the clover was cut and then delivered to each member's farmstead, where it was either used fresh or preserved for later use.

As of mid-1972 the number of persons employed by the Komárov cooperative was thirty-nine. The ratio of men to women was roughly one to one, as it has always been. Reflecting a countrywide tendency, older people predominate, the average age of members of the cooperative being around forty-eight years:

	Below 20	20–29	30–39	40–49	50–59	60 and above	Totals
Men	1	3	2	4	6	2	18
Women	2	4	4	4	5	2	21

Since then the number of full-time cooperative employees has further decreased.[2]

[2] Related figures indicating countrywide tendencies and characteristics may be of interest to show how the rural exodus is reflected in the shrinking agricultural population and the changing age distribution of agricultural workers. While the mean figure of inhabitants of the Czech Socialist Republic rose from 8,893,000 for 1948 to 9,842,000 in 1971, the average number of persons employed in agriculture fell as follows:

1948	1953	1960	1965	1968	1971 (Preliminary Figure)
1,321,000	1,103,000	906,000	800,000	752,000	718,000

The percentages of persons, by age groups, permanently active in agriculture in Czechoslovakia as a whole are given for selected years in the table below:

Age	1935	1955	1959	1965	1967	1969
15–19 years	13.3	7.8	5.4	4.3	3.9	3.4
20-49 years	59.0	53.5	51.0	49.9	52.9	56.2
50-59 years	14.6	24.2	27.8	26.1	22.9	20.3
60 years and over	13.1	14.5	15.8	19.7	20.3	20.1

Recent ratios of males to females permanently active in unified agricultural cooperatives in the Czech Socialist Republic are as follows:

Sex	1960	1970 (Preliminary Figures)	1971 (Preliminary Figures)
Men	42.4	45.7	48.4
Women	57.6	54.3	51.6

Twenty-three members of the cooperative had reached retirement age by 1972. Of this number thirteen were men and ten were women. For men normal retirement age is sixty, and for women without children fifty-seven, but it can be as low as fifty-three for those who have brought up five or more children. Retirement income depends on the earnings received during active employment and the length of employment. The minimum among the members of the Komárov cooperative amounts to 445 Kčs per month and the maximum to about 1300 Kčs—in general, approximately 50 to 60 percent of the individual's average earnings during the last five or ten years of work, whichever is higher. In addition, each retired member of the cooperative is entitled to the yield of grain and potatoes from twenty-five ares (0.62 acres), equal in area to the personal private plot.

Free medical services are available to employed persons and their families in all sectors of the state-run economy. In addition to retirement pension and medical services, all employed persons are entitled to a variety of welfare benefits generally based on average income and length of service. These benefits include disability payments, widows' and orphans' pensions, sick pay during illness, health resort vacations, and funeral expense grants (1000 Kčs).

Maternity benefits currently amount to a flat 2000 Kčs at the birth of a child and 90 percent of average daily earnings for a total of twenty-six weeks. In order not to lose any income, women normally resume their full duties in the cooperative when these benefits are exhausted. Since by reason of its small size Komárov does not have the usual nursery facilities available in all larger communities, care of the child is taken over by older members of the family who have retired from active farm work.

Paid vacations vary in length according to age and length of service, normally with a minimum of two weeks and a maximum of four weeks. In the Komárov cooperative, vacations were uniformly three weeks long until 1972. The expectation is that in the future they will follow whatever is the practice for industrial workers.

Since the consolidation of the several cooperatives, the Komárov villagers have felt some apprehension. They have been concerned that the increased hierarchy of the central management in Vlastiboř might put an end to the close relationships which the members of the Komárov Unified Agricultural Cooperative had come to enjoy among themselves. Since the compensation of the members of a cooperative depends ultimately on its productivity and since Komárov was operating with above-average efficiency, it is also feared that the consolidation may result in reduced benefits. There is some evidence that this may indeed be so. For example, the Komárov members of the new cooperative expect to pay 40 percent more for a quintal (220 pounds) of wheat and 50 to 75 percent more for a quintal of potatoes, which they used to purchase from their own cooperative for 100 Kčs and 20 Kčs, respectively. Particularly disconcerting, however, was the drop in the monetary value of the work unit for 1972 and the lack of any indication that this was due to merely a temporary readjustment.

Although it is conceivable that such measures could have some effect on the earnings of the Komárov farmers, there is every reason to believe that the postwar period of sacrificing agriculture to heavy industry is over and that the furtherance of agricultural production through rationalization, mechanization, professionalization, and incentive giving has become the foremost concern of the government. Earnings of villagers have been slowly but steadily rising, and to slow down the rural exodus, the government is committed to improving the lot of the agricultural worker through various benefits not available in the rest of the economy.

Notwithstanding all this, agricultural employment and membership in unified agricultural cooperatives carries low prestige among the young Czechs, who are urgently needed to replenish the aged and rapidly aging population of farming villages. These young Czechs seem to care little for the heavy outdoor work involved in farming or the episodic distribution of free and work time inherent in much of agricultural production. But least of all are they willing to give up the life-style that a city has to offer despite its inevitable inconveniences, which in most cases are considerable. In Prague, where 8 percent of the country's population reside, commmuting to and from work adds at least an hour on the average to the workday, and shopping is more frequently than not a test of patience. By contrast, family housing in the village is rent-free, commuting by bus or car to work, which some must do, provides an occasion for social gossip, and periodic visits to towns for major shopping serve as a welcome diversion.

Among fifty selected occupations in a recent (1967) study of occupational prestige structure carried out on a representative sample of 1431 respondents, chairman of a unified agricultural cooperative ranked eighteenth, tractorist or combine operator twenty-sixth, and member of a crop production group forty-seventh; first was minister (high state official) and last, fiftieth, was parking lot attendant. Results of two polls, one taken in 1937 and the other in 1966–1967, reveal that although in terms of social utility farming was ranked at the top in 1937, by 1966–1967 it had slipped to eighth place (behind physician, university professor, scientific research worker, engineer, miner, secondary school teacher, and locomotive engineer, but ahead of nurse, architect, mason, and minister). Considering the Czech appetite and fondness for good beer and rich food, the poor showing of agricultural occupations is startlingly ironic.

Agricultural production, which in earlier times placed a great many different demands on the farmer and his helpers, has increasingly become an assortment of specialized activities. Large-scale field crop production and feeding and caring for a large number of livestock or poultry justify a high degree of mechanization and specialization, which formerly could not possibly have paid for itself, even on a large farm. Some of the postwar changes in the organization of education reflect the needs of socialized agriculture. Vocational secondary education is provided by a system of vocational schools that offer a four-year program combining general education with vocational training and practical work experience. The passing of the final state examination earns the student a diploma that qualifies him for either employment or higher education. Every effort is made to train specialists who can provide more effective technical management and improve production at a faster rate than has so far been the case.

In short, we are currently witnessing the Czech peasant's ultimate passing from the scene. Perhaps most telling is the belief of the Komárov villagers that not only is a return to private control of agricultural land practically unthinkable, but that it is probably also undesirable. What feelings of attachment to the land still remain after a generation of socialist approach to land tenure have been largely rationalized away by the compensating advantages that members of cooperatives have begun to accrue after the bleak period of the 1950s. One of the perceived advantages is the lessening of risks borne in the past during every growing season by the small- and medium-sized peasants. This was expressed anecdotally by a seasoned old villager: "Before the war, when a storm was gathering and clouds were moving toward the village, everyone was running *into* the fields; nowadays, when people see threatening clouds, they tend to run *from* the fields home."

The members of the cooperatives are becoming agricultural "specialists" employed in the highly differentiated aspects of livestock production or crop production, primarily those involving the use of various kinds of farm machinery. Thus, while formerly the peasant managed all aspects of his private farming operation, today he is well on the way to becoming a link in a chain of increasing complexity. The centuries-old view of land and weather, of crops and livestock, all as part of an indissoluble whole, is rapidly giving way to the industrial worker's or bureaucrat's fragmentary and compartmentalized conception of production or employment.

Czech vocabulary has kept pace with these socioeconomic transformations. The common term for "peasant," *sedlák*, attested in Czech writings as early as the beginning of the fourteenth century, has become anachronistic and has been replaced by the term *zemědělec*, "one who works the land." Steadily gaining currency, however, is another term applicable to the majority of workers in the socialist agricultural sector—*družstevník*, "member of a cooperative." And with the increasing division of labor and specialization found in agriculture, there is a further tendency to refer to an agricultural worker by the specific occupational title which he or she holds, for example, *traktorista* or *traktoristka*, "male or female tractorist." In short, the recent changes in the status of the primary food producers have brought about corresponding shifts in the Czech lexicon. The term *sedlák*, "peasant," has simply fallen into disuse, and the peasantry, both as a class and as a repository of traditional values, have virtually disappeared from the scene.

6 / The village as a community

Originally, the concept of community (*obec*) comprehended all of the so-called neighbors—the first settlers of a Blata village and their descendants. Other meanings gradually came to attach to the word as traditions and times changed, but the primary sense was rooted in feelings of neighborliness. The management of community affairs and the use of the land held in common rested in the hands of the adult males who were "neighbors." They dealt with matters including the upkeep of village roads, contracts with communal employees, the maintenance of the local school once it had been established, and the like. Their decisions were of course subject to review by the appropriate authorities and, prior to 1848, by the lords to whom the land ultimately belonged.

The common lands, which were held jointly by the neighbors, usually encompassed about a third of the total village territory and included meadows, pastures, some forestland, ponds, a smithy, and the herdsman's cottage. In Komárov, such lands amounted to slightly less than a fifth of the entire peasant acreage. As a rule, once a year each neighbor was assigned a portion of the common land to do with as he saw fit. It was felt the land ought not to be unused and that it should at least serve for pasture. Even though an attempt was made to benefit equally all those eligible, this was not always easy to accomplish. When it came to assigning portions of the common land to individual neighbors, therefore, one of two methods was employed. If it was unlikely that the assignments would favor any one villager over others, they were made according to the numbers under which farmsteads were recorded in the land register. Tradition has it that during the eighteenth century, before Komárov farmsteads had been assigned numbers, allotments were made in clockwise progression beginning with the farmsteads in the eastern portion of the village common and, once the full circle had been completed, continuing concentrically out from the settlement. If the portions of the common land to be assigned were of unequal value, lots were drawn to determine the priority of choice. Individual peasants were assigned numbers by the appointed village head or, after 1848, by the village mayor, and the youngest farmer was asked to reach into a bag and draw out small wooden balls with matching numbers.

The privilege of using the village common land carried with it certain obligations. Among them were the responsibility of caring for the village poor if there were any, the upkeep of public thoroughfares, the maintenance of the local school, and the like. A law promulgated in Bohemia in 1867 stipulated that village common land be considered principal property of the community, but for all practical purposes the neighbors were permitted to retain the right to its use. It was at that time that the term "old holder" (*starousedlík*) was first used. In point of fact, the old and established peasant families had the option of purchasing some of the village property and incorporating it into their holdings. Since the original hereditary holdings were long strips of land running from the village common toward the village boundary, the allotments purchased for younger sons of well-to-do farmers grew progressively smaller, particularly as the population was peaking during the second half of the nineteenth century. Finally, by virtue of an act passed in 1919, what was left of the original common land became the property of the community as a whole, but its use by old holders did not cease until 1932. What this act did, in addition to putting an end to some of the old customs, particularly the ceremonial admission of a new member among the village neighborhood, was to shift control over the common land from the old holders to the village administrative officials and ultimately to an agency of political authority.

A farmer became a "neighbor" by birth, marriage, or purchase of a farmstead. In the latter two cases he was ceremonially accepted among the rest when he arranged a feast for them and contributed an acceptance fee to the community treasury. Those few who made Komárov their home by marrying into a local family generally came from the surrounding area and were well known to the villagers. Only one farmer is said to have married in from a distance—a man who came from the Chodsko region near Domažlice. The family name, not common in the Blata but frequently found in Chodsko, seems to confirm it. There is no record of any outsider ever establishing himself in Komárov by virtue of having purchased a farmstead. On the whole, then, in-migration into Komárov— at least during the last two centuries, for which full records are available—was negligible.

In its secondary meaning, the concept of community referred to those who enjoyed the right of domicile in a particular place. This right was granted a person after a period of adult residence of at least ten years. Essentially a medieval institution but made into law in 1863, the right of domicile guaranteed basic maintenance at public expense to those persons who were unable to work or were destitute. Customarily, what had served at one time as the herdsman's dwelling became the village poorhouse. In Komárov it was a very rare occurrence for anyone to require support from community funds: informants recall only two families ever claiming such support, both during the first quarter of the present century. The right of domicile came into general use at the beginning of the current century and was universally accepted after 1918. After World War II, when health and pension benefits were extended to all of the country's citizens, the right of domicile was abolished as superfluous.

Lastly, the term "community" came to refer to a group of people who lived in a particular locality and there exercised their citizens' rights. This is the concept that is still current today.

Before 1848, the village head (*rychtář*) for centuries was primarily the representative of the lord of the domain. Even though he and the aldermen assisting him were generally appointed from among the candidates submitted by the community, they were invariably individuals whom the lord found suitable. It followed that in the course of time a measure of alienation tended to develop between the villagers and these officials, particularly as their administrative and judicial authority grew.

After 1848, the administration of the community passed into the hands of the mayor, who was assisted by four aldermen. All these officials were elected by secret ballot and by men only until 1918, when women gained suffrage. Before the establishment of Czechoslovakia in 1918, the mayor and the aldermen were invariably chosen from among the larger old holders. Following World War I, farming cottagers occasionally came to hold administrative offices; since they were in a distinct minority, however, their influence was only slight. Instead, the village administration began to feel the influence of political parties. During the First Republic, this influence was exerted primarily by the Agrarian party, whose candidates for local offices—just as was the case for candidates from some of the other parties represented—had to be approved by the higher party echelons. Since the establishment of the cooperative in the 1950s, when class (but not social) distinctions were erased, decisions have been made by elected function-aries who for the most part are Communist party members. The slate of candidates for these offices is checked in advance for approval by party and state authorities. The administrative head of Komárov is the chairman of the local national com-mittee (místní národní výbor). He is assisted by ten village representatives, two of whom currently are women. The present officials, who serve for a period of five years, came into office after the election held in November 1971, in which 126 Komárov voters, eighteen years of age or older, participated.

In the past, the social differentiation between the farmers and the farming cot-tagers was clearly marked. The richer peasants enjoyed the privilege of more prominent pews in the parish churches of Hlavatce or Soběslav, choice tables in the village inn, and their families claimed better cemetery plots. Marrying from a peasant farmstead into the house of a farming cottager was a rare occurrence. Following World War I these distinctions began to blur, and once Komárov made the transition to cooperative farming they disappeared completely. In fact, in the 1950s it was a definite advantage to be of modest economic background. For example, elective village functions, at least initially, were closed to members of the larger peasant families. What new social distinctions have developed seem to be neither permanent nor insurmountable, even though they play their role in the village microstructure. They are the distinctions between those who are members of the Communist party and those who are not, those who hold offices and the rank-and-filers. Party members and functionaries have been known to claim and enjoy certain advantages in work assignments, compensation, and distribution of goods temporarily in short supply. For that matter, favoritism of this kind existed also in the highly politicized atmosphere of the First Republic.

Still more evident was the social distance between farmhands and their employ-ers. Farmhands were recruited primarily from among the young members of the families of farming cottagers, although occasionally from the families of small farmers if there were many children. The time of hiring and discharging was at Christmas.

The relationship between the head of a farmstead and his hired help was strictly patriarchal. Just like members of the family, farmhands were provided with five meals a day and a place to sleep. The help ate at the same table with the family, and after work at night they were expected to be in bed not later than the farmer's teenage children. If there was reason to suspect unacceptable behavior after hours, the farmer or a village officer responsible for law and order would make a night inspection of the quarters where female help were lodged. A male farmhand caught visiting there was routed out immediately and then collected early next morning and made to put in a long day's work, under close supervision, on roads or ditches.

In addition to food and lodging, farmhands received compensation both in cash and in kind. In the 1850s, for a year's work a male farmhand typically received 18 guldens, a pair of pants, and in some farmsteads a shirt. The average compensation for female help was 12 guldens, a skirt, two blouses, two aprons, and a kerchief. By the 1880s compensation for males amounted to 25 guldens and a pair of pants, for females 18 guldens and the same outfitting as earlier. Before World War I, a male farmhand received about 70 Austrian crowns; after the war, 1200–1500 Kč (Czechoslovak crowns) but nothing in kind. Compensation for females amounted to about 10 percent less.

It was also the custom to give the help a large cake (a long pastry woven from strands of leavened dough and baked) at Christmas, an Easter cake and eggs at Easter, and on special occasions—weddings, christenings, dedication feasts, and harvest home—some extra cash and food. The female help were usually given time off the last three days of the year so that they could visit their parents, and the male farmhand responsible for the livestock could expect a small cash gift following the sale of an animal. But all such extras did little to offset the very meager wages. In order to make a little additional money to spend on amusements, both the help and the older children would sometimes "skunk out" (dělat schoře, from dělat, "to do, act as," and schoř [regional form for tchoř], "polecat") the farmer of some grain, which they sold surreptitiously to merchants in Soběslav, Veselí, or Bechyně. The farmer usually knew what was going on, but as long as these minor thefts did not exceed a tolerable amount, he closed his eyes to them. (For that matter, pilfering has not been limited to the past, though today the implications are much more serious, since collective or national property is involved.)

At times, simple quarters were provided for a married farmhand and his family, and for the labor he, his wife, and their older children contributed they were given the use of a small field. There were reportedly three such cases in Komárov between 1900 and 1910. From the point of view of the farmhand, this sort of arrangement was highly desirable. Least desirable was to have work for the harvest season only. A hundred years ago, such day laborers received 2 Austrian crowns per day, meals, and a loaf of bread. If the work was done in their own village, workers usually claimed their daily loaf during the winter when possibilities of employment were very scarce and money even scarcer.

In general, although the real wages of the farmhands had been going up, they continued to fall behind the wage increases in other occupations and were certainly not commensurate with the growing incomes of the farmers. It is no wonder that by the end of the century the complaint was frequently heard that good help was hard to come by. Given a choice, a girl was much more likely to work as a maidservant in the city, where she could expect a lighter work load and better pay than in the village. The following excerpt from a letter written in the 1890s by a village hired girl to her girl friend (or relative?) employed in a city is typical:

When you visit here, Katie, bring along the kerchief for me; I'll pay you for it, because I want to buy it anyway so it'll come in handy. I won't be able to make it to the church fair [*pout'*] because the farmer is building a barn—we have masons and carpenters here—[and] he is using up much money and nothing is left over for us; you're more likely to get hold of ten crowns than people here [to get] a few hellers [100 hellers = 1 crown] from the farmers. Don't be angry with us. . . .

The hiring of help continued until the establishment of the cooperative, when the institution of hired farm labor disappeared completely.

Until recently, the people of Komárov had devoted themselves almost exclusively to agriculture. Historical records give no indication that any home industry or crafts were ever carried on to an extent that would have exceeded strictly local needs. Family members of small farmers did engage occasionally in nonfarming services for others. In such cases, one party earned some needed additional money and the other received prompt service for less than he would have had to pay had he engaged someone from outside the village. Today, with nationalized communal repair shops in Soběslav and other nearby towns understaffed and slow, this practice not only continues but is on the increase. Men who are skilled in masonry, carpentry, or the repairing of electrical equipment or automobiles manage to supplement their regular wages quite handsomely through extra work done in their spare time.

In the past, the relatively few nonfarming members of the community varied somewhat in number, reflecting the slowly changing needs of their fellow villagers. The most profound shifts occurred during the past half century, and are indicated below.

In terms of families or individual persons, the data available from Komárov for the early 1920s yield the following figures:

Farmers   22 families
Farming cottagers   12 families
Farmhands resident at Hope   4 families
Farmhands of both sexes employed
   in the village   22 individuals
Widowed and orphaned persons   6 individuals
Nonfarming members of the
   community (for example,
   forester, smith, shopkeeper)   5 families

TABLE 5.   SOCIAL MICROSTRUCTURE OF KOMÁROV DURING THE
MID-1920S, IN PERCENTAGES

	Males	Females	Totals
Farmers	14	14	28
Farming cottagers	6	6	12
Farmhands and youth between 16 and 18 years of age	8	12	20
Other working persons (teacher, smith, innkeeper, and forest and estate Hope employees)	2	2	4
Subtotal of persons of productive age	30	34	64
Children below 16 years of age	11	15	26
Superannuated persons	4	6	10
Subtotal of unproductive persons	15	21	36
Total of all persons belonging to 41 farmsteads	45	55	100

Except for harvesttime, a significant number of the farming cottagers worked at a sawmill in Sudoměřice—six males during 1926, but only one or two during the subsequent economic crisis.

The latest count, as of 1972, reflects the current tendency to seek employment outside the agricultural sector:

Employees of the cooperative	39
Persons employed elsewhere (nearby industry, forest administration)	43
Retired persons	37
Children below 15 years of age	48
Students and apprentices	4
Others	10
Total	181

Of the total of 181 Komárov inhabitants, children up to fifteen years of age account for 48, men for 67, and women for 66. This ratio is far more favorable than that for the Czech Socialist Republic as a whole, where males constitute only 48.4 percent and children up to fifteen only 22.6 percent.

Just as in German, French, and other European languages, in Czech a person may be addressed in either the familiar or the formal, polite form. The familiar makes use of the personal pronoun *ty* ("thou") and of the second person singular form of the verb (compare the German *du hast* and the French *tu as*). The formal, or polite, form employs the personal pronoun of the second person plural, *vy*, and the corresponding form of the verb (compare the German *Sie haben*, which is the third person plural form, and the French *vous avez*). Villagers of the same social standing addressed each other by the familiar form and by their family names or by references to the houses in which they lived. Only friends, relatives, and former schoolmates used first (Christian) names or childhood nicknames. Old people and those belonging to other social groups were addressed in the polite form, but without "Sir" or "Mister" (*pane*, vocative). Strangers, unless they were clearly of the lowest social class—beggars, vagrants, and so on—

were spoken to in polite forms and usually addressed as "Mister" or "Sir." The same form of address was accorded to townspeople, officials, and others of the kind. Priests were addressed as "Reverend Father" (*velebný pane* or *důstojný pane*, vocatives), sometimes with their full title added. Farmhands were addressed by their given names and the familiar forms if they were young, or the polite forms if older. In turn the farmer and his wife were addressed by the help as *pantáto* and *panímámo* (both vocative forms, meaning literally "mister father" and "mistress mother") or *strejčku* and *teto* (both vocative forms, meaning "uncle" and "aunt"). The choice between the two depended on the background of the speaker. Boys were addressed by the familiar form until reaching conscription age, girls until their engagement, but generally not after they reached twenty. Until 1918, members of the regional nobility—the former domain owners—and officials from outside the village were frequently addressed as *jemnostpane* (vocative form, meaning roughly "gracious lord"). Except for the last case, the forms of address have changed little, but for the most part the title *pan*, "Mister, Sir," has been replaced by *soudruh*, "Comrade." Party members address each other in the familiar forms even when they are merely acquaintances.

To identify individual villagers, it was the custom to give the family name and the house number, or a distinguishing nickname derived from the person's residence if there were several people of the same name in the community. Thus, one might speak of "Honsa from (number) twenty-nine," or one might make reference to his house, which is known as *u Kundrátů* (at the Kundráts)," even though the Honsa family has lived there for several generations. Besides his or her given name, every villager thus had two names—the official family name as well as a name *po chalupě*, that is, "after (his, her) cottage." To refer to a farmhouse, one used the house number or the family name, frequently with a specific topographical designation such as "across from the smithy," "at the end of the village toward the forester's house," "(number) fifteen, on the road to Klečaty," and so on.

7 / Family and friends

Both the manner in which an individual household operated and the way in which the institution of the family was viewed doubtless underwent change in the course of centuries, but few events could have affected it as profoundly as did the transition to cooperative socialist farming, when both men and women became specialized employees of a large-scale agricultural enterprise. How earlier innovations, such as the abolition of the labor obligation and the change to intensive farming, influenced family outlook and functions it is impossible to tell, though one may suspect that they, too, had a marked effect.

According to archival records, in 1787 the labor obligation of individual farmsteads amounted to 107 man-days with the use of a team of oxen or 108 man-days without it. Of these totals, 65 days were to be worked off between Saint George's Day (April 24) and Saint Gall's Day (October 16) and the remainder during the winter. It appears unlikely that the modest needs of the estate Hope could have exhausted the manpower locally available and, as a consequence, a number of Komárov peasants must have had to discharge their obligations on other noble estates, most likely in the neighborhood of Bechyně, or wherever else they may have been directed. By no means did all of the farmers fulfill the labor obligation themselves. The wealthier peasants passed the duties on to their farmhands, while the smaller farmers and farming cottagers sent their older or adult children. In some cases well-to-do peasants may even have paid off their obligation in cash. But whether it was fulfilled directly or indirectly, the labor obligation must have been a source of constant pressure and irritation to the individual farming family.

Until 1848, military service was not compulsory, but every community was periodically required to provide a small contingent of able-bodied young men. It was not unusual when recruitment was going on to "catch" young farmhands, who at such times tried to hide from the village officials. Sons of peasants avoided military service by working for a noble estate, since after three years of such employment, they were exempt.

During the period of individual farming, the head of the family was the husband, but the moving spirit was his wife, and the social standard of the family depended primarily upon her qualities. Even if her husband managed the farm poorly, a sound farmwife was able to keep the farmstead going. On the other hand, an inefficient farmwife could easily bring a farm to ruin despite the best efforts of her husband. This was the case largely because the woman was in a much better position to oversee the performance of the help than was her husband, who spent much of his time working in the fields away from the farmyard. Not least in importance, the duty of bringing up children who would continue in the tradition rested primarily upon the woman. Before making basic decisions concerning the family and the farmstead, the farmer invariably consulted with his wife and never took action without first hearing her opinion. For all these reasons, the community tended to be more tolerant of negative qualities in a man than in his wife.

Aside from the division of labor, which has already been discussed, there were a number of customs that defined the role and status of each sex in certain situations. In day-to-day life, for example, women served at table and never sat down with the men at meals. They stayed completely out of dealings that were normally transacted by men. A number of tasks were reserved strictly for females, and any male assuming these would have been subject to ridicule not only by his male friends but by the village women as well. Among such tasks were sewing and the mending of clothes (although leather items were sewed by men), care of children, and cooking. Only when the farmwife was ill and there was absolutely no one to replace her would a man consider assuming her duties on a temporary basis. Quite to the contrary, a woman could take on the chores customarily performed by men—plowing, harrowing, or minor repairs in the farmyard—without losing the respect of others. In fact, in the eyes of the villagers she inevitably gained recognition as a highly capable person. These attitudes are reflected to the present day.

The contribution in cash and kind that a woman (or a man, if he married into the family) brought to a household was considered joint property, whether the agreement was oral or in writing. Local courts generally recognized oral agreements even before the second half of the nineteenth century, when written agreements came to be drawn up. It is difficult to say how property settlements would have been handled in a divorce case, since such a situation never occurred in Komárov. Judging from exceptional cases in the villages peripheral to the Blata proper, it would probably have depended on the grounds for divorce. Generally in such cases a substantial part, if not all, of what was originally brought in by the party was taken out again. The woman usually resumed living with her parents. At present, property matters assume much less importance, and decisions are made by the court. But even today—in contrast to the big cities—divorce is rare in the Blata villages.

The low incidence of divorce has been due, first, to Komárov's strict Christian moral principles. Public pressure in the small community effectively discouraged any departure from the established moral norm. Second, the exercise of parental control over the selection of marriage partners helped avoid mismatching. Marital infidelity was, and still is, considered a most serious breach, with transgressions by women judged more severely by the community than those by men. In the eyes of the villagers, unfaithfulness would have been sufficient grounds for an immediate parting of the ways. Premarital relations were tolerated if they were without consequences and did not become a matter of undue attention or give rise to scandal. In any case, the great majority of young men and women married those with whom they had been intimate. Promiscuity apparently did not exist in the past, and today it is considered a kind of prostitution.

The favorite social activity for women was feather stripping. Stripping feathers involved plucking the soft barbs and down from the stiff feather shafts so that they could be used in feather beds and pillows. In the wintertime this activity took place almost daily, the women moving from one household to another. As they stripped feathers they visited together and entertained themselves with such traditional genres as folk songs, legends, and folktales or with popular contemporary songs, the relating of personal experiences or movie plots, and the like. As one might expect, talk frequently centered on discussion of local affairs or happenings in other villages; occasionally unpleasantness resulted when someone indiscreetly repeated outside what had been said at one of these gatherings behind the person's back. The farmwife in whose house the feather stripping took place was expected to treat all those who assembled. Coffee and pastry were served, and sometimes a small glass of sweet liqueur as well. It was not uncommon for older men to participate in these sessions. Feather stripping as a regular activity lasted until the 1940s; today such gatherings are held much less frequently.

Until the 1950s, the centers of male social activity in Komárov were the two village inns. One was frequented almost exclusively by the landed farmers, the other by farming cottagers, farmhands, and occasional visitors to the village. The place to learn the latest village gossip, as well as what was happening in the outside world, was the inn of the farming cottagers. Except during the period of peak activities, both inns were visited regularly in the evening. Only the peasants with larger holdings could afford to stop in during the day. A great deal of discussion of community affairs took place, enlivened by singing and card games. In good Bohemian tradition great quantities of beer, drunk from large metal steins (máz, sing.) holding a quart and a half each, were consumed on these occasions. To shun the inn was most unusual. Any man who did so would have been considered tightfisted and unsociable.

Many personal arguments and complaints were settled in the inn; in other communities such disputes might have ultimately involved a lawyer. The two parties, with a few beers under their belts and an interested audience at hand, would reproach each other with as many references to past disagreements as they could possibly think of—and the memory of the Blata peasant is said to have been remarkably keen. Finally one opponent would say, "Let's wash it all down with a drink!" and everything betwen the two would be forgotten from that time on.

For some years now there has been only one inn in the village, and it remains the place where men like to gather to talk over a glass of beer whenever their schedules permit. The attendance is so regular, in fact, that on those special occasions when the young people come in for a dance, the inn becomes uncomfortably crowded. To take care of the situation, a small hall is currently being added.

In the spring, the young people of both sexes, regardless of economic background, congregated in the evenings on the village common whenever the weather permitted. Much singing took place, as well as much teasing between boys and girls. Old-timers consider these gatherings among the most pleasant memories they have of their young years. The custom of meeting on the common began to decline after World War I, while the get-togethers in the inns continued undiminished.

Other opportunities for mixed activities came with the carnival season, harvest home, dedication feasts, and certain festive family occasions. Added to these after World War I were film showings and, later still, meetings of various village organizations and of the Unified Agricultural Cooperative.

While television has negatively affected the social life of the community as a whole, it has tended to strengthen relations among close neighbors and friends. As long as only relatively few families had television sets, as was the case toward the end of the 1950s, friends and acquaintances gathered together to watch. Even today, when a television receiver can be found in nearly every house, it is customary to watch in the company of others.

For half a century or so prior to the establishment of the cooperative, parents tended to transfer the farmstead to their children after reaching the age of about sixty. But a hundred years ago, when a fifty-year-old man and a forty-year-old woman were considered old and worn-out, sons took over the management of the farmstead correspondingly earlier. The heir was customarily the oldest son or, if there were no male descendants in the family, the oldest daughter. The second son of the more landed farmers was expected to study in Soběslav to become a teacher. If the son (or daughter) married early, the old and the young couple spent several years running the farm jointly, after which the old couple retired. In such cases, the son invariably managed a substantially greater portion of the farmstead than did his father.

The rights that the retiring farmer and his wife were entitled to for the rest of their lives go back to medieval custom. Until 1848 these rights were subject to the lord's purview, although their extent was partly defined by law. Invariably the principle on which retirement rights were based was rooted in the necessity of not exceeding the economic potential of the farmstead. As a rule, rights were tied to the particular farmstead, which meant that even new owners, unrelated to the retired couple, were responsible for carrying out the obligations to them.

In the Blata, the arrangements made by the retiring farmer usually consisted of the right to room, medical care and board in the case of physical disability, rations from the farm's yield, and various services and minor privileges, such as having his allowance of grain hauled to the mill for grinding, being able to keep poultry and a cow in the farmyard, and the like. After 1918, cash payments were usually made for part or all of the retirement ration previously received in kind. But room and certain other privileges were never exchanged for cash payments. Cases of serious disagreement between the old and the young were the exception in the Blata, rather than the rule—even if many Czech novelists dealing with the peasant scene used such conflicts as their favorite plots. The retired farmer and his wife helped the young couple as much as they were physically capable of doing, and it was not unusual for them to carry on for a time with most of the agricultural activities. Frequently they reserved a part of the farm for their own use, especially if there were still teenage children to be taken care of. The authorities did not favor such an arrangement because it tended to weaken, temporarily, the productivity of the farm. Retirement arrangements disappeared with the establishment of the cooperative, when all older persons became entitled to a pension. Most pensioners today help out in the cooperative to offset the shortage of agricultural manpower as well as to supplement their modest retirement income. Some devote much of their time to hobbies, for which they had little time before.

Compensation arranged for the younger siblings, who had to yield their rights in the farm to the firstborn son, varied with circumstances. Since daughters marrying out were entitled to a dowry in lieu of a share in the farm itself, such arrangements primarily concerned the younger sons. If one of them left the village to study to become a teacher, it was assumed that the expenses incurred in supporting him during his study were sufficient compensation. However, among the wealthier peasants he could generally hope for a lump sum of money at the time his parents retired or when the heir of the farmstead was married. In theory, each child was entitled to an equal share of the value of the farmstead, including the fields that belonged to it. If there were many children in the family, the shares were likely to be relatively small, and there was a tendency to encourage one of the younger sons to become a priest. It was expected that he would then not claim his full share, and this was usually the case, even though on occasion siblings would be unpleasantly surprised.

To take a specific case at the turn of the century: the total value of one of the largest Komárov farms was estimated at 30,000 guldens, and there were three children to be considered. An even share for each child would thus have been about 10,000 guldens. However, upon his marriage the heir assumed the care of the retired farmer and his wife as well as the payments on the mortgage and any interest on outstanding indebtedness. Considering these obligations, he received one half of the total value, while his two siblings each were to receive half of the remainder, or 7500 guldens. Part of the compensation was usually paid to siblings immediately after the wedding of the heir, the rest according to agreement in two or more installments—one perhaps a year later, the second after three, five, or sometimes even ten years. There were no fixed rules, arrangements being suited to the particular circumstances of each family.

Judging from the parish registers, after 1790 the average number of surviving children per family was only rarely more than three. But given the mortality during the nineteenth century among children below fourteen years of age (at least 50%), the number of births must have been substantially higher than three per family. Since the 1890s, child mortality has been steadily dropping, and today it stands at a very low figure indeed: for Komárov, below 3 percent during the first year of life and about one-fifth of 1 percent for those one to fourteen years old—averages slightly higher than those for the Czech Socialist Republic as a whole. During the last hundred years the number of births apparently was controlled by such practices as coitus interruptus and the empirical utilization of female fertile cycles. Mechanical contraceptive devices were considered immoral, and reportedly even today their use is somewhat limited.

In the past, from a very early age children were expected to help in the household and around the farm to the extent of their ability and strength. Among their first chores usually was herding the geese, and later, at about the age of ten, the cattle. Still later they helped with the haymaking and with harvesting in general. Girls were asked to assist the farmwife and to help in watching and taking care of their younger siblings. Occasionally, the peasants with larger holdings hired young herders from among the poorer families to work from spring until pasturing had to be discontinued in the fall. Some of the herders were pupils over twelve, who were partially excused from school attendance during pasturing season. As of 1919, however, compulsory school attendance admitted no exceptions.

For children, sharing the duties in pasture was an occasion for various collective activities—games, singing, wood carving, and the like. Other than at these times, and on Saturday afternoons, Sundays, and holidays, there were few opportunities for children to enjoy themselves as a group. During the 1920s, various ball games became popular, soccer in particular, even though it was not approved by school authorities until the late 1930s (earlier it had been considered a rude sport, detrimental to the physical and mental development of a child). However, the small size of the village and consequently the relatively few children of the same age made it impossible for a stable team ever to develop. Local branches of the Sokol, a national sports society concerned primarily with gymnastics, were established in Bechyně, Sudoměřice, Soběslav, and Veselí. Still today, because of Komárov's uneven numbers of young people, those who show talent in one sport or another must seek recognition in one of the sports clubs of the nearby towns, primarily Soběslav.

Among themselves children used the familiar form and addressed each other by their given names or nicknames. When speaking to their parents, or other relatives, the custom was to use the polite form and the appropriate kinship term of address. The same held true for all adult members of the community, whom the children usually addressed by the terms *pantáto* or *panímámo*, "mister father" or "mistress mother," as appropriate. Today the situation is analogous, but the vocative *pane*, meaning "Sir," "Mister," is used to address adult nonrelatives by the younger people, and the vocative *soudruhu*, meaning "Comrade," by the older ones. One peculiarity of the Blata is the use of the terms *bratřině* and *sestřině* for male and female second cousins.

Under the jurisdiction of the Hlavatce school, the first school in Komárov was begun in 1791. According to archival records, although thirty-seven children were within the ages of required school attendance for that year, not one showed up. It is not surprising that the teacher from Hlavatce assigned to the Komárov classroom had difficulty collecting the compensation in cash and in kind due him from the villagers. In fact, because the parents depended on their children over ten years of age for a variety of essential chores, school attendance remained highly irregular until the 1870s. When the Komárov school became independent of Hlavatce in 1869, and coincidentally when all teachers became state employees, a stricter regime went into effect. As a result of fines imposed upon parents, attendance improved substantially; however, during the warmer months teenagers continued to be excused during part of the day to help out on the farm.

After completing the five grades of primary school, children attended three years of secondary school in Soběslav or, more rarely, in Bechyně. Prior to 1918 they walked. After World War I, bicycles came into use, one bicycle frequently serving two pupils. In exchange for farm products, the parents of some of the pupils arranged for their children to live with townspeople during the week through the worst of the winter. Upon completion of their compulsory school attendance, children of farming cottagers and small farmers usually began an apprenticeship in a trade. Those of larger farmers returned to farm duties or continued with agricultural studies in Tábor, which offered a four-year course with a diploma and a two-year course; winter courses were also given and after World War I were also offered in several other communities in the vicinity of Komárov.

Some of the children from well-to-do peasant families enrolled in the teachers college in Soběslav, others in the gymnasium in Tábor or České Budějovice. Schooling in the latter city offered some advantage because boarding facilities, founded by Bishop Jirsík in the 1870 s, were available there for Catholic children recommended by their local parish priest. Some few individuals continued with university studies in either Prague or Vienna (after 1918, only in Prague). To have children who were studying carried a great deal of prestige.

Today, the Komárov school serves about a dozen pupils in grades one through four, after which they attend classes in Hlavatce for five additional years. The current trend seems to be to seek employment immediately upon graduation. The fact that the pay differential is only slight between those with additional schooling and those without it no doubt contributes to this situation. Most of those who continue to study after the compulsory nine-year school obligation choose a field other than agriculture; those remaining faithful to an agricultural career are in a distinct minority.

As already noted, neighbors were old, established members of a community as well as, more specifically, those residing in the immediate vicinity. In communities such as Komárov, where individual family dwellings were adjacent and their inhabitants had known each other since childhood, the institution of neighborhood played little part—the whole village in fact constituted a neighborhood.

When a pig was slaughtered, nearby neighbors invariably received larger shares than those more distant. Announcements of an engagement, wedding, or death in the family were communicated to close neighbors first; to do otherwise would have been judged as deliberate slighting. The fact of living in a neighborhood naturally affected the ties of friendship among children of the same age, who saw more of each other than of others living farther away. If tragedy struck a family, everyone in the community lent a helping hand regardless of distance, class, or social distinction. But the fact of being neighbors did have a special importance in the enacting of annual customs or when special family events were observed. Thus, in caroling, it was considered proper form to visit the neighbors first.

Apart from the neighborhood of farmhouses, there was also a neighborhood of farmlands—fields and meadows. Good relations among those whose lands adjoined were very important indeed, for any trespassing was difficult to control and even more difficult to prove. An unfriendly neighbor might toss the rocks collected from his own field onto those of his neighbor, or let the weeds of his poorly cultivated land infest the neighborhood. He could remove some of his neighbor's dung onto his own field, or steal sheaves from an adjacent field at harvesttime. He might even plow away a narrow strip of his neighbor's field, a most serious offense.

It was thus the desire of every farmer to be on the best possible terms with his neighbors, whether within the settlement itself or beyond it in the village lands. For all these reasons, villagers exercised strict selection of marriage partners and of those expecting to move in, and made every effort to maintain and enforce the accepted norms of community life. But precisely because the expectations were so high, there was always the possibility of some disagreement or quarrel that on occasion could end in the courtroom. Again, no such cases are attested for Komárov, but they did occur now and then in peripheral villages of the Blata.

Godparentship, relationship by blood or affinity, and friendship had their importance primarily in the life and dealings of individuals and families. Secondarily, they were reflected in community life, as when a larger group of relatives or friends used their influence to promote their interests in the community—to elect a mayor or an alderman, for example. In general, kinship, godparentship, and friendship carried more weight than the simple fact of being a neighbor. This was noticeable not only in those traditional activities that transcended the confines of an individual family but also in the case of persons who suffered a sudden misfortune and needed immediate financial or other assistance.

Somewhat similar to neighborhood groups were informal groups that began to develop in the 1860s, once the oppressive rule of the Austrian Interior Minister, Alexander Bach, who prohibited such activities, came to an end. Among these groups were the volunteer fire brigade, which functions to the present day; a reading circle together with an amateur players' guild, in existence between 1918 and 1949; and a savings association, first founded in 1908 and functioning, with some interruptions, to the present. Some villagers were members of various organizations in the nearby towns, particularly in Soběslav and Bechyně. These groups helped promote acquaintances and friendships among those members of the Blata communities who shared similar interests.

In conclusion, the families of Komárov were tightly knit until the 1950s, as required by the farming activities in which they were engaged, and due to the fact that active village contacts with the outside world were relatively limited. The villagers were reserved but friendly. A generation of changes has left its mark on the cohesion of both the family and the community, however, with many of the young people seeking and establishing friendships on their jobs outside the village. The age-old pattern of plodding work has given way to the more nervous rhythm of the twentieth century. But a friendly visitor to the village is still received as a welcome guest and made to feel at home.

8 / Nonfarming villagers and outside visitors

For a long period during the days of individual farming Komárov had two communal employees, a herdsman and a smith. Each worked under contract, an oral one until 1867 and subsequently a written one. Agreements with the two employees were concluded annually on Saint George's Day (April 24) or on Whitmonday, although their term of service began on Saint Gall's Day (October 16) and ended on Saint Andrew's Day (November 30) of the next year. The contracts were negotiated early in order to give the men time to find other employment if for any reason either of them was not to continue for another year. Contractual negotiations were concluded publicly before the chief administrative official of the village, the occasion providing an opportunity for the farmers to make whatever remarks they considered appropriate concerning the quality of the services they were receiving. Each communal employee made the request for his contract by means of a fixed formula, which ran roughly as follows: "Neighbors, I beg you to grant me the opportunity to make my living and earn my bread among you." Once the contract was made out and signed, the employee shook the official's hand, saying "May God grant you good fortune." Following the ceremony, the two men were obliged to treat the members of the community, for which each provided a quantity of beer and threescore eggs. For their work, both employees were paid by individual farmers according to the services rendered them. In addition, the village provided them with free housing —for the smith in the village smithy, and for the herdsman in a cottage set aside specifically for him.

The smith was expected to produce all the iron items needed by the farmers— plowshares, shovels, forks, spades, hoes, iron harrows, and the like—and to take care of all wagon and door ironwork. In addition to housing, the smith had the right to use a portion of the communal fields and meadows about two hectares (five acres) in extent, to mow and collect for his own use the grass from along the public roads and thoroughfares, and to have his fields plowed and his harvest brought home by the village farmers.

On Saint Gall's Day the smith settled with each farmer individually, subtracting whatever advance payments had already been made and collecting the remainder in either cash or victuals. The sharpening of plowshares whenever they needed it was customarily paid for in a lump sum—by a farmer of large holdings with about one and a half bushels of grain (rye or wheat), by a middle farmer with about two pecks (about half a bushel), and by a farming cottager with a peck at the most. After he had collected from his village customers, the smith was obliged to serve the neighbors a hearty meal of roast goose. This event, to which the neighbors always looked forward, took place as a rule on Saint Catherine's Day (November 25).

Around the turn of the century, the character of the smith's activities slowly began to change. Increasingly he was called upon to repair farm machinery, and later still, various kinds of power engines. From 1932 on, his compensation was in cash only and on delivery, but his perquisites of housing and the use of a modest amount of farmland continued. Today the position that the village smith once held is included in the cooperative, and consists primarily of the maintenance and repair of power machinery.

The herdsman's job was to tend the cattle in pasture and to ring the Komárov chapel bell three times daily: at six in the morning, at noon, and at eight in the evening. He was also expected to treat sick cattle, to geld, and to help the cows in calving. For his services he received grain equal to about 500 gallons.

Accompanied usually by his wife and older children, the herdsman made his collections three times a year, making rounds with a wheelbarrow into which individual farmers poured an amount of grain corresponding to the number of head of cattle under his care. Each cow or heifer counted as one head, and three sheep or three swine also as one head. Collection dates were fixed: Saint Matthias's Day (February 24), Saint James's Day (July 25), and Saint Andrew's Day (November 30). To cheat the herdsman during his collection was unheard of, and anyone attempting to do so would have lost all standing in the community. The herdsman kept some of the collected grain for his family's use, but the major part he sold in town to merchants. His income from such sales was reportedly twenty to twenty-five guldens. For his bell ringing he received a loaf of bread per week and the right to use from one-half to one full hectare (approximately one to two and a half acres) of communal fields and meadows. Subject to agreement with the smith, he was entitled to some of the grass from along the roads. Additional rewards were due him if he had the keeping of the communal bull, boar, ram, or buck. He further received a fee for arranging the covering of female animals. It was his duty to treat the Komárov neighbors with a roast of mutton on Saint Andrew's Day.

According to local tradition, the herdsmen were the descendants of Swedish soldiers who settled in the area after the Thirty Years' War and married women from the village. This is said to be the reason the herdsmen and their descendants never held other jobs. While it is impossible to confirm this belief by archival evidence, it is significant that most of the herdsmen's names were Švejda, which appears to have been derived from the Czech equivalent for "Swede," Svéd.

All of these practices and arrangements began to change about a hundred years ago when, as a result of the transition to intensive farming, there were fewer and fewer sheep and the pasturing of cattle was coming under the personal supervision of each individual farmer. The herdsman began to serve more as a communal herald and servant. After rolling his drum, he would read the proclamations of the village council as well as other public announcements in front of each farmstead. He also ran errands for the community and for individual peasants, and continued with the bell ringing. His caring for what few sheep still remained in the village ended about the time of World War I, but he went on providing limited services for cattle until the last war. From 1927 on, he became the owner of the stud bull, which brought him some needed cash.

Until 1932, a part of the herder's compensation continued to be paid in kind. From that year on, his contract ran according to the calendar year, and he was paid entirely in wages. Like the smith, he still retained his perquisites of housing and some farmland. After World War II, need for the herdsman ceased entirely, and his quarters became the village firehouse and the office of the local national committee.

The function of the village secretary was customarily filled by the local teacher, who received additional compensation for the work. The functions of the village mayor and aldermen were honorary, but although those who held the offices were not paid, they doubtless derived some advantages from their official positions. Today the position of village secretary is filled by the secretary of the local national committee, and there are also salaried administrative employees of the cooperative. The former functions of the mayor are handled by the chairman of the local national committee, and the duties of aldermen by the members of the committee.

In addition to the innkeeper, who is today an employee of the people's consumer cooperative, the village also had a resident gamekeeper and forester. At one time, both were in the employ of the noble estate; today they work for the state forest administration. Members of the community were anxious to stay on good terms with the forester in order to receive his friendly consideration when it came to buying timber or collecting forest fruits or firewood. Essentially this relationship holds to the present day.

Finally, during the second half of the last century Komárov had one or two embroiderers. Reportedly they were the daughters of farming cottagers, who had been taught by their mothers. Because of their exceptional skill and good taste, they were able to develop embroidery into a full-time occupation. Demands for their work came from nearby towns as well as from Komárov.

The estate Hope employed a steward and several farm workers. In earlier times, these were probably sons of farming cottagers from Komárov and other nearby villages. Relations between Komárov and the noble estate were never particularly friendly; however, there was a tendency on the part of both the villagers and the estate to live in peace. The owner of the estate and his manager were well aware that the villagers, numbering more than 200, could do much more harm to the estate with less than ten employees than the other way around. As the estate was not particularly well equipped—its livestock in 1810 amounted to only 2 horses, 6 oxen, 2 bulls, 18 cows, and 5 calves and heifers—it was in no position to offer serious competition to the self-sufficient local farms. Then, too, the morale of its employees apparently was never particularly good. After 1918, the help consisted of members of four resident families. When Hope was expropriated in 1923 as a result of the postwar land reform, some of these families left the area. Those who stayed received three to four hectares (seven to ten acres) of farmland each and a portion of the buildings. These buildings still house three families, but the barn and the land belong to the cooperative and are used to house and pasture young cattle.

After 1850, Komárov was regularly visited by the mail carrier from Soběslav and the gendarmes from Bechyně (today members of the public safety corps), a chimney sweeper, and also on occasion a veterinarian. The master chimney sweep and his journeymen came from Bechyně; today the chimney sweeps who come to Komárov are members of the Soběslav communal enterprise. Until the 1950s, it was the custom at New Year's for the letter carrier and the chimney sweep to go from house to house giving their good wishes and leaving a small calendar. In turn, it was appropriate to give each a small cash gift and treat them to something to drink or to eat. Today, however, one tips the letter carrier only if he brings good news or money. It is no longer the practice of any of the neighbors who happen to be in town to collect all of the mail for the rest of the village, which was always done with no expectation of any reward.

Among those who visited the Blata villages, whether on a regular or irregular basis, were Gypsies, beggars, and itinerant jobbers of various kinds. Medieval documents mention several of these categories, stressing the inconvenience such visitors caused the villagers and the criminal activities for which some of them were held responsible. But by far the most unwelcome and feared visitors of all were the armies that moved through the countryside. In this respect, the Blata was relatively fortunate, having been affected only during the Thirty Years' War and the Napoleonic Wars.

Regular visits by wayfaring jobbers seem to have begun rather late—about the second half of the eighteenth century, in particular after the abolishment of serfdom in 1781 and the issuance of the Peddler Patent in 1787. Both itinerant peddlers and beggars visited Komárov, and members of each group had their set routes and days. The peddlers included glaziers, who invariably found enough work setting windowpanes; ragmen, who collected rags, leather, paper, bones, and bottles; tinkers, almost exclusively Slovaks from the region of Trenčín, who managed to keep busy during the period that earthenware was in use; gelders, who arrived during the spring and fall, usually from Moravia; and pig dealers, primarily from Hungary and Poland, who visited in the spring and sold farmers suckling pigs for fattening. Peddlers from southeastern Europe carried baskets on their backs and sold such small items of everyday use as pocketknives, mirrors, and the like, all of cheap and inferior quality. For the most part they were Serbs and Croatians from poor regions of Bosnia and from the area of Kočevje in Slovenia. The house-to-house sale of pigs stopped altogether after 1918, and gelders and tinkers appeared only rarely after that year. As enameled ware, iron or aluminum pots and pans began to replace earthenware, there was less and less work for the tinkers. The visits of glaziers also diminished.

Most of the beggars were older people, sometimes physically handicapped, who considered their profession to be begging and were not looking for work. They were required to have official permission from the appropriate authorities to beg. Usually they were given one or two kreuzers—after 1918, ten to twenty hellers (*haléřů*, gen. pl.)—and on occasion also food or some old clothes. During the economic crisis of the 1930s they were joined by the unemployed, who, although they accepted gifts of money or food when no employment of any kind could be found, were nonetheless eager to work, unlike the beggars.

Among the irregular visitors to the Blata villages were Gypsy tinkers, who arrived with carts and were surrounded by numerous members of their families. Reapers coming from southern Slovakia, where harvesting had been completed, or from the Bohemian foothills, where it had not yet started, offered their services during the peak period of harvest. Poles were brought in at the beginning of this century to help with harvesting on Hope's farmlands.

A special kind of itinerant was the wandering musician. Most of these strolling players knew little about music, and their simple playing of tunes was designed to cover up the real purpose of their visit, begging. Until World War I, they were largely violinists, clarinetists, bagpipers, and zitherists; after the war they tended to be accordion players. Much less frequent visitors were itinerant puppeteers, artists, acrobats, and others, since these preferred to draw on the larger crowds to be found in the cities. Only at annual dedication feasts did a dozen or more of them make it a point to gather in the village and put up their tents and stands.

The strict prohibition at the beginning of World War II of all house-to-house peddling and begging put an immediate end to such activity. It did not resume in 1945, partly because there was a steady demand for workers, whether with or without skills. Until the 1960s, harvesting brigades from cities took the place of the reapers, and mobile units of cooperative stores supplanted the peddlers. Mobile cinemas replaced the performances of traveling artists and by the end of the 1950s offered regular weekly programs. Among the latest cultural innovations have been mobile libraries that visit villages on a regular schedule and draw a respectable readership.

Between the wars, a few unemployed persons as well as relatives and friends who lived in the cities came to help at the time of harvest or haymaking. Those who had originally come from the villages knew how to help efficiently and worked hard, if only not to be laughed at behind their backs; but others were not used to the long working days and intensive output of energy. From the point of view of the farmers, their services were of limited value.

During both wars, the villages were visited by people from the big cities, who came to supplement their meager food rations with illegal purchases of such scarce commodities as butter, eggs, flour, and meat. As a rule, these were acquaintances or relatives of the farmers, who were thus assured that they would not be reported to the authorities. It was virtually impossible for a stranger to buy from the farmers; a few unfortunate experiences with informers had taught them better. This reserved attitude toward strangers on the part of the farmers no doubt contributed to their reputation as greedy and selfish people.

Tourism has only recently become an important social institution, although tourists began discovering the Blata as early as the end of the nineteenth century. At first they were, for the most part, members of the nationalist-minded intelligentsia who were motivated by the desire to find what they considered to be the uncorrupted culture of the folk. During the years preceding World War I they were joined by folklorists and ethnographers. Komárov old-timers estimate that at the beginning of this century some fifty tourists visited the village every year, arriving on foot or by bicycle. By the 1930s, this number had risen to several hundred. During the last decade or so, private cars and organized bus expeditions, even from abroad, have brought several thousand outsiders every year to the Blata villages for several hours' visit. The fact that Komárov is served by a good highway has no doubt encouraged this development. In turn, the visits of tourists have stimulated efforts to repair and restore the facade of those buildings representative of valuable folk architecture.

Good friends and relatives of the Komárov farmers enjoyed visiting occasionally, and some of those who had children came regularly to spend their summer, Christmas, or Easter holidays. Up until the last war it was not the custom to inform the village folk ahead of time, but today—except in the case of intimate friends or very close relatives—arrangements are made in advance by correspondence. It was considered appropriate for the guest to bring small gifts for the members of the farmer's family, or a larger gift for the entire family. The guest, as he well knew, was judged according to the gift he brought. During the period of individual farming it was further expected that those who came to visit for a longer time would help with the household or farmstead chores. The duty of the host, on the other hand, was to feed the visitors well and on their departure to pack some food for them to take back. This provided an occasion for the reciprocal judging of the host. Frequently the gifts exchanged exceeded the means of the givers, who very much wanted to "show off."

The length of a visit was determined by its purpose. It was not supposed to exceed the duration of the festivity or observance that ostensibly brought the guest—a christening, wedding, dedication feast, the slaughter of a pig, and the like. Courtesy visits were not to last more than half a day, and it was taken as inconsiderate if they were made during the period of urgent farm work. Those who visited and made sincere efforts to help were of course welcome for any length of time.

9 / Contact with the outside world

Despite some of the differences in landholdings and individual interests among farmers, the community of Komárov acted as a whole and, in a broader sense, as a member village of the Blata region. To be sure, there were occasional quarrels between individual communities as to which was entitled to a better stand of timber or peat bog, or whether administrative authorities had shown partiality in a particular decision concerning the region. Too, there were occasional "wars" between Komárov teenagers and those of neighboring villages over the boundaries between adjoining pasturelands, forest areas rich in berries, and the like. And now and then fistfights broke out between the locals and the visitors during dances or other social gatherings. Yet none of these incidents was serious enough to weaken the awareness of and pride in belonging to the larger Blata community. Toward the end of the nineteenth century these feelings of pride were no doubt enhanced by the ambitious ethnographic exhibition (*Národopisná výstava českoslovanská*) held in 1895 in Prague, in which the Blata villages were represented by an especially chosen group of villagers wearing traditional folk costumes as well as by extensive exhibits of material culture. Nor was there any lack of regional cultural activities. The museum in Soběslav, established in 1897, held frequent exhibits and supported or issued publications concerning the Blata villages, such as annual or monthly bulletins and catalogs of exhibits. Indirectly, interest in local folk traditions was furthered by those born in the region who subsequently distinguished themselves in Czech cultural, political, or commercial life. To some extent many came to consider the Blata as a folk cultural reservation, and even today some thought is being given to making ethnohistorical monuments out of Komárov and Zálší. Thus far, at least, many of the older farm buildings have been protected. Because the Blata villages belong to a depopulating region, there has been little danger that an influx of indifferent outsiders might erase what local color and sense of tradition still remains.

The villages to the west, south, and east of the Blata proper belonged to the larger Blata region. The life-style and culture of their inhabitants did not significantly differ from those of the Blata proper, yet there was little contact between the two groups of villages. Except for seeing relatives, there was little if any reason for visiting back and forth. Among these peripheral communities, Dolní Bukovsko to the south had the reputation of being the local Gotham. There were many stories told of the folly of its inhabitants, mayor, and village council. One such tale runs as follows:

The market day in Dolní Bukovsko had always been Thursday, but the people came to feel that Saturday would suit them better. They decided to send a deputation of citizens to the emperor in Vienna to request permission for the change. Before saying good-bye to their families and setting out on their journey, the men chosen to go grew beards in order to look more distinguished. In an inn where they stayed one night they were joined by a barber. He was a rogue who had nothing better to do than to shave them smooth as they lay fast asleep. When the members of the delegation awoke the next morning, they looked around in amazement. When each failed to recognize any of the others, all were convinced that they had become separated from the rest and had lost their way. So they all set off separately for home, having accomplished nothing.

Just how and when these humorous tales originated it is impossible to say. For the past seventy or eighty years they have been kept alive through written rather than oral tradition. The folk designation of Dolní Bukovsko as Kozákov, or Kozárov, which was actively employed until about a hundred years ago, may have been derived from the name of a village that ceased to exist during the Middle Ages, probably about the time Dolní Bukovsko was founded in the early fourtenth century. But other explanations are also plausible. A region north of the Blata, near Tábor, was and still is called Kozácko. The region is noticeably poorer, both in soil and in the appearance of its villages. The folk costume differed from that of the Blata, which was much more ostentatious, particularly in the case of the women. The Blata folk regarded Kozácko with scorn. To call a person from the Blata a "Kozák" or "from Kozácko" was considered an insult. Contact between Kozácko and the Blata was provided by those looking for seasonal work in the richer region to the south, but marrying into the Blata was an exceptional occurrence. A bridegroom or bride from Kozácko was subject to all sorts of slighting and was never quite considered equal. This feeling persisted until the end of the 1930s; at present, being from Kozácko is at most a subject for innocent teasing.

Except for those who studied in cities, the contacts of Blata villagers with outsiders were limited to only a few places: České Budějovice and Tábor, where girls from poorer families served as housemaids and where some of the young men were assigned for their military service or prepared for university studies; Prague and Vienna, where a few farmers' sons attended the university, masons and carpenters found seasonal work, and poor girls served as maids; and pilgrimage towns, Příbram in particular.

There was likewise little contact with members of other nationalities. From the beginning of the Slavic settlement of Bohemia, the Blata and the surrounding areas had always been Czech-speaking. Again, except for students attending universities, what contacts with foreigners did exist were solely on an individual basis. During the Austrian-Hungarian Empire, these were German-speaking state officials and representatives of private firms, Jewish merchants of nearby towns (Soběslav had a fairly strong Jewish minority), and some itinerants. The feeling toward foreigners of a lower cultural standard was, and still is, one of social distance and disapproval. To marry a member of such a group was unthinkable and no such case was ever recorded in Komárov. Germans and Jews were disapproved of on the basis of nationality and religion—an attitude fostered by a millennium of Christian tradition and the nationalistic and anti-Semitic policies of the Czech bourgeoisie of the nineteenth century. Yet socially it was not necessarily inappropriate to marry a well-to-do German official or Jewish merchant and, even considering the small population of Komárov, marriages with them did occur. At least such cases were tolerated by the villagers, although they considered these liaisons somewhat exotic. During the Nazi occupation of 1939–1945, the attitude toward the Germans took a noticeable turn for the worse, while that toward the Jews improved as a result of the persecutions which they were made to suffer. What additional contacts the men of the villages made with other nationalities during military service in World War I or compulsory labor assignments during World War II were individual experiences and did not figure significantly in the attitude of the village as a whole.

As for the villagers' view of cities, they tended to see primarily the advantages that cities had to offer, even if at the same time they considered their own contribution of primary importance to society. Thought to be among the attractions of urban life were the regular working schedule and the choice of one's employment, health insurance and retirement plans, recreational and cultural facilities, the variety of consumer goods to choose from, and, best of all, the relative freedom and privacy the individual was able to enjoy. Little thought was given to the concomitant disadvantages of urban living. In contrast, the farmers noted the disadvantages of village life: the fragmented and irregular work schedule with its excessive demands during peak periods, the lack of cultural and social opportunities, and the relentless social pressures that were brought to bear on members of the tight-knit community. The pull of the cities continues even today, particularly among younger people, although villages have been modernized, health and pension insurance extended to farmers, and working conditions regularized. Appreciation of the relative peace and cleanliness of the rural environment may be found in only a few individuals.

The feeling toward authorities and officialdom of all sorts was and still is one of mistrust. This attitude applies not only to administrative organs of the state—local, district, and regional national committees and their antecedents in earlier times—but to courts and service arms of the government as well—railroad and bus transportation, postal service, and the like. The villagers consider officials as sources of directives and prohibitions and collectors of levies, and as those who are supposed to help the individual but who are hardly able to accomplish what he feels needs to be done. Overlooked is the fact that one of the functions of state authorities is to coordinate and administer according to valid laws and that the petitioner is not always in the right. Peasants furthermore regard bureaucratic procedures as superfluous and officials as an element maintained at the expense of those who work hard manually. Official visitations in the villages are therefore viewed with suspicion, and during the last two wars they generated fear. Surprisingly deeply rooted are the memories of serfdom and the labor obligation of the past. It is understandable that the economic and administrative changes of the 1950s evoked strong analogies with feudalism and that less than fully competent functionaries were compared with feudal stewards.

In judging the various professions, the villagers of Komárov pay highest respect to all specialists in the agricultural sector and in forestry and fishfarming, and to teachers or researchers who are concerned with agricultural economics and engineering. Next figure teachers, physicians, miners, and workers in the chemical industry. Last are bureaucrats, professional politicians, and professional soldiers. Even though surveys of this kind were not made until recently, the testimony of old-timers suggests that fifty years ago the evaluation would have been very much the same.

10 / The wedding

The most important single event in the life of a Komárov villager has always been the wedding. Before the introduction of the socialist cooperative farming system, the success of the individual farming enterprise depended heavily upon the character, personal qualities, and work skills of both the bride and the groom, and on the initial contributions of their families. The circumstances and arrangements that led to a marital union were therefore of the utmost concern not only to the two marriage partners but to their families and even to the community as a whole. Villagers were eager for every single household in the community to cooperate willingly and actively with the rest for the sake of the common prosperity of all. During the three-field system of land cultivation, the close cooperation of all villagers had been an absolute necessity. But even during the subsequent period of intensive farming, the villagers took great care both to insure that marital unions augured well for the future of the farmstead concerned and to prevent anyone from joining the community who was considered unsuitable. If objectionable qualities in one marriage partner, although negligible in themselves, were to be reinforced by similar qualities in the other, the resultant life-style of the new family might have had undesirable consequences for the whole village.

To preclude the development of such a situation, most parents began the search for a prospective spouse for their son or daughter before he or she reached a marriageable age. Markets in nearby towns, pilgrimages, and the various festivities for which people from the region gathered in great numbers all served as good opportunities for such looking about. The house-to-house peddler or itinerant craftsman occasionally served as another helpful source of valuable information.

The most efficient means of securing a suitable partner, however, was to enlist the help of a professional go-between. This was customarily a trustworthy older man known for his wit, eloquence, and a wide range of acquaintances in the area. Very often his function was hereditary. The go-between was expected to arrange for the introductory meeting between the prospective partners and their parents, negotiate the marriage agreement between the two parties, and sometimes even to assume charge of the wedding festivities. In addition to being generously treated during the wedding feast and sent off with substantial quantities of festive food, he also received payment for his services—given in cash or grain or both—commensurate with the means of the newlyweds and their parents. Toward the end of the nineteenth century this payment amounted to anywhere between twenty and one hundred guldens, and on occasion could be even more.

Komárov did not have its own go-between. From the turn of the century through the last war, the people of Komárov and most of the other Blata villages were likely to use the services of Mr. H., a resident of Soběslav. The villagers had little opportunity or time to make regular visits to the various Blata communities. But the marriage broker, whose stock-in-trade was the intimate knowledge he possessed of the socioeconomic status of all his potential clients, made it a point to stay in close touch with several villages and their adjacent settlements. However, what he learned in the course of his activities as go-between he was obligated to keep strictly to himself—any abuse of this trust would have lost him all further clients.

Once the marriage broker had made a suitable selection of partners and both families had agreed to his choice, it was necessary to arrange the terms of the marriage union—that is, how much the bride was to bring to the marriage, how much the groom, how much the compensation of the younger siblings by the groom or the bride was to amount to if they were to lose their share of the farmstead, what the terms of retirement were to be for the old couple, and the like. Wedding arrangements did not always work out at this stage, sometimes because of the inflexibility of one or the other set of parents concerning only a relatively minor matter—for example, a difference of one cow or one hundred guldens. In such cases, the search for a partner had to begin anew. The personal feelings of the prospective bride and groom carried little weight—the rule was that parental wishes must be obeyed. This tradition could prove a heavy burden on young people who met during a pilgrimage, while attending church on Sunday, or at a dance, and became interested in each other without their parents' knowledge. If one or the other was judged unsuitable—primarily from a financial standpoint—the acquaintance had little opportunity to flourish into a permanent relationship. Only exceptionally did a child disobey, usually when the partner selected by the parents proved completely unacceptable because of an excessive age difference or some undesirable physical trait.

The larger the farmstead, the greater the capital needed and the more necessary it was for the partner who was marrying in to bring along an adequate contribution—in money, furnishings, or livestock. This was particularly essential whenever there were several siblings who eventually had to be paid off. Before World War I, a bride marrying into a large farm was expected to bring in at least 1000 to 2000 guldens as well as household furnishings. That this was a tidy sum indeed and good evidence of the prosperity that large farmers of the Blata achieved can be seen from the fact that a hundred years ago a cow cost thirty to forty guldens, compared to about 10,000 Kčs today.

Since financial transactions of this magnitude could hardly be left to oral agreement only, by about the 1860s marriage contracts came to be drawn up with increasing frequency. One such contract concluded in October 1861, and certified as approved by the appropriate authorities in October and November of the same year reads as follows (here given in literal translation, with names and villages omitted):

Marriage Contract,

which was negotiated on the day and in the year recorded below and concluded as further detailed, between [Name], owner of a farmstead in [Village], represented by his guardian [Name], a retired farmer from [Village], as the bridegroom, being the party of the first part, and [Name], the underage daughter of [Name], owner of a farmstead in [Village], represented by this her father, as the bride, being the party of the second part:

I

The betrothed make to each other a promise of marriage, with this contract to become fully valid when it has been approved by the appropriate superordinate authorities and the marriage of the betrothed has been concluded.

II

All property, which the betrothed already hold in their possession, or which they gain or inherit in the future, shall become property held by both parties in common.

III

In the event that one or the other party of the prospective marriage partners dies within six years from the present date without leaving issue, the party surviving the deceased shall become the sole heir of the estate, but shall pay out one third of the estate to those designated by law as closest relatives of the deceased. In the event of the death of one or another party of the betrothed after six years without leaving issue from their marriage, the surviving party shall inherit after the deceased the entire estate, save for one fourth of the inheritance, according to Article 1253 of the Civil Code.

In the event that children result from this marriage, the succession of inheritance shall follow the valid laws. [Unless otherwise specified by a marriage contract, testament, or other legal document, the succession of inheritance was as follows: first—spouse, children, parents, and siblings; next—grandchildren, grandparents, uncles and aunts, and cousins; last—other relatives according to consanguineal or affinal distance.]

IV

The father of the bride, [Name], assumes the obligation of giving his daughter [Name] from his own property on behalf of him and his wife 2800 Austrian guldens (in words—two thousand eight hundred Austrian guldens) as dowry, which he shall pay out in full and in cash to the bridegroom [Name] as follows:

(a) even before the conclusion of the marriage   1000 Austrian guldens,
(b) within a quarter of a year after the marriage 1000 Austrian guldens,
(c) in four years counting from the present day
    the remainder of   800 Austrian guldens,
which amounts to the entire cash dowry of 2800 Austrian guldens.

Further, [Bride's father's name] submits to giving the prospective marriage partners for their farmstead, and delivering to them upon request, a pair of oxen in the value of 140 Austrian guldens, two cows in the value of 60 Austrian guldens, one new wagon with appurtenances in the value of 30 Austrian guldens, and 10 head of sheep valued at 20 Austrian guldens.

V

On the other hand, [Bridegroom's name], with the consent of his guardian [Name], by virtue of this contract causes the farmstead owned by him in [Village] and recorded in the register of deeds under number [Given], with all the lands and appurtenances pertaining thereto, and with all the rights and obligations which already rest on it, or may legally fall upon it in the future, to become property jointly held by his bride [Name] without any restrictions whatsoever, for a price of transfer in the amount of 1200 Austrian guldens, in words—one thousand two hundred Austrian guldens.

VI

Inasmuch as the bride [Name] by virtue of this contract acquires joint ownership of farmstead No. [Given] in [Village], she shall be excluded, together with her former heirs, from any claim to the dowry.

VII

This contract shall be duly entered in the records, and any transaction which may be made now or in the future on its basis, must be duly entered upon the books.

The contract was first signed by all four individuals mentioned in it, as well as by witnesses, and then was approved and signed by officials representing the appropriate authorities.

The bride's dowry expected by farmers of small- and medium-sized holdings and farming cottagers was, of course, correspondingly smaller. Among the farming cottagers, in fact, the important considerations were that the bride know how to sew and embroider and the groom be skilled in a craft that was locally useful— in particular, masonry, carpentry, cabinetmaking, or tailoring—as well as in farming.

If two young people became acquainted directly and had reason to hope that their parents would not object to their marrying, the young man announced to the girl, "I will come to visit you and yours." If she was agreeable, on the next Sunday or holiday the young man arrived with one of his older male relatives, who in this case assumed the function of the go-between. If the parents of the girl were willing, the discussion of financial matters took its customary course. When both parties came to a mutually satisfactory arrangement—and according to older informants this was so in more than 90 percent of the cases—a request was made for the banns to be read in the parish church or churches of the marriage partners, which for those resident in Komárov was Saint Andrew's Church in Hlavatce. If the marriage took place against the wishes of the parents, the tendency was invariably to have the ceremony performed somewhere other than in the local parish church. Since the end of World War I, it has been possible to arrange for a wedding anywhere, and many a Komárov wedding ceremony has been held in Soběslav or Veselí, which offer more elaborate settings.

If the parents of one of the partners were no longer living, others substituted for them in the following order of priority: father's brothers and sisters, mother's brothers and sisters, godparents, and more distant consanguineal relatives such as grandparents, cousins, and the like. If not even the latter were available, a respected older villager or the go-between served; if a bride or groom happened to be under legal age (twenty-one before 1949, eighteen afterward), the legal guardian or at times even the parish priest might be called upon. In these circumstances, the financial negotiations were said to be easier to transact.

Once the reading of the banns was formally requested, arrangements for the wedding were put in charge of a master of ceremonies, known as the *družba*, usually an older, respected male from the area who spoke well. It was his responsibility to see that the wedding arrangements and the ceremony itself were conducted properly and to the enjoyment of hosts and guests alike. Even though the function of the *družba* was an honorary one, it was expected that the families of the newlyweds express their appreciation of his talents and time with a gift in cash or in kind, depending on their means. After World War I, when this function lost much of its former importance, it came to be filled by a local relative, occasionally even a woman.

After the second banns, the first cakes were baked, which were then taken around to the potential wedding guests by a member of the household in which the newlyweds were to reside. Occasionally this task was taken care of by the master of ceremonies, or by him and the designated family member. While presenting the cakes, an invitation to the wedding was issued by one of several fixed formulas—for example, "Mr. [Name], the bridegroom, and Miss [Name], the bride, send you their greetings and beg you not to be ashamed to attend their wedding," or "Mr. and Mrs. [Name], the parents of the bride [the bridegroom], send you their greetings, wish you everything good, and beg you to come to celebrate the merrymaking of their daughter [son] [Name]," and the like. Whenever it was the master of ceremonies who issued these invitations, he employed longer formulas embellished with all sorts of witty turns of phrase.

After the third banns it was the custom for the invited guests to send some sort of contribution toward the wedding feast. The feast was customarily celebrated in the house of the bride and the obligation to arrange for it fell on her parents. As a rule, however, the negotiations with the groom's parents included some arrangement for their contribution as well. Customarily their share was to supply flour and beer. During the first half of the nineteenth century the invited guests commonly contributed millet, gingerbread for grating (to be sprinkled over cakes and other dishes), and eggs. Later, other foodstuffs were sent as well. If the bride was from a poor family of farming cottagers or farm laborers, the guests would help with a financial contribution toward the expenses of the feast, and after the wedding the bridesmaids collected among the guests "for the bride." Such a girl might receive a fair sum of money to help the young couple get started, reportedly as much as 100 guldens.

There were a number of customs and beliefs in the Blata according to which days of the week and months of the year were judged suitable or unsuitable for weddings to take place. Most commonly weddings were celebrated during carnival season, that is, between Epiphany (January 6) and Ash Wednesday, the first day of Lent. Unsuitable for weddings were the periods of Lent, Advent, and Christmastide. The people of Komárov paid heed not only to the attitude of the Church but to certain practical considerations as well. It was generally assumed that soon after the wedding a child would be conceived. If the wedding was celebrated during carnival season—a period of relative inactivity for the farmer—a child was likely to arrive at a time when farming activities had been completed and the supplies from the harvest were at their most plentiful. On the other hand, a wedding during Advent would have held the unwelcome possibility of the birth of a child during the peak agricultural activities, and Lent weddings were restricted by the Church. May was considered an inappropriate month as the period of childbed might fall during the beginning of the busy spring period. If it was necessary for a wedding to take place during an unsuitable period—for example, as the result of the bride's pregnancy—it was always a short ceremony quietly performed.

Unlucky for weddings were Friday (Christ's day of death), Monday, and Wednesday—the odd days of the week. Sunday was avoided for practical reasons. Those few who did schedule a Sunday wedding were likely to be suspected of attempting to cut short the wedding merriment in order to save money. Most commonly, weddings were celebrated on Saturday, making it possible for the guests to enjoy themselves well into the night. At present, as a consequence of the five-day workweek, many weddings take place on Friday. The earlier prohibitions or restrictions on certain days and periods of the Church year have become irrelevant. But the tendency to avoid planning a wedding at the time of intensive activities in the fields still continues.

On the eve of the wedding the bridesmaids met at the home of the bride to make garlands for the female participants and to tie rosemary twigs with streamers for the males. There could be as many as ten bridesmaids, but regardless of how many or how few, the number had to be even.

On the day itself, the bridegroom and his party arrived early enough at the bride's house to have breakfast, consisting of soup and gruel. As they entered her home, they passed through the so-called green gate, a festive entrance arranged from freshly cut saplings arched over with ribbons and such inscriptions as "Lots of luck," "Best wishes," and the like. Soon after, guests began to gather, each being welcomed by the master of ceremonies with great pomp.

When everyone had gathered, the master of ceremonies brought the bride from the chamber where her trousseau had been assembled. It was considered proper for the bride to weep and pretend reluctance to leave the chamber, which served as the symbol of her childhood home. Next the master of ceremonies requested the parents' blessings for her and her future husband. At this point the bride thanked her father and mother for having brought up and cared for her, and the parents of both gave the couple their blessings. Those assembled were served cakes and brandy, each guest presenting his own glass flask (*pryska*), customarily decorated with a painted design. Even the onlookers who usually gathered for larger weddings were offered a drink with which to toast the wedding couple. Once the toasting was completed, the wedding party was loaded onto decorated wagons—the bride and her bridesmaids in the first, the groom and the groomsmen in the second, the remaining older guests and the musicians in the rest—and the party proceeded to the church, followed by the younger members and some of the onlookers on foot. Along the way, musicians—at the very least a fiddler, bagpiper, and usually a clarinetist—played songs appropriate to the melancholy occasion of the bride's leaving her home. The wedding party sang the first stanza of each song in two- or three-part harmony, the musicians then repeating the tune without the voice accompaniment. Even though weddings could have taken place, in theory, with the vicar's permission in the Komárov chapel, no such case is remembered. After the church ceremony the party returned to Komárov, again with the musicians accompanying them. Since it was the custom for the newlyweds to abstain from so much as tasting any of the food served at the wedding feast, they went on ahead to have something to eat while the rest of the guests made a stop at the inn for some early dancing.

Unless the wedding feast was held at the village inn, it took place at the home of the bride. The wedding meal customarily consisted of a fixed sequence of courses. Beef soup was served first, followed by boiled beef with thickened gravy, gruel of millet (and later of wheat farina), and peas, all of which were sprinkled with grated gingerbread purchased in Soběslav. Next came roast meat, usually beef, and at large weddings also poultry with sweet thickened gravy. Finally, a variety of sweets and cakes was brought out, including the enormous wedding cakes, or řičice, which could be as large as one and a half feet across. These cakes, culinary works of art, were prepared in large quantities and decorated by the farmwife. They were cut and distributed among the wedding guests except for the one made especially for the bride, who kept it intact until it fell apart. Originally guests drank brandy, but by about the 1880s beer began to be used more and more often. Wine was served at only the richest weddings—true also of coffee—and was saved for the very end of the feast.

During the feast, the guests were entertained with speeches and songs from the master of ceremonies and the groomsmen. The speeches were stereotyped, drawing largely on the various cheap editions of wedding speeches that appeared during the nineteenth century. Most of them were based on a book published by František Jan Vavák at the very beginning of the nineteenth century, *Smlouvy neb chvalitebné řeči svatební* (Agreements, or Praiseworthy Wedding Speeches), for which he drew on still older sources. After the feast, a dance took place in the inn, but before the bride could make her appearance there, she had to submit to the custom called the "bonneting" (*čepení*). Until the end of the past century, the bride and her bridesmaids each wore an ornamental crown, the symbol of an unmarried girl. At this point in the celebration, the women took off the bride's crown and other ornaments, put a bonnet in their place, tied a veil to the bonnet and bound the bride's head with an ornamental headband. This arrangement was to be worn by the bride during the entire first year of her marriage whenever she left her home. The custom of bonneting began to disappear about the beginning of the present century and has been reenacted only in those few cases in which the young couple and their parents wished to celebrate a traditional wedding.

After this ceremony, they took the bride to the inn; not until the groom had bought her with some money, however, would they turn her over to him, amid general rejoicing. The amount paid varied from one or two guldens to as much as fifty guldens if the groom happened to be well off. The customary joke was to offer the groom first an old woman, next a younger married woman, and finally his new bride. Afterward, dancing occupied the night until the small hours.

On the second day the groom, accompanied by his party, came to claim his bride, taking both her and her trousseau off to his home. The trousseau was loaded onto a wagon or wagons in such a way as to make the most ostentatious showing possible, since all the village judged the marriage portion of the bride according to the appearance of these wagons. From the beginning of this century, the bride more likely than not, spent the first night with the groom, and both then went to fetch her trousseau on the second day.

Upon reaching her new home the bride was welcomed by the groom's mother or, if she was no longer living, by a close female relative, and another feast began. In the evening, there was still another festive meal at the time the women were enjoying themselves arranging the feather-filled bedcovers on the newlyweds' bed (*stlačky*, pl.). At noon on the third day, the young couple themselves put on a reception, or "friendly dinner," for relatives and closest neighbors. Thus the wedding festivities were concluded, usually on Monday.

The aftermath of weddings, however, lasted several weeks. Soon after a girl married into Komárov from a more distant village, it was the custom for her to invite other married women from the neighborhood or village to a special treat of cakes and sweet liqueur. If there was a recently married woman among the invited guests, she was warned in advance by the others to be ready to "buy herself out." At the party, the women took one of her slippers and decorated it with ribbons, refusing to give it back to her until she had made a gift of some money to help pay for the food served. If there were several such women, they all were invited, and with the money they contributed still another party was arranged.

Weddings in the families for farming cottagers were naturally less elaborate, but they, too, lasted three days and followed the same general pattern. A "small" wedding, generally that of a widower or widow or of an older couple, lasted a day and a half. A "quiet" wedding did not exceed one day and was conducted with no music or singing. Such a wedding, concluded during Lent or Advent, when the Church ruled out conspicuous merriment, was almost always the result of the bride's advanced state of pregnancy. Quiet weddings occurring at other times of the year could come about because a young couple insisted upon being married despite parental objections, and as a result there was no one to undertake the preparations and arrangements for the full-blown festivities.

Since the last war, the situation has been similar only up to a point. Weddings are large, "small," or "quiet" for much the same reasons as before, but whatever their nature, many of the traditional customs are no longer observed. Young people become acquainted at work or at social activities. Once a couple decides to marry, they themselves set a date for the wedding that fits conveniently into their vacation plans or the like. Some of the wedding decorations are now bought ready-made, and the bonneting, the festive toasts, and function of the master of ceremonies, if they are employed at all, assume only token form. There are generally two weddings now, the first a civil one, the second in church. Since the beginning of 1950, the former is required, the latter optional and up to the couple. Before that time, from 1868 on, either type was legally valid. Despite the fact that religious feelings have noticeably weakened, civil ceremonies alone are still the exception. Instead of wagons, the wedding party makes use of automobiles, and live music has been replaced by records and tape recordings. The bride's trousseau is no longer displayed for everyone to see as in the past, since under the present distribution of wealth it has less economic importance, but there is no lack of awareness of the property involved. It is not at all rare for a bride to receive as a gift from her parents a savings account of 20,000 Kčs or the equivalent in furnishings. The food and drink correspond to contemporary tastes, but the sequence of courses is much the same: beef soup, sometimes cold or warm hors d'oeuvres, beef with bread dumplings, roast beef, poultry, sweets, and coffee. Beer and wine are served with the meal, brandy being used only for toasting. Occasionally the festive meal is served in a restaurant of a nearby town. Those few who wish to impress everyone arrange to have the wedding in a location of historical importance such as the city of Tábor or the castle at Hluboká near České Budějovice, in which case the wedding dinner is likely to take place in a nearby hotel. The dinner is paid for by the bride's parents, with the family of the groom contributing.

The age at which young people marry has not changed significantly since 1790, as the parish registers of births in Hlavatce indicate. As a rule the bride was, and still is, between seventeen and twenty-one years of age, the groom twenty-three to thirty. It is considered wise and appropriate for the man to have completed his military service before marrying. ·Women over twenty-two and men over thirty are considered to have passed the marriageable age.

One type of marriage found during the period from about the middle of the past century until the last war occurred occasionally in the Blata: girls from larger farms became welcome brides for teachers and for officials from the regional estates belonging to the large landowners. Since these men did not marry until they had received a decent salary and a permanent appointment—no earlier than at about thirty—the age difference between husband and wife in these cases was usually ten or more years.

Until the middle of the past century, marriage partners came almost exclusively from the farming families of the Blata and the surrounding regions. Because the landholdings of the South Bohemian nobility were quite extensive, it was usually not necessary, even before servitude was abolished in 1781, for a bride or groom to ask permission to leave the feudal domain to marry. The cases of "marrying in" or "marrying out" involved partners belonging to different patrimonial domains or the daughter of a small farmer marrying into a craftsman's family in the nearby town, or, conversely, a young man from such a family marrying into a farmstead.

At present, choices seem more limited than earlier. Komárov is a purely agricultural community and those who have not developed a genuine liking for farming in their youth are not likely to marry within the village, be they women or men.

In other respects, circumstances have changed much more profoundly. Before World War II it was exceptional for the bride to be pregnant. Today, about one out of six weddings is the result of a premarital pregnancy. As late as the middle of the past century it was the custom for a girl who became pregnant before marriage or who was known to be casual about sexual relations to be made to stand in front of the church "with a fiddle," a pair of short wooden boards with holes only large enough for a woman's wrists, analogous to the stocks or pillory, but light enough to carry about. While the informants do remember the phrase "with a fiddle" (s housličkama, dialectal for the literary form s housličkami), the meaning has escaped them; they now think that such a girl was expected to play the violin. As visitors to church passed by a girl whose wrists had been locked into the "fiddle," she was expected to tell them, "Welcome to church; I have sinned carnally." And after the Mass, as people were leaving, she was to say, "I greet you with God's word—where can I ever put down this fiddle?" The women used to sing derisive songs during the wedding of such a girl, and cases are remembered in which matters ended before the judge. For the most part these customs had faded out by the end of the last century.

In sum, weddings have always been the gayest events in the otherwise evenly paced social life of Komárov, and the villagers continue to look forward to them with great anticipation. While the importance attached to launching the bride into marriage with deliberate ostentation and substantial gifts has not diminished but has simply assumed new forms, nearly all of the old local customs, among the most colorful in Bohemia, have been discarded. Now that the parents no longer play a crucial role in the events leading to weddings, and relationships between young people of opposite sex have become greatly liberalized, Komárov, along with other Czech villages, has inevitably gone the way of cultural uniformity.

11 / Birth and death

Within a year of the wedding, as a rule, a child was born. If this was not the case, the villagers were likely to make fun of the husband by telling him that he was "sterile" or "weak." A childless marriage was considered punishment from God, or at least a grave misfortune. In the Blata villages it was in fact quite exceptional. It is of interest to note that when it did occur, the fault was not one-sidedly assumed to lie with the woman. Only in the case of older people— when widows and widowers married, for example—was the lack of children in a marriage accepted by the community without comment.

Until the 1950s births always occurred at home. There was a general dislike of maternity homes, and as late as the 1930s and 1940s the prevalent attitude was that only unwed mothers and women of ill repute went to such places to give birth. At present, only about one out of eight babies is born at home, primarily because the mother unlike most continues to work until delivery just as did women in the past, and there is not always sufficient time for transporting her to the nearest maternity center, located in Tábor, some 18 miles (30 kilometers) distant.

Until the end of the past century, it was the custom for female relatives to set up a "corner" (*kout*) in the main room for the woman about to give birth; this consisted of a bed hung with one or two heavy sheets to afford her privacy. These sheets were richly decorated with embroideries representing various Christian symbols believed to give protection against evil forces. It was thought that without such coverings a great storm would come about during the birth and take away both mother and child. During pregnancy, the woman was expected to take great care not to let herself be frightened by certain animals (frogs, snakes, weasels, and others), not to get burned (otherwise the child could have a birthmark), not to step over certain objects (frogs, snakes, human excrement, and anything else people detested), and not to eat certain dishes (strongly seasoned food in particular). Dark beer was recommended to insure that the mother would have plenty of milk. Hard and steady work was believed to guarantee that the child would grow to be healthy and industrious. These recommendations are still considered valid and followed today.

During the actual birth, the woman's mother or mother-in-law was present. If neither of these was still living, one of her aunts or an older experienced woman of the village attended her. A midwife lived in Zálší, but before she could be called and brought to the village the baby had usually arrived. Fortunately, not even the oldest informants can recall a single case of a complicated birth in Komárov.

Christening took place on the third day after the birth and involved the selection of godparents, a process to which the Komárov villagers attached a great deal of importance. Anyone from the village was eligible for godparenthood. To refuse to serve was a grave insult, as it was to refuse anyone who offered to stand as

The special pot, koutňák, *in which chicken broth used to be taken to a woman in childbed. (The specimen shown is at least a hundred years old. Height is 11 in. Photograph from the archives of the Institute for Ethnography and Folklore of the Czechoslovak Academy of Sciences.)*

godparent. By the same token, the community found it difficult to accept as godparent anyone from a distant village or town, a person completely unknown to them, or someone not respected. On the other hand, to secure as godparent an esteemed and highly situated person from outside the village was considered an honor for the child, the family, and the village. It was likewise not uncommon for a wealthier farmer to serve as godfather for the children of his farmhand, or to act as best man at his wedding. The personal and economic obligation felt by a farmhand so honored generally proved of advantage to the farmer, making him surer of his helper's continuing services.

The child's name was decided by his parents, in consultation with the god-parents. The child was usually named after a godparent, though sometimes the name was used as a second Christian name and so recorded on the birth certificate but otherwise never used. Only when the name chosen was strikingly unusual or unsuitable did the priest exercise the right to talk the parents out of their choice.

Quite commonly there were two godparents, a godfather and a godmother (usually a married couple), but one sufficed. One or both carried the child to church for christening, and they were expected to pay the fee for the ceremony. After the christening, the godparents were invited to a festive meal. In turn, custom demanded that for a month or so they send the new mother various foods. The most favored was boiled chicken in strong broth, carried in a special pot (*koutňák*).

The godparent was morally obliged to give the child a gift of money as a christening present (until 1918, usually a silver gulden), and to care for the child in the event it later lost its parents. The godchild's attitude toward his godparent was like that toward his parents—respectful. The parents consulted the godfather on all of the important decisions in the life of the child, and if necessary the godparent acted in the child's behalf. More recently, when legal guardianship was instituted, it was usually the godfather who was designated guardian. Godparents gave gifts to their godchildren on birthdays and name days and brought them pictures of saints and other souvenirs from pilgrimages. Godchildren, in turn, were obligated to visit their godparents on the godparents' name days and at Easter and New Year's to give them their best wishes. If the godfather was struck by misfortune and if the godchild in the meantime had become head of a farmstead, it was expected that he care for his godfather as if he were an actual parent. Although the institution of godparenthood is still observed, it has weakened considerably, and the mutual obligations are no longer as strongly felt as they were earlier. The relations between parents and the godparents of their children were never of any special significance.

During the six-week period after birth, the woman remained confined. She was not allowed to work, to leave the child, or to visit the inn. The belief was that if she left the baby for a short time the mythical "wild woman of the woods" would substitute her own child for it, and that a visit to the inn would give rise to a fight. At the end of the period of her confinement the mother attended church for the churching (*ouvod*, dialectal for the literary form *úvod*)—a ceremony in which a woman who has given birth is received in the church with blessings and thanksgiving. The mother and her child were wrapped in a sheet, in some families made and decorated especially for this occasion. Accompanying her were the child's godparents and her closest relatives, who were afterwards invited to a festive meal. Not until after the churching could the mother resume her regular chores and have sexual relations with her husband.

Until they were at least a year old, infants were never dressed in new clothes; otherwise, it was believed, they would wear out a great deal of clothing when they were older. For the first six weeks babies were wrapped in swaddling clothes. After that period they were dressed in long gowns made from old clothing.

While the circumstances associated with childbirth have changed a great deal since the last war, many traditions surrounding the ending of life have persisted into the present. Until the end of the 1930s it was common practice to arrange for the sacrament of extreme unction to be received by anyone who was nearing death. Even those few among the Komárov villagers who were known to be unbelievers or "heretics" did not refuse to receive the last rites. On such occasions the women of the village, at least the older ones, customarily gathered together and, following the administration of the sacrament, knelt down and prayed for the dying person. Among the old women this custom has survived to the present. It was believed that if the person had been a great sinner it would be difficult to light candles, and that once lit, they would burn only weakly and give faint light. During the last hours of the dying person, the closest relatives—usually his children—walked around him carrying a lighted candle that had been consecrated. It was also the custom to open the windows in order that the soul upon its release from the body would not have to leave the room by way of the chimney and become black. When death occurred, the surviving members of the family told all of the domestic animals on the farm that the farmer, or the farmwife, was with them no longer. Today these customs are observed by only a minority of the villagers, and extreme unction is administered in utmost privacy.

After death, the body was laid on a board, washed and dressed before rigidity set in, and put into a coffin. If the body was to be buried in a shroud, the woman who sewed it was not supposed to make knots in the thread for fear they might pinch the dead person; nor was she to bite off the thread as she was sewing, since if she did so she might soon lose her teeth. During the past century it was still customary to bury married people in their wedding attire. The whole village came to say good-by to the deceased, and it was the rule that each sprinkle the body with holy water. Even the few unbelievers, who did not say a prayer or put a picture of a saint into the coffin, would not refuse to comply with the custom of sprinkling. Three fronds of grain were dipped into the font of holy water and then used for sprinkling. Before the funeral proper, guests were treated to something to eat, particularly if they had come from other villages. The custom of sprinkling the body and treating guests continues today.

On carrying the coffin from the house, it was necessary to touch the doorstep with it, usually three times, thus permitting the dead person to say good-by to his home. Outside the house one of the survivors took leave of the village in the name of the deceased and begged forgiveness of any whom he might have wronged. The funeral procession commonly stopped for the same purpose in front of the chapel and wayside crosses along the route. The coffin was preceded by a priest. If a woman had died, the coffin was carried to the cemetery by women, that of a man by men. A coffin bearing a young person was carried by young men and preceded by girls dressed especially for the occasion by wearing garlands on their heads. The first girl was attired in white, the one behind her was dressed in black and carried a candle, and those following were again in white. Otherwise, the color of mourning was black, although some informants claim that in the distant past it used to be white.

Komárov did not have its own cemetery. Most villagers were buried in the Hlavatce cemetery, about 4 miles (6 kilometers) to the north, but some of those women who had married into Komárov were taken back to the cemetery nearest their former home.

When the weather was bad, or when a death occurred in winter, the funeral procession used a wagon. If the horses refused to move, it was said that the dead person was unable to say good-by to his home. At the cemetery, the usual church rites were held. It was considered the duty of the closest relatives to lament over the body and to bid the deceased farewell in a loud voice. Otherwise the people of the village would talk. After the funeral, all participants were invited by the relatives to the inn. Although the music was gay, the rhythmic "stamping in" (*zadupávání*) of the deceased, a form of dancing practiced as a festive diversion in many places elsewhere in Bohemia, was not the custom in the Blata. The pallbearers and the girls who accompanied the coffin were treated to some brandy mixed with honey.

Even today few villagers are buried without the assistance of a priest, but several aspects of funerals have assumed a modern form. Immediately upon death, the body of the deceased is now regularly taken to Soběslav. After it has been prepared in the mortuary for burial, it is returned in a coffin to the home. Farewell ceremonies to village friends and to the dead person's house take place much as they did in the past. Afterwards the body is taken to the Hlavatce cemetery, with automobiles replacing the earlier processions on foot or in wagons. The observances over the grave have remained relatively unchanged, and the reception afterwards continues to be held. Only a very few Komárov villagers are cremated; when they are, the proceedings are held in České Budějovice.

Although much has changed in Komárov since World War II, and despite the fact that the role of the Church in the religious life of the villagers has greatly diminished, the simple yet fundamental faith of the past has remained largely unshaken in the presence of death.

12 / Traditional observances and beliefs

The many customs and observances that marked the passage of time for the Blata villagers were closely tied to the cycle of the church year as established for Roman Catholics by the Council of Trent during the sixteenth century, with slight modifications following the First Vatican Council (1869–1870). In addition, the traditional activities of the villagers were also affected by the various secular reforms and decrees originated during the reign of Maria Theresa and Joseph II. The account that follows of Komárov customs and observances as of about a hundred years ago is arranged chronologically according to the church year beginning with Advent Sunday, four Sundays before Christmas. Since the end of the last century many of these traditions have gradually fallen into disuse, and today some of them have been completely forgotten except by the very oldest members of the community.

During the season of Advent, when the mood is of anticipation of Christ's birth, older people attended morning mass in Hlavatce or Zálší, and some few even in Soběslav. They carried with them hymnals and, since it was still dark around six in the morning, candles with which to light their way. The mystical atmosphere of the Advent services with their medieval hymns had a strong emotional impact on the people, and even those few who were not regular churchgoers usually made the effort to attend at least Sunday mass at this time. To a lesser extent, this has remained true to the present.

There were several traditional events during Advent that helped to shorten the period before Christmas, eagerly anticipated by everyone but most of all by the children. On the eve of Saint Barbara's Day (December 4), it was the custom for the so-called Barbaras (*Barborky*, pl.) to go about from house to house dressed in white with apples and nuts for good children and raw potatoes for naughty ones. The visiting of the "Barbaras" was done in complete silence. The size of the group depended on the number of single girls in the village between the ages of fourteen and twenty. However, if there were fewer than four in the proper age-group, even younger girls or young married women were asked to participate. At the beginning of the present century the custom began to change. Today, it survives in only a few neighborhoods, where a household may expect the visit of just one "Barbara," occasionally accompanied by an "angel."

On the eve of Saint Nicholas's Day (December 6), children looked forward to receiving gifts from their parents. Fruit and candy, shoes or smaller items of clothing, and, since the 1940s, toys or books, were all put on the windowsill to be found there by the children the next morning. It was the custom to leave the presents in the window for several days so that neighbors and other villagers could judge the economic well-being of the parents or, alternately, the behavior of the children. Children who had been guilty of wrongdoing, who had flagrantly disobeyed their parents, or who had not lived up to the minimum standards of the village, received little, and sometimes even nothing at all. Informants claim that presents not commensurate with the economic and social standing of the family were a much more severe form of chastisement for the child than any sort of corporal punishment could have been. On the other hand, parents plainly attempting to economize on their gifts to children who had not misbehaved were talked about by other villagers and considered miserly. This holds true to the present day. Even though presents are no longer placed in the window, the quality or quantity continues to be a criterion by which visitors judge the generosity and economic standing of the family.

Until the 1920s it was customary on the eve of Saint Nicholas's Day for several young people dressed in costume to visit the various farmhouses. One was dressed as Saint Nicholas (*svatý Mikuláš*), with a long white beard, chasuble (outer vestment), and a bishop's miter (headdress) and staff. Some, usually four in number, were dressed as devils, and one as a "she-goat," with a wooden goat head having a movable lower jaw attached to a pole and carried horizontally by one of the boys. The upper fixed jaw was covered with the skin of a hedgehog. Saint Nicholas would admonish the children, who had to say a prayer, and then give them gifts, while the devils and the "she-goat" clowned about and teased the women and young girls. But as early as the beginning of the century another group began to make the usual rounds, a threesome consisting of Saint Nicholas accompanied by a devil and an angel, and this was the one that ultimately prevailed and does the visiting to the present. This group also praised the children or reprimanded them, according to prior instructions from the parents, and then left presents. Today the custom tends to be practiced by arrangement among close friends and neighbors so that several threesomes may be making the rounds of the village at the same time. Between 1918 and 1945, a Saint Nicholas party was now and then arranged in the school. Older students were dressed as the threesome for the occasion, and the celebration included a dramatic scene, often with pedagogic intent. With Christmas and its gift-giving less than three weeks away, presents brought by Saint Nicholas are usually fruit and sweets rather than practical gifts, and for adults occasionally a bottle of liquor of better quality than they would ordinarily buy for themselves.

On Saint Lucia's Day (December 13), Komárov houses used to be visited by the Lucias (*Lucky*, pl.). These were older women wearing white headcloths who made the rounds looking for women who might be spinning on that day. When any were found, the Lucias slapped the spinners' hands with their own hands or with twigs. The visitors were treated in a friendly fashion and given some pastry and brandy. This custom was discontinued at the time of World War I.

Customs marking Christmas changed radically betwen the 1870s and 1890s. Before that time, strict fasting was observed on Christmas Eve until the evening meal, which was simple but substantial: a thickened soup; "black Jake" (*černý kuba*), a mixture of dried mushrooms and groats; sweet puree, sometimes made of fruit (mostly pears), sprinkled with gingerbread; pastries, usually fluffy buns (*buchty*, pl.) made from leavened dough with a sweet sauce; and fruits and nuts. Every member of the household had to be present around the table for the evening meal, and great care was taken to make sure that there were an even number of people. If the household consisted of an odd number of members, a farmhand was "borrowed" from neighbors. The meal was preceded by a common prayer, which was led by the farmer. All of the domestic animals were given something from each of the courses served. After dinner, fortunes were told. Lead was molten and poured into water, and the future was interpreted according to the shape of the hardened metal. Walnut shells holding small lit candles were floated in dishes of water, and anyone whose shell sank, extinguishing the candle, was believed to be going to die within the year. As many pieces of bread or cake as there were people at the table were put on a stool, each piece assigned to a particular person. The dog was then brought in and permitted to take one piece. The one whose piece of bread the dog chose was supposed to die within the year. And there were still other customs predicting death. A favorite practice of marriageable girls was to throw slippers over their heads in the hope that they would land pointing toward the door, a sign that the owner would marry within the year. The girls also shook trees in the garden with the words, "I shake, I shake the elder; let me hear from you, dog, where my beloved is today." The next sound of a dog barking supposedly signified the direction in which the "beloved" lived. A gift of food, a slice of Christmas cake with a piece of apple and a nut, was given to the well, with the one who tossed it in crying, "Here, well, have this for Christmas Eve!"

The Christmas tree, introduced in Bohemia during the 1820s, came to be widely used about a hundred years ago. Simply decorated, it became the outward symbol of Christmas, together with the serving of carp as the main course on Christmas Eve. There were three different ways of preparing the carp: breaded and fried; in sweet black sauce (*na černo*); or boiled in water with vinegar (*na modro*). Fish soup took the place of the thickened soup, and pastries were replaced by a special Christmas cake, a large loaf of braided leavened dough (*vánočka*).

Gifts, previously exchanged on Saint Nicholas's Day, are more and more often saved until Christmas Eve, to be found under the Christmas tree. They have tended to become ever more expensive and ostentatious. Currently, gifts of money are quite common, designed to serve as the basis for saving toward a refrigerator, an automobile, or some other substantial item for the family or individual.

The three Christmas holidays—Christmas Day (December 25), Saint Stephen's Day (December 26), and Saint John the Evangelist's Day (December 27)—are still remembered as the period of former Christmas festivities, even though the extent of the Christmas holiday period has now been somewhat reduced. Some friends and neighbors still visit each other, caroling on Saint Stephen's Day. Children are given pastry, fruit, and sometimes even money, while adults offer each other something to drink; on occasion, what began as a friendly visit turns into a drinking bout. Until the end of the 1940s caroling on Saint Stephen's

Day had a definite economic aspect: those making the rounds for the gifts of money or foodstuffs were the children of the poorer farming cottagers or farmhands.

Through the end of the last century the twelve days between Saint Thomas's Day (December 21) and New Year's Day, or between Christmas Day and Epiphany (January 6), were used as a means of prediction for the weather during the following year, with each of the twelve days representing the corresponding month. However, throughout the year there were many ways of prognosticating the weather and other conditions having to do with farming activities, most of them related to a particular saint's day. Examples are "If a goose walks on ice before Saint Martin's Day (November 11), it will walk in mud after Saint Martin's Day; if a goose walks in mud before Saint Martin's Day, it will walk on ice after Saint Martin's Day" and "If the leaves have not fallen off the trees before Saint Martin's Day, a severe winter will follow."

New Year's Eve (December 31) has always been celebrated exuberantly with food, drink, and dance, and still is today. Formerly, parting with an old year and the welcoming in of a new one was observed in individual households or among very close neighbors. Today, the tendency is for the younger people to drive to town to attend a special New Year's party at a hotel or restaurant, while older people generally sit up in front of the television set until midnight.

For the main meal on New Year's Day it is still common to serve pork for luck and lentils to keep the family in money. Even though few would admit it, the superstition concerning the first person met on that day lingers on: for example, meeting a child or a young person means luck, an old woman unpleasantness. As for the first extraordinary activity or event on New Year's Day, stepping into excrement means poor luck for the entire year, while finding a coin connotes good luck in the year ahead.

The official end of the Christmas season was Epiphany (January 6), referred to in Bohemia as the Day of the Three Magi. This was the day on which the Christmas tree was customarily discarded. It used to be observed festively with much food and drink, but since the end of the last war it has become a workday and celebration has ceased. The custom for children to go about from house to house caroling also has virtually disappeared, though at one time it was the rule for a group of children to go from door to door singing, "We three Magi, we've come to you. . . ." Until 1870 the caroling had the character of a collateral school activity, and it also served a distinct social function. The teacher accompanied the children from house to house, beginning with the farmers who were best situated economically and socially and ending at the gamekeeper's station and the estate Hope—the most distant points from the village. On behalf of the group the teacher chalked on the door of each house the sign K + M + B— *Kašpar* (Caspar) + *Melichar* (Melchior) + *Baltazar* (Balthasar)—and the appropriate year, and then sprinkled the door with holy water. A rhymed reminder that a gift was due was recited by the children, for example:

> Reach, farmer, very deep [into your pocket],
> So that your hand won't ache within the year.
> The one who gives us nothing,
> He is from Stingytown.

The main function of the teacher was to present a short play. The full play, with at least nineteen parts, was performed, reportedly, in a Soběslav inn until 1875. In the village a simpler version was used, with fewer parts and shorter roles. Performances took place in the main room of the more prosperous households. The content followed the Gospel story: first the shepherds and then the Three Magi paid homage to the Infant Jesus and brought him gifts. When the Three Magi, under instructions from the angels, refused to tell King Herod the whereabouts of the Infant, Herod ordered all newborn babies murdered. The play ended with Herod being taken by the devils to hell. Afterwards the teacher and performers were rewarded with gifts of food or money. In Komárov this play was performed until the early 1880s. Some boys still continue caroling rounds in their neighborhood, but they no longer chalk the doors with the initials of the Three Magi.

The entire carnival season was marked by feasting and dancing. Until the 1880s the frequent dances were attended by all of the villagers and followed a fairly fixed pattern. The farmwives and older women sat along the walls of the largest room of the inn, while the boys stood together in one corner and the girls in the opposite. The farmers sat at a table in the small adjoining room or in the main room where the dancing took place. Until 1848 the evening's dancing was opened by the village head, who first admonished the boys not to get into fights and then wished everyone a good time. Later this function was performed by the mayor or, if he happened to be unavailable, by the first alderman. The music was simple: either two fiddlers, a fiddler and a bagpiper, or a fiddler, a bagpiper, and a clarinetist. The dances played were short, with individual stanzas repeated several times. The first ones to dance were the farmers and their wives. Later on, when spirits had become high, boys one at a time would step before the musicians, throw them a coin, and then sing a tune, which the musicians would pick up. Soon everyone was dancing, and the second time around all joined in singing the whole song or the refrain. The greater the swaggerer, the more money he threw. While the usual amount was a silver coin, amounting to twenty kreuzers (100 kreuzers = 1 gulden), there were those who put up as much as a gulden or two.

By the 1880s the traditional musical ensemble was replaced by a small brass band consisting of a clarinet; one or two flügelhorns; sometimes a type of saxhorn or tuba, such as a baritone, euphonium, or helicon; and percussion. If a band was not available, an accordionist together with a fiddler, a clarinetist, or a flügelhorn player—and from the 1920s, on the phonograph—provided a satisfactory substitute. While the composition of the band has changed little if any over the years, its repertory has changed markedly. No longer does one hear the folk songs that used to be shared by young and old alike. The program played today includes a mixture of current hits, spirited pieces in duple time, and a wide variety of dance music. As the antiphonal style of singing was disappearing, a new custom began to make its appearance during the carnival dances. This was the custom of having a "solo" dance played, a number performed exclusively for that individual or couple who had requested and paid for it.

To break into a solo dance was considered a gross offense and almost invariably resulted in a fight. But this was not the only source of potential trouble.

Fights also occurred when boys visiting from other villages repeatedly danced with local girls or when one of these boys paid more conspicuous attention to a particular local girl than was considered appropriate.

Both of the Komárov inns, which were relatively small, were full to overflowing during the traditional carnival dances, particularly when many visitors from the neighboring communities came to join in the merriment. A great many villagers, mainly children, the teenagers, and the poorer members of the community, did not manage to squeeze in and crowded together outside next to the windows or else sat in the windows, where they voiced their opinions on everyone present. Misunderstandings frequently arose when a child repeated something he had heard from adults at home that was not meant for public consumption.

Carnival season culminated during Shrovetide, the three-day period immediately preceding Ash Wednesday. On Sunday after mass the youth of the village, accompanied by musicians, went from house to house collecting contributions for the band and for snacks to be enjoyed along with beer. The procession included several masked figures—usually a bear, an old woman carrying a basket on her back with an old man in it, a Jew, and several "runners" (*laufři*, pl.). The runners were humorous masked figures who ran around the edges of the procession keeping the group in order. In the afternoon the band began the carnival merriment. People danced through the night on Sunday, again Monday evening until morning, and on Tuesday evening until midnight. Tuesday's dancing was dedicated to farmers and farmwives. The carnival season was "buried" amid joking and teasing at midnight on the eve of Ash Wednesday. It was generally represented by a fat man, with the ceremony mocking a church funeral service.

Carnival celebrations of the last hundred years in Komárov have been limited almost exclusively to dancing and drinking. The tendency developed for various clubs or associations—the volunteer fire brigade, for example—to put on the dances for the purpose of financing their normal activities during the year. Quite frequently a club would arrange for a dance in a village where it was not actually organized, although some of its members may have lived there. These masked balls, however, have nothing in common with the original folk masquerade. Such masked processions ceased to occur toward the end of the last century, and present attempts to revive the custom are not always successful. While the Unified Agricultural Cooperative of Vlastiboř has been giving the necessary time off to those wishing to participate, the young people of Komárov, most of whom are employed in industry, have not been so lucky. For that matter, many of the village young people prefer to attend the masked balls organized in the cities, where the bands and the program are more "sophisticated."

Ash Wednesday, when the faithful received in church the sign of the cross on their foreheads in blessed ashes, was regularly observed until 1918. During the early years of the First Republic the church ritual virtually disappeared, but by the mid-1920s the older people were eager to receive the blessing again, and the custom continues to the present.

In addition to accompanying carolers on January 6, the village teacher walked with the children on their rounds on Saint Gregory's Day (March 12). The patron of school children from medieval times, Saint Gregory was regularly commemorated until 1870, when teachers became state employees and their participation prohibited. One purpose of the Gregorian declamations or plays, as they were called, was to entice children to attend school; the other was to collect contributions for the teacher and the school. A part of what was collected was distributed among those pupils who took part in the house-to-house performances.

Before World War II, all villagers wore dark clothes during Lent. Strict fasting, however, was observed only by some of the older people. The most outstanding custom of the Lenten period was the "carrying out of Death" and the "bringing in of summer" on the fifth Sunday in Lent. The ceremony was performed by school children, girls in particular. "Death" was a figurine made of straw and stuck on a pole, with decorations of colorful pieces of paper or cloth, or blown-out eggshells. It represented the dying winter, and the children carried it through the village while singing a simple song that began with the words, "We are carrying Death out of the village, and a new summer into the village." Once having made the rounds, the children took Death to the creek, dumped it into the water, and hurriedly ran away, as it was believed that the one who was last to leave the scene would die within the year. Next the children walked through the village with "summer," symbolized by a small decorated tree and in some cases a figurine representing a baby. This time they sang, "Death we carried away for you, a new summer we've brought [to you]." It was during this round that the children received presents from the farmwives—cakes, money, and the like—which they divided among themselves. The tradition, widespread in Bohemia, died after World War I, and attempts to revive it were unsuccessful.

Easter was the most festively celebrated period of the year. It was preceded (and still is) by a thoroughgoing cleanup of all farm buildings in preparation for the busy season ahead. Outwardly, Easter was characterized by special dishes prepared and served only at this time and by various activities of magical significance.

Easter cakes (*mazance*, pl.) were baked—round wheat loaves with the sign of a cross cut in their tops—and on Maundy Thursday some gruel made of millet was served with honey. During the course of this century the sweet gruel has been replaced by simple pastry made from wheat dough, "Judas cakes" (*jidášky*, pl.). These are made in the shape of two linked horseshoes, and are sweetened with honey. A special kind of poultry stuffing, made of crumbs, eggs, butter, and nuts, and frequently with some smoked meat added, is prepared in great quantity and baked in a large pan all by itself. On Easter Sunday and Monday, a roast lamb or kid was invariably served. Today, when sheep are not easily available, any good cut of meat will do, but veal is generally preferred. Pastries, made from more elaborate dough, were baked in the shape of a lamb and eaten following the main meal.

Easter activities included the coloring of eggs, either hard-boiled or emptied of their contents. Today, decorations on eggs are frequently made by transfer printing or with artificial colorings, but some people continue to employ methods common fifty years ago. In those days onion skins, saffron, or blueing were widely used for coloring, and decorative patterns were either scratched on the colored egg or applied by the lost-wax process, also known as *cire perdue*. The coloring of eggs has always been the task of girls and retired farmwives.

On Good Friday, "moving the soil"—that is, engaging in any kind of agricultural activity—was strictly prohibited. To do so, it was believed, would cause the soil to yield a poor crop. Among common magical activities were the cleansing of the body in the running water of a stream and the "extirpation of evil" from the house and fields by means of pussy willows blessed during the church service on Palm Sunday. The pussy willows were placed behind picture frames and doorframes, near the ceiling of stables and the barn, and stuck into the fields. Having been blessed, they were believed to protect the farmstead against evil forces. Repeating before sunup on Good Friday the Lord's Prayer and the Hail Mary five times under a garden tree was also considered effective against evil. Sweepings from the house were burned or at least thrown onto the manure pile. During the reading of the Passion in church on Good Friday, women were supposed to be at home twisting thread, since clothes sewn with such thread were thought to protect the wearer against the evil eye or malevolent supernatural beings.

Easter was the time when children began their spring games with marbles, tops, and hoops. A favorite activity was looking for treasures at the same time that the Passion was being read on Good Friday, for it was believed that at that time the earth opened up to reveal its treasures. Several games were played in which Easter eggs were used very much like marbles. On Maundy Thursday and Good Friday the boys observed another custom, moving noisily through the village with wooden clappers. Most of these wooden rattles were small, but now and then the boys constructed one so large that it had to be carried by several of them or moved about on a wheelbarrow. While most of the traditions observed by the adults died out around the end of the century, children's Easter games continued until quite recently. Before the 1940s the presence of the majority of villagers at Easter services was quite common. Today, only older people, mostly retired, participate. The one custom that has persisted to the present is the boys' switching of girls on Easter Monday with braided willow twigs until the girls present the boys with Easter eggs.

Dating back centuries and practiced through the period of individual farming were a great many customs associated with certain spring farming activities. For instance, about the time of Saint Gregory's Day (March 12), it was believed appropriate to plow the fields; cabbage and turnips were to be sown on Saint Mark the Evangelist's Day (April 25) and transplanted on Saint Vitus's Day (June 15); the time for the sowing of flax was Saint Adalbert's Day (April 23); and potatoes, planted before the end of April, were supposed to have been hoed and plowed before Saint John the Baptist's Day (June 24). All of these dates, as well as others that closely correspond to optimum agronomic periods, still basically hold, but their connection with specific days of the church calendar has weakened considerably, and, for the youngest generation, has almost completely disappeared.

Short-term forecasting of weather was based on the observations of natural phenomena: rings around the moon or low-flying swallows meant rain, the croaking of frogs good weather, red evening sky after sunset a gathering wind, and the like.

When threatening hailstorm clouds were approaching, incantations were sometimes recited by those believed to have special power to repel them. These individuals went into the fields with a loaf of bread or a wicker basket of grain and, facing the approaching clouds, recited a magic formula. More frequently, however, the church bell or a horn was sounded to avert potential disaster to the crops.

The night before Saints Philip and James's Day (May 1) was marked by the "burning of the witches," a custom observed to the present day. In recent times the "witch burning" has become primarily an amusement engaged in by the village young people. Old informants had heard or read of various magical beliefs associated with this tradition, but considered them superstitious nonsense. Among these was the belief that ferns bloom only during the night before Saints Philip and James's Day and that whoever found such blooms would have access to hidden treasures.

An important activity was the erecting of maypoles on May Day (May 1). Every boy put up a decorated tree in front of the house of his favorite girl, or else used the opportunity to take revenge on her for refusing his attentions or for preferring a boy from another village. In such cases, the boy or a group of boys placed a straw figurine in front of the girl's house or on top of the roof. By the end of the nineteenth century, the custom of individual maypoles and straw figurines had died out. Forest management authorities objected to the theft of young trees, and the jokes with straw figurines sometimes gave rise to complaints that could even end up before the judge. Today only one maypole is erected, in front of the chapel or in the middle of the commons. The whole village is present, and this celebration of May Day is combined with the observance of Labor Day (May 1). Recently a different kind of horseplay has developed between the boys from neighboring villages—stealing each others' maypoles during the night, or at least cutting off the upper decorated portions. For this reason the Komárov youth guard their maypole through the night, and in addition sink it deep into the ground and wrap several feet of the pole just above the ground with metal sheeting to make sawing difficult.

Another period rich in traditions was the season of Pentecost, or Whitsuntide, commemorating the Holy Spirit's descent on the apostles. This period began with Whitsunday, the seventh Sunday after Easter, and was primarily a time of activities for young men of the village. Until the beginning of this century it was customary to take part in the "walk with the king" or in the "beheading of the king," each varying somewhat from village to village. In the former tradition, everything centered about the "king," who on Whitmonday walked from house to house accompanied by other young men. The "king" was a youth elaborately attired in a long white shirt and several colored silk kerchiefs. Usually he had to be of a certain age (most often sixteen) and could not have served earlier as "king." If there was no one of the right age in Komárov, a younger or older youth became "king." The one chosen, however, had to be a serious youth who could go through the entire proceedings in a dignified manner, never breaking into a smile. In front of each farmhouse the one who best knew how improvised a witty distich concerning those who lived there—for example, "The fence at the [Name]s' is broken; their daughter no doubt is anxious to be married," or "The turf around the [Name]s' house is green; the farmwife is a good cook indeed," and the like. The group with the "king" received a gift of money or food, which they later divided among themselves. As they moved about from place to place they were accompanied by many of the villagers, who amused themselves by judging the appropriateness of the comments. If it happened that the "king" and the boys unjustly criticized or slandered someone, there could be unpleasant consequences, for it was the older members of the village who made the decisions concerning the young in such matters as military recruitment.

The "beheading of the king" involved a similar activity. On Monday the boys again took the "king" to every farmstead, this time improvising a simple play or "selling" straps that they had previously prepared from the bark of pines. The main purpose of these activities was to receive gifts. Once all the farmsteads had been visited, the group carried out the "beheading" on the village common, with the "executioner" cutting the "king's" paper crown or an old pot from his head with a wooden sword. Just before the execution the group again improvised opinions concerning the individual households or the villagers. If there was a farmwife who failed to give them what they considered an appropriate gift, they made up verses critical of her. Once again, troubles frequently arose when some of the villagers felt offended. The authorities, until 1849 those in the noble's employ and subsequently the judicial authorities in Bechyně, came to take an unfavorable view of these customs because of such occurrences and occasionally issued a prohibition, to which the village youth usually paid little attention.

Until the 1880s, the younger farmhands, too, had a "king." It was he who brought the livestock first to pasture on Whitmonday. The one to become the "king" retained the honor a full year, at which time he had to defend the title or yield it to another.

During the night from Whitsunday to Whitmonday—and on occasion at other times as well—boys and farmhands engaged in various tricks. The most common were nailing shut a door to a house, taking apart a wagon and putting the pieces on the roof, hanging a doghouse in a tree with the dog inside, suspending a tied goose in a bucket from a straw rope hung between roofs, covering the opening of a chimney, throwing into the pond milking stools or tools not properly put away, posting various placards with amusing announcements on walls, and the like. These practical jokes continued until the 1950s, when they were prohibited as contrary to the spirit of socialist coexistence. Since there were few young boys in the village, everyone knew who the perpetrators were, and that made matters even worse.

The last traditional observance before harvesttime was the feast of Corpus Christi (the second Thursday after Whitsunday), honoring the Eucharist. Birch twigs, pussy willows, sweet flag, and other plants used in Corpus Christi observances were stuck into the fields or under the roof of the farmhouse to guard the property against lightning, fire, or other misfortune. Wreaths worn by young girls in the procession of Corpus Christi were dried and used for protection against lightning. Some of these customs are still followed, though not openly.

Among the traditional summer and autumn observances, two stand out— harvest home (*dožínky*) and the dedication feast (*posvícení*). Harvest home was observed on the last or next to last Sunday in August, depending on the progress made in bringing in the crops. Each farmer and his wife put on a feast for their farmhands and other helpers, that ended in a communal dance at the inn. Sometimes the last sheaf was decorated, and a special harvest-home wreath was woven for the farmer and his wife. The harvest festival was strongly encouraged by the Agrarian party during the First Republic under the slogan "The Countryside —One Family." It continues to be observed in a somewhat different form even today, when the function of the farmer and farmwife is assumed by the chairman of the cooperative and his wife or some other high official of the cooperative. Funds for the feasting and dancing come from the cooperative, but it is considered appropriate for functionaries to contribute to both from their own pocket.

Usually on Saint Bartholomew's Day (August 24), soon after harvest home, children would bring home branches with berries from a rowan tree, which their parents would hang on the house. According to an informant, this observance was to commemorate the saint's escape from the hands of his pursuers. When he was to have been stoned to death, Saint Bartholomew took refuge in a particular house. His enemies secretly marked the house with a wreath of rowanberries in order to find it again, but when they returned the next morning they found every house similarly marked. Specially prepared butter, which the farmwife churned before sunup on Saint Bartholomew's Day, was believed to have healing power when applied as an ointment to sore parts of the body.

The dedication feast was once again an occasion for a thorough cleaning of the farmstead. Following the regulation issued during the reign of Joseph II that only one dedication feast could be held a year, this not earlier than Saint Gall's Day (October 16), the celebration customarily took place on the Sunday following Saint Gall's Day. While it is observed to the present time, the "small" feast commemorating Bohemia's patron saint Wenceslaus (September 28), which was marked by the serving of the popular roast goose, has been discontinued.

The dedication feast lasted two days and much food and drink were consumed. Animals were butchered and cakes were baked in quantity. The farmers bought barrels of beer. Relatives and friends from neighboring villages were invited by farmhands and the children several days before the feast. But anyone who happened to come by was given plenty to eat and drink.

On Monday afternoon all of the farmhands met at the inn for a "pleasant hour" (*pěkná hodinka*). They had the right to dance and drink until the small hours of Tuesday morning. The dedication feast is still festively observed today, but with fewer young people in the village, the "pleasant hour" is no longer held.

All in all, from the rich assortment of traditional annual customs, the tendency has been to retain those that had the most attractive external form and that provided opportunity for collective celebrations in the household as well as for the village as a whole. Observances directly associated with church rituals were to disappear faster than those serving to enhance family prestige and economic standing. In part this was so because the Church became weakened by the secularist policies during the First Republic and later came under vigorous attack by the postwar regime in the 1950s. And in part it was the result of the opening of the village to the outside world. While older people have retained much of their old faith and continue their participation in the major Church observances throughout the year, young people have adopted the casual attitude or neglect characteristic of the urban scene. It is no wonder that enthusiastic participation in local religious events and the customs surrounding them has been eroding and that the villagers' feeling of belonging to a spiritual community has lost much of its former intensity.

To determine the extent and nature of the traditional beliefs in supernatural beings presents difficulties, since it is almost impossible to separate supernatural beliefs that developed locally from ideas derived from reading fairy tales. During the past hundred years the collections of Božena Němcová (1820–1862) and Karel Jaromír Erben (1811–1870) have been included among the standard books read in Czech schools, and as a result every villager became acquainted with their contents at a very early age. Among the supernatural beings that populate these fairy tales are the water sprite (*vodník*), a male being supposed to inhabit and haunt the water, nymphs, will-o'-the-wisps, forest ghosts (*hejkalové*, pl.), fiery men, the revenant (one who returns after death or long absence), the snake supposed to live under the doorstep and act as the household spirit, and goblins. Today villagers of whatever age consider belief in any of these beings as superstitions that may have been accepted by their ancestors but at present have no other function than to serve as fanciful reading material for children. According to old records, the Blata villagers at one time believed in the power of the water sprite, the household snake, and goblins, but toward the end of the last century they reportedly began to be ashamed of these superstitions and claimed not to have any knowledge of them.

Yet there are various minor superstitious practices, many of which are still very much alive and in daily usage. Bad luck for an entire day may be brought about by meeting an old woman as the first person of the day, having a black cat cross one's path from the right, seeing a nun, stepping out of the door with the left foot, and other omens. Good luck, in turn, follows the meeting of a child or a pretty girl as the first person of the day, seeing a chimney sweep, stepping out of the door with the right foot, and the like. Clothes should not be thrown on the bed but put away without delay, for otherwise one's work will not proceed well. One should not whistle in living quarters because doing so brings poverty. A screech owl or a crowing hen forebodes a death in the household or among relatives, which is also denoted by such unusual occurrences as the sudden stopping of the clock for no apparent reason. Farmwives disliked anyone to bring gallnuts into the farmstead, claiming that if they did the hens would stop laying eggs. Associated with these superstitions are the beliefs in lucky and unlucky days or periods for the performance of certain activities, and the belief in omens of good and bad luck—for example, a horseshoe or a four-leaf clover on the one hand, excrement, rope from a hanged man, or a piece of wood from a coffin on the other.

Today people still wall a small coin into the foundation of a new house, and many nail a horseshoe onto the frame of the window or the door, or on the doorstep. Very commonly, drivers use as amulets in their cars such items as a figurine of a small pig or monkey, a horseshoe, a four-leaf clover, or the like. These superstitious practices are only in part traditional. Many are learned from radio or television interviews with favorite singers and actors and then passed on from one individual to another. These fashionable superstitions come and go, a situation by no means peculiar to the Blata.

Folk medicine in Komárov follows closely the practices employed elsewhere in Bohemia. Its rational aspects are based on school instruction, popular medical handbooks, and herbals. Every family makes use of various herbs for medicinal purposes, to a great extent quite in accord with contemporary pharmacological practice. To induce sweating, tea made from the flowers of the linden (*Tilia cordata* and *Tilia platyphyllos*) or an infusion from common elder flowers and fruit (*Sambucus nigra*) is used; for a cold, a decoction of dried dog rose hips

(*Rosa canina*); for stomach and intestinal colics, an infusion of dried centaury leaves (*Centaurium umbellatum*); as a gargle or in a compress on wounds, an infusion of dried chamomile flowers (*Matricaria chamomilla*); and for poorly healing wounds, crushed plantain leaves (*Plantago lanceolata*). Such practices become irrational only when blind faith in the healing power of herbs causes refusal of other medicines, the aid of a physician, or hospitalization. Similarly, people sometimes overestimate certain modern preparations, antibiotics in particular. Cases of failure to complete a course of antibiotic treatment in order to save the preparation for future emergencies are far from rare. In such circumstances antibiotics assume the role of the medieval "miracle cure," a kind of universal remedy. There are also instances in which old medicines that have lost their potency and may even be dangerous are used for ailments that are only superficially similar to the one for which the medicine was originally prescribed. What this amounts to essentially is a modern form of imitative magic.

During the nineteenth century and through the 1920s, there were two kinds of folk doctors in the Blata—herbalists and exorcists. The former made rather rational use of herbs that they themselves collected, largely on the basis of herbals and popular medical guides. A particularly well-known herbalist was Mrs. H. of Bošilec, a village southwest of Veselí. Her knowledge was valued even by physicians, who made no attempts to discredit her.

Little is known, on the other hand, about exorcists. They were visited secretly and no one was willing to discuss what procedures they employed or how much they received for their services. The exorcists themselves never discussed their practices, which were prohibited by law.

The widespread use of folk healers can be explained partly by the fact that until recently there were too many patients per physician in rural areas and also by a general feeling of mistrust toward doctors. Very likely this mistrust came about because doctors were generally not called to attend sick persons until it was too late for them to be of help. Dislike and distrust of hospitals was the result of biased reports concerning the conditions there and the notion that hospitals were only for poor people and beggars (which was largely the case at least until the middle of the nineteenth century). Adding to the mistrust were exaggerated reports in newspapers and magazines concerning the miraculous effects of new drugs and surgical methods. The patient accordingly expected to be helped immediately and was naturally disappointed and discouraged when he was not. Responsibility for the lack of success was then attributed to the physician and the hospital—again a situation not peculiar to the Blata.

Today, with health care and hospitalization virtually free, and rational scientific knowledge in every field widely disseminated, the traditional reluctance to make use of modern medicine is rapidly disappearing. About the only serious obstacles are the inconveniences of having to travel to the nearest town and then being subjected to a long wait in the office of the health service.

13 / The Church and the state

Two sharply defined ideologies have affected the outlook on life of the Komárov villagers. The first was the Roman Catholic faith, its militant Counter-Reformation stance fading steadily during the last two centuries, and its influence further moderating after 1918 and again after the Second Vatican Council. The other was dialectical materialism, at first Stalinist in both explication and application. Older villagers have been exposed to both these opposing ideologies through the influence of school, church, various training courses, and a highly politicized press, as well as in their dealings with those in authority.

Concerning very early times we have scarcely any information. We do know, however, that the influence of the Roman Catholic Church has been continuous since the original settling of the area during the thirteenth and fourteenth centuries. For a long period canon law was also the state and international law, and such church records as registers of births, confessants, marriages, and deaths were the only reliable sources of vital statistics concerning the populations of the various feudal domains. Despite the fact that the villagers of the Blata came into contact with the forces of the Reformation during the fifteenth and sixteenth centuries through Hussitism and the Bohemian Brethren (a Christian body established in 1467), its impact was generally weaker in southern Bohemia than elsewhere in the land. However, the people of the area were aware of the South Bohemian Hussite tradition, and it continues to be a source of pride, particularly as Jan Hus (John Huss), Jan Žižka, and other Hussite reformers or warriors were either from the Bohemian South or developed a close relationship to it.

There must frequently have occurred interesting clashes as well as convergences between these two antagonistic approaches to Christianity. Officially, Hus, Žižka, and their followers were always presented by the Roman Catholic Church as heretics who brought the Czech nation to the brink of ruin. On the other hand, the Church found it expedient to respect the local outlook and mood, and priests who were sent to administer South Bohemian parishes were reportedly instructed with this in view. Any priest who unduly offended the sentiments of his parishioners would have lost the trust of those whom he was attempting to shepherd. It was therefore not unusual for the parish priest to assist with the festivities commemorating Hus or Žižka and praise them publicly from the pulpit as examples of patriotic Czechs. More recently, such expressions of religious tolerance were supported by the goodwill and patriotism of the bishops of České Budějovice.

The attitude of the Blata peasants toward Christianity was largely rationalistic, and after 1848 even self-confident. One informant went so far as to assert, "I can manage to survive without their teaching, but they cannot without my bread." The Church and its representatives were seen by the peasants as the bearers of Christianity, who were paid to profess, spread, and uphold the teachings of Christ, and who therefore deserved their respect. The relationship of the peasants toward the clergy was largely determined by the personal characteristics of the clergymen. Some were considered kind and understanding and the people took to them well; others were little liked or even actively disliked. The occasional nonobservance of celibacy was generally tolerated: the obligation of priests to remain celibate was never looked upon with any particular favor by the peasants. Father H., a well-liked priest who served Komárov as well as other communities toward the end of the nineteenth century, had seven daughters by his housekeeper, a situation that he made no attempt to hide. One of the informants, now deceased, recalled with no sense of shock how she once met him happily rubbing his hands together and declaring, "Well, I have just married off another girl."

With regard to Christian ideology, the villager was exposed to the fundamental teachings of Roman Catholicism in school during certain periods reserved for religious instruction. What little he learned there from the catechism and biblical history was usually mechanically memorized and rather poorly understood. Thus he acquired only superficial knowledge and appreciation of Christian philosophy, despite widespread emphasis on practical morality and external church activities. There was little interest in or occasion for going beneath the surface in either Komárov or the Blata in general, which produced none of the lay Bible students and folk scripturalists characteristic of eastern Bohemia. Nor were there ever any attempts in the Blata to interpret the Scriptures in a highly individual manner as was the case elsewhere in Bohemia, where such attempts occasionally led to popular chiliastic movements.

Since there has never been a church in Komárov—only a chapel consecrated to the Visitation of the Virgin Mary—mass has usually been said in Komárov only once a year (on July 2), and virtually all ritual activities in which the villagers participate have taken place outside the community. Komárov's parish church (Saint Andrew's) was located in Hlavatce, but many people preferred to walk to Zálší, Soběslav, or even Bechyně to church on Sundays and holidays. Zálší was closer than either Hlavatce or Soběslav, and Masses were regularly said there. The advantage of going to Soběslav was that until World War II some stores there were open on Sunday for the benefit of their village customers.

The farmers of Komárov and their wives usually attended the early mass. Afterwards, the women went home to prepare the festive Sunday noon meal while their husbands engaged in discussions in front of the church or stopped at the inn. The children and young people, the aged, and the farmhands attended High Mass around ten. The afternoon vesper service was attended by everyone.

Regular church attendance in nearby towns or villages provided welcome opportunities for meeting other members of the community or region and exchanging opinions with them, keeping informed about the current concerns of the Blata communities, looking for or appraising marriage partners for children, and most of all for being exposed to a variety of cultural innovations. Many a project of potential benefit to the community as a whole went through its initial planning in front of the church on Sundays. Information would be gathered by the farmers during the morning; at the noon meal the situation might be discussed with the farmwife, the retired farmer, and sometimes the adult children and farmhands; and finally, in general discussions before and after vespers, plans were often worked out and arrangements decided upon.

Until about the time of World War I, all of the people of Komárov took part in the church rituals; these held considerable attraction, and their external forms had profound influence on the villagers' feelings, thinking, and esthetic sensibilities. The various obligations that the Church imposed upon or expected of them included attendance at mass on Sundays and on holy days of obligation, confession and Holy Communion at least once a year, and optional participation in the stations of the cross and various pilgrimages. The whole community attended early morning masses during Advent, midnight mass on Christmas Eve, services on Candlemas Day and at Easter, and processions on Rogation Days and on Corpus Christi. The Advent hymns (*roráty*) and the carols during the Christmas season were especially enjoyed because of their ancient tunes and simple yet poignant texts.

Until the 1880s it was customary between the two morning services for the farmers to climb to the choir loft of the Soběslav church and sing carols with secular introductions, as in the following example:

> Our village magistrate has handsome horses,
> I would pay a thousand guldens for them,
> Indeed, I would pay that much for them;
> Yet I would rather have his daughter,
> His daughter, daughter, little daughter,
> The magistrate's Nannette.

Until the time of World War I, the Blata farmers gathered on Christmas Day in the choir loft after the early Mass and without accompaniment sang a song glorifying the Eucharist. It was over twenty stanzas long and began with the words,

> Come and supplicate, all of you farmers,
> And all of you plowmen
> Who are cultivating the fields,
> Supplicate and you will receive blessings.

During Lent, until the end of the nineteenth century, people dressed in dark clothes, and on Fridays regularly attended in large numbers the stations of the cross and the sermon that followed. In the Blata villages, including Komárov, morning services were held in the village chapels on Maundy Thursday through Holy Saturday between five and six in the morning. On Easter Sunday it was customary to go to confession in Hlavatce. The arrangement of going to confession on different days according to age, sex, and domicile was a survival from the time of the Counter-Reformation, during the second half of the seventeenth century, when attendance at confession was obligatory and served as a population count and a check on each person's attitude toward the Church. In those times, attendance was certified on a small piece of paper. Individuals who did not fulfill their confessional obligation were investigated as heretics. The modern analog is the judging of people's political attitudes by whether or not they decorate their windows with flags on state occasions, participate in political meetings, wear buttons in their lapels, and the like.

The remaining church services, in which participation was optional, were attended for the most part by elderly people. It was at least a half hour's walk to Zálší, and even more to Hlavatce. At times when farming activities demanded the full attention of the farmer and his helpers, it was neither practical nor advisable for the able-bodied to take the time to attend.

Collective participation in pilgrimages was not only an expression of faith but carried social prestige as well and was an important means of self-realization. Until 1914 it was a social necessity to make a pilgrimage to Mariazell in Austria at least once in an individual's lifetime. On foot the journey there and back took fourteen days, but at the end of the century train excursions began to be organized. After World War I, as a result of the political rearrangement of Europe, pilgrimages to Mariazell ceased. Next in importance was the pilgrimage to Svatá Hora, near Příbram, which took five days and was invariably made on foot. To save their shoes from excessive wear and their feet from blistering, the pilgrims used to walk barefoot or in socks with reinforced soles. The local people of Příbram welcomed the pilgrims with special greetings, fanfares played by brass bands, and girls attired in festive clothes. Some individuals made the pilgrimage to Svatá Hora as many as thirty times. Among the places in southern Bohemia to which pilgrimages were made were the Church of the Miraculous Virgin Mary in Římov, the Church of the Assumption of the Virgin Mary in Bechyně (August 15), and the Chapel of the Most Holy Trinity in Křemešník, near Pelhřimov. Very popular were the pilgrimages to Prague on Saint John of Nepomuk's Day (May 16), made by train after the 1870s. The tableaux that occurred whenever the small processions of arriving villagers met the main procession are still remembered in full detail by those old informants who participated. They describe how each secondary procession was required to ask permission to join the main stream of pilgrims. Twice permission was denied, but on the third asking the smaller procession was at last permitted to join, and the entire group then moved forward together.

The only pilgrimage annually observed in Komárov itself was the so-called Hradec pilgrimage (hradecká pout') on the second Sunday of July. Pilgrims from Jindřichův Hradec walked in a procession to Bechyně, with the Komárov villagers joining them on the way. On that morning, mass was read in the Komárov chapel, and in the evening there was music for dancing, which the young people enjoyed. This annual festivity is observed to the present day, except of course for the pilgrimage itself, which would be considered out of place under present conditions.

After World War I the hold of the Church began to loosen rapidly, but the first fissures had become evident as early as the 1870s with the establishment of the teachers college in Soběslav. Some of the younger sons of Blata farmers went to Soběslav to study and there became influenced by evolutionist materialism with its attendant atheism; they were also affected by the other intellectual currents to which a fair portion of teachers had become receptive. However, any views which they took home with them, or other quasi-religious notions deriving from industrial civilizations such as spiritism and theosophy, made little if any impression on the Blata peasants, who were equally unreceptive to anti-Christian or anticlerical organizations advocating cremation, agnosticism, and the like.

Since the 1950s, those eagerly seeking to advance their political careers have openly proclaimed their aversion to the Church and to Christianity as an idealistic world view in order to better their politico-social profile. The number of active churchgoers rather rapidly fell to about 10 percent to 20 percent of the total village population. However, quite recently these figures have gone up again slightly—the result of certain relaxations in church–state relations, the reforms of Vatican II (mass said in the vernacular, for example), and the modernizing of religious instruction for those school children who specifically request it. The partial return to religion may also symbolize the quest for some firm point of reference in a world in which standards of judgment have been shifting with disconcerting rapidity.

Although Christianity was the official state ideology of Austria-Hungary, the militant efforts of the Czech patriots against Vienna did not appear to be directed against Rome, and the striving for national independence had little effect on the attitudes toward the Church in the purely agricultural villages of the Blata. The democratic liberalism of the First Republic was not concerned with establishing a new ideology or with changing the old one. Instead, the molding or redirecting of people's views was attempted primarily by the various political parties, which began to assume a very active role in the life of the young republic.

In Komárov, a purely agricultural community, the Agrarian party understandably had by far the greatest influence even though the number of organized party members was very small indeed. There is no question that the Agrarian party—the largest political party during the First Republic—had the interest of the landed peasants very much at heart and strove for the improvement of every aspect of agriculture. It took great interest in its registered members and was able to attract them with such external trappings and activities as festivals, band concerts, and a riding organization. These were what the villagers saw, and not the signs of political conservatism evident in the party's readiness to pit the village against the city, or the fascist tendencies that the Agrarian party came to display in its foreign policy orientation. To the peasant the political direction of the high party echelons was of little importance as long as it did not encroach upon his interests. Some of the small farmers and farmhands were said to be inclined toward the Social Democratic party, but on the whole the attitude of the farmers toward politics was always reserved, and political meetings generally proved unproductive simply because hardly anyone ever bothered to attend them.

The attitude toward fascism, which employed the most brutal means of coercion and oppression during the period of the Nazi occupation (1939–1945), was uniformly negative. When someone did actually collaborate with the occupying Germans—and there appears to have been no such case in Komárov—it was not out of sympathy with the methods and aims of fascism but because of the resulting personal advantages. In a strictly rationed wartime economy these could of course be considerable. The Blata peasants judged severely but justly those who did cooperate with the enemy: persons with education—teachers, officials, and those who went to study in German universities while Czech universities were forcibly closed—were held in greater contempt than those with a minimal educational background or the poor.

The attitude toward historical and dialectical .materialism as the ideology of socialism is somewhat controversial. The harsh pressure on the villagers after 1948 to join the cooperative system, as a result of which the three largest farmers in Komárov were turned out of the community as kulaks (prosperous peasants who refused to cooperate with the efforts to collectivize) and their property expropriated, and the uninformed farm policies handed down by those ignorant of local conditions and usages could scarcely generate enthusiasm or acceptance. Sympathy for the expelled kulaks did not grow out of any particular affection on the part of the other villagers but came about because the community had lost valuable workers and storage areas, and because their farm buildings, unused and unattended, began to deteriorate; to date many of these have not been put to regular use. But there is no question that compassion played its part, too, aided by the memory of Nazi persecution and the indirect remembrances of the serfdom and the labor obligation of the distant past. Some of the external features of contemporary socialist management have been seen as but a variant of feudal legal norms. Among these similarities are the difficulties encountered when one wishes to resettle, change employment, emigrate abroad, or enroll for university study; the periodic screenings of individuals and groups for attitude and loyalty toward the government; the cult of personality; the more or less compulsory work brigades; and the practical impossibility of securing redress of the decision of party and state organs. From the peasant's point of view, the philosophical system underlying the socialist form of government itself appears to be completely irrelevant. None of the local political functionaries managed to go beyond the superficial understanding of socialism acquired from popular brochures, short-term courses, and working meetings called to discuss and solve concrete problems. The villagers realized very quickly that these officials were often more concerned with deriving personal advantages and prestige—the power to be able to "rule," to manipulate others—than with the establishment of true socialism and its ideological foundation. On the other hand, the villagers were equally quick to appreciate the rapid electrification of communities and the establishment of telecommunications, improvement and construction of roads, and the advantages brought about by the transition to cooperatives. Among these benefits were health and pension insurance, child allowances, fixed working schedules (even though this was largely in theory since a labor shortage forced most agricultural workers to work overtime, for which they received additional compensation), the right to paid vacation time (taken for granted in other sectors of the economy), group excursions to theaters and other cultural events as well as to places of special interest, and help provided by work teams of students and military personnel during harvest.

Members of the older generations—those born prior to 1918—are of the opinion that the present system uprooted the old order without replacing it with something more valuable. However, the wisdom and equanimity gained through a lifetime of hard labor in the fields have resulted in their being able to view the contemporary arrangement with indulgence and tolerance, even if they have found adapting difficult. A certain apathy or ambivalence can be detected in the views of the middle generation, particularly among those who were affected by the Nazi occupation, the political events of the 1950s, and most recently the events of 1968. Their attitude may best be characterized by the comment of one of the informants: "What am I really to believe? What once was white later became black, then green, and today again is black or even yet some other color. What I was once praised for I am today harassed for, and the other way around." Members of the youngest generation seem to react against the views of their elders, which understandably leads to occasional conflict with the established ideology and its spokesmen. That, of course, is a trend currently found elsewhere in the world as well.

There are three categories of nontraditional observances—those decreed officially, those assumed voluntarily, and those enjoyed spontaneously. Included in the first category are state celebrations and legal holidays. During the Austro-Hungarian monarchy the birthday and the name day of the emperor were both celebrated, while during the First Republic the birthday of President T. G. Masaryk (March 7) was a holiday. Such holidays were received with universal delight by school children, for whom they meant a welcome relief from the routine of a regular school day. The attitude of adults was reserved: only individuals who had developed an emotional bond with those who were honored celebrated the occasions.

The second category includes countrywide festivities officially established but accepted spontaneously and voluntarily. Everyone understands their meaning and feels himself emotionally involved in their observance. Among these are May 1 (Labor Day), an official state holiday after 1919 but celebrated by some from 1891 onward; October 28 (Proclamation of Czechoslovak Independence [1918], Day of Nationalization [1945], and Passage of the Law Concerning Czechoslovak Federation [1968]), observed as a state holiday from 1919 on; and May 9 (Anniversary of the Liberation of Czechoslovakia by the Soviet Army [1945]), celebrated as a state holiday after 1945. The popularity of these holidays is due at least in part to the fact that since they are legal holidays, all nonessential work is suspended. During the times of individual farming, the significance of these days was somewhat blunted for the farmer, who at the very least had to take care of the daily chores concerned with cattle and other domestic animals, with no opportunity for equivalent time off at other periods to balance out his work. Considered of lesser significance was another state and church holiday observed during the First Republic—July 5, Saints Cyril and Methodius's Day—because it fell within a period during which the farmer was particularly busy. September 28, the day of Saint Wenceslaus, the beloved patron saint of the Czechs, also came at a busy time, but it was traditionally celebrated nonetheless with the "small" dedication feast, though often on the following Sunday rather than on the day itself.

Among days recognized internationally, Mother's Day was celebrated on the second Sunday in May during the First Republic, but is no longer commemorated. Since 1948 two other days have been observed—International Women's Day (March 8) and International Children's Day (June 1). They receive mention in the newspapers and are marked in schools and some places of employment by a speech or a brief meeting. If they are observed by individual villagers at all, they have an intimate family character.

Finally, among festivities in this category were parades in which members of certain organizations were expected to take part, appropriately attired for the occasion. In Komárov these played a very minor role because of the small size of the village. Only the members of the Sokol and of the volunteer firemen's corps used to be seen in their festive uniforms on legal holidays, and the firemen on Corpus Christi.

Among the spontaneous observances were the commemorative activities honoring Jan Hus on July 6. Reportedly these became widespread after about the 1860s. It was the custom to build bonfires and sing patriotic songs. Prior to 1918 these activities involved certain risks, since the gendarmes were instructed to search out the instigators and break up their meetings by scattering the fires. Since Czechoslovak independence in 1918, when July 6 officially became a commemorative day, enthusiasm seems to have subsided, although the setting of bonfires was kept up quite regularly for some years. The Nazi occupants prohibited these activities for their own reasons, and since World War II, commemorations have occurred irregularly and with less and less frequency; July 6 has once again become an ordinary day. The moving spirits behind these celebrations were the youth and the teachers of the Blata region. With the exodus of many young people into cities and the closing of the teachers college in Soběslav in 1955, bonfires honoring Jan Hus have become a thing of the past. Yet during the First Republic, Komárov was known among the villages of southern Bohemia as the home of the most enthusiastic July 6 celebrations.

14 / Arts and crafts in the Blata

The desire of the Blata villagers of a century ago to be surrounded by objects pleasing to the eye extended to various aspects of their material culture—houses, house furnishings, attire, ceremonial textiles, earthenware, and many others. Decorative objects were largely the work of artisans located in nearby towns, while embroideries were of local manufacture, as were certain objects of wood and iron produced by local village carvers and smiths. However, some few items—paintings on the underside of plate glass, laces, and certain kinds of ceramics—were brought in from other regions, in some cases quite distant. For example, paintings under glass came from the hilly region of southeastern Bohemia and from Šumava (Böhmerwald), laces from Stříbrné Hory (known today as Ratibořské Hory) near Tábor, from the Krušné hory (Erzgebirge), and the Český les (Böhmerwald), from Sedlice near Blatná, and from the region of České Budějovice. Special kinds of ceramic wares, such as stoneware pitchers, originated in Muskau and Bólesławiec (at present in the German Democratic Republic and Poland, respectively) and were purchased through middlemen in Votice north of Tábor. Factory-made earthenware was manufactured in České Budějovice, Klenčí, and Týnec on the Sázava (in Týnec only until the end of the 1850s). Many of these imported articles became so common in the Blata that informants are frequently of the opinion that they were produced locally. Occasionally even the labels of a museum display perpetuate such erroneous provenience.

Perhaps the most characteristic feature of esthetic display was the folk costume of the Blata. The men's costume ceased to be worn during the 1850s, the women's and children's (essentially miniature versions of the adult costumes) towards the end of the century. Their design, however, is well known from museum collections and contemporary accounts.

In 1824, Antonín Polák, a parish priest in Veselí on the Lužnice, gave the following description of the regional folk costume:

> The town of Veselí dominates a region which because of its many marshes is referred to as the Blata, and its inhabitants are called accordingly [Blaťáci]. Those who live in the town are dressed in the urban style, but the peasant garb is worth noting.
> The men wear a cloak of green cloth with clasps, ornamented on the collar, back, and sleeves with multicolored silk. On their heads they wear a cap of otter fur or a low black hat with a medium-sized brim and a rich assortment of

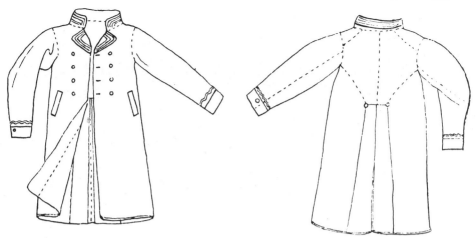

Figure 8. Coat worn by the men of the Blata about the middle of the nineteenth century. (After Drahomíra Stránská, Lidové kroje v Československu, Vol. I, p. 183.)

broad ribbons. Others are now beginning to wear a simple cap, dyed in black, similar to a nightcap, and on top of it a somewhat pointed hat with a flat brim and an ornamental velvet band with golden fringe. Their legs are covered with blue woolen socks and their feet with shoes fastened by brass buckles or leather straps. Others wear boots, and they dress in coats with wide collars [reaching partway down their backs]. Their vests are made of green cloth and have a tight row of shiny buttons. [The pants of that time, which Polák fails to mention, were made of leather, rough linen, or dark cloth, gathered below the knee.]

The women wear purplish red woolen stockings, short skirts of homespun serge, green, blue, or garnet in color, with numerous creases in the back and bordered with a broad band at the bottom. Their aprons consist of two multi-colored kerchiefs, sown together with distinctly visible stitches. They wear a comfortable bodice [a tight-fitting sleeveless waist of cloth or silk] with shiny buttons, and also a green or blue waistcoat with shiny buttons and frequently with a broad ornamental band bordering the sleeves. They cover their heads with a cap and headband and a white, richly embroidered veil, whose narrow ends are tied together in a knot on the left side of the face. The bulk of the veil hangs down from the shoulders in rich folds. When walking to town, they carry either the so-called Prague basket [woven from willow twigs] over their [left] arm or a [woven] bag covered with black leather and embroidered with various [floral] designs. Those who are unmarried are dressed in the same way but wear no cap or headband. Around their neck the women wear a finely embroidered collar. Their shoes are lined with red leather.

All villagers entertain themselves with singing, accompanied by a bag-piper and a fiddler, who reinforce the tune by gaily stamping their feet in time with the music.

This account was probably furnished in response to a comprehensive survey of Bohemia that was then being privately undertaken (but never completed or published) and described the early phase of the women's costume of the Blata. The later phase, roughly from 1850 to 1890, was characterized by the introduction

A group of married women (with heads covered), single girls (one with a garland), an old married man, and a single young man—all in the costumes worn in the Blata during the second half of the past century.

of certain elements of urban attire and an almost excessive ornamentation with embroideries, laces, and a greater variety of colors.

Embroideries, specimens of which are preserved from as early as the beginning of the eighteenth century, were applied primarily to veils, aprons, headbands, and the bed-curtains (*koutnice*) that were hung in the corner of a room where a woman lay in childbed. Among the embroidered textiles, the oldest are on coarse homespun cloth, decorated in red in cross-stitch or plaited stitch. The ornaments, of Renaissance character, are based on stylized flowers. More recent embroideries, perhaps from the middle of the eighteenth century, are done on fine cloth in yellow, red, or other silk according to patterns traced out beforehand. The ornaments of these items are in a more rococo style and generally represent stylized blossoms and hearts. Bobbinet was commonly used for background material. In the final phase of this period many embroidered articles were decorated with fish scales (mostly from carp) and gold thread. Almost every village had one or two professional embroiderers who did piecework at home for others and also taught young girls the art of needlework. Some of them, like

Terezie Ritterová from Soběslav (ca. 1760–1830), were known well beyond the Blata region.

Gables of houses facing the public thoroughfare were commonly provided with niches for statuettes. These were usually carved of wood, but some were made of clay in local ceramic workshops. As a result of the interest of collectors and museums after the last war, they have almost completely disappeared. The saints most commonly represented were Saint Florian, whose protection was sought against fire; Saint John of Nepomuk, who was believed to give protection from damage by floods; and the Virgin Mary, intercessor for domestic happiness and protector of the family. All were portrayed in their usual hagiographic likenesses: Saint Florian as a Roman knight with a pail; Saint John as a priest in a cassock with a surplice, stole, and biretta, and sometimes with a circle of stars around his head; and the Virgin Mary as a madonna of the Mariazell type, that is, with a crown on her head. From the 1870s, the Virgin Mary of the Lourdes type also was used. While most of the carvings of the saints, all from the last century, were made locally, it is difficult to establish whether they were done by individual farmers or by the few semiprofessional craftsmen found among the Komárov farming cottagers who engaged in part-time cabinetmaking or carpentry.

Among the wooden objects locally manufactured were supposed to have been pegs used to tighten binders for sheaves of grain or for planting. When decorated by whittling or notching in relief and then inlaid with poured tin, these pegs were given by young men as love tokens to girls at the time of engagement, for name days, and the like. Strictly utilitarian pegs, of course, were unadorned.

Every man knew how to work with wood and every woman how to sew. The absence of these skills or incompetence in them put an individual on the fringes of the community. People used to say that a young man unable to work with wood was unfit to become a successful farmer, and a girl unable to make herself an apron or a bonnet was incapable of running a household. While truly creative talent was limited to only a few individuals, the fact that others tried to imitate the best specimens of various decorative items at least encouraged creative activity, for which the present times offer little incentive.

Ceramic products were made by professional potters in Soběslav, Bechyně, Týn on the Vltava, Veselí, and Dolní Bukovsko. The most valuable from the artistic viewpoint is earthenware made in Soběslav. It is ornamented with stylized flowers and leaves in the rococo style, with lines, drops, dots, and similar shapes typical of the decorative technique that utilized a cow's horn. The horn was filled with glaze, which flowed slowly through an opening made by cutting off the tip. Most distinctive are platters, bowls, pitchers, and the special pots used to hold strong chicken broth prepared especially for women in childbed. Preserved specimens of earthenware span a period of approximately 1790 to 1914, at which time the ceramic works were closed.

Ornamentation of the smith's products, which had to do primarily with house doors and farm wagons, was largely limited to cold-hammering, but there were some instances of sculptural ornamentation that were forged while hot. The smith found himself busy at times when a particularly attractive iron mounting made its appearance in the village: what one farmer had was soon desired by

Two married women in the embroidered costumes worn in the Blata about a hundred years ago.

others. This was true of other types of items as well, whenever their decorative function was strikingly noticeable. Yet the possession of such objects did not serve as a criterion of social or economic class. The daughter of a farming cottager had the same festive costume as a girl from a farmstead, and sometimes it was even more elaborately decorated. The less intensive farming operations in her household must have left her and the other women of the family more time for needlework.

Today it appears that the relationship of the villagers toward various art forms is almost exclusively one of consumption, and that the chief criterion of artistic effectiveness is the degree of realism. The reasons do not have to be sought very far. In a society in which it is relatively easy and inexpensive to treat oneself

Decorated pegs—turned, carved, and inlaid with poured tin—used in the Blata as love tokens. (Specimens are about a hundred years old. Overall height is 12 to 16 in. Photograph from the archives of the Institute for Ethnography and Folklore of the Czechoslovak Academy of Sciences.)

to well-recorded and reasonably well-reproduced music or dramatic performances, the individual considers his own active participation in the creative process superfluous and uneconomical. And in a village community that continues to be largely absorbed in its own narrow problems and busies itself with day-to-day farming activities, it is difficult to expect understanding of and appreciation for artistic principles other than realism, which alone seems to have meaning for the villagers. Their attitude toward other artistic conceptions of reality—with the exception of those that are simply variants of realism, for example illusionism or naturalism—is one of disinterest and in extreme cases can be wholly negative. Our informants reacted to representative samples of nonrealistic modern music or paintings and sculpture with such comments as "I don't understand it," "it is beyond my comprehension," "it looks (sounds) like the creation of a madman," "that's screeching and scraping rather than music," "she is squeaking as though someone were cutting her throat," and the like. Only a relatively small minority of respondents were willing to admit that "there may be something to it" and that their failure to appreciate it might well be due to never having been taught how to listen to or view with understanding anything that is not straightforward or representational.

Even the music of the old masters is largely unappreciated by the people of Komárov. The majority clearly prefer small dance forms and the compact, straightforward sound of a brass band or a folk music ensemble. Knowledge of Blata folk songs continues to be fairly extensive throughout the entire community re-

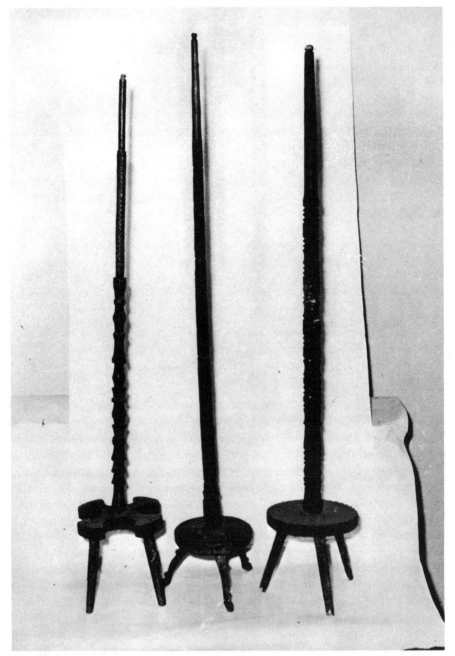

Carved distaffs from the Blata. (Specimens shown are about a hundred years old. Overall height is 40 to 50 in. Photograph from the archives of the Institute for Ethnography and Folklore of the Czechoslovak Academy of Sciences.)

gardless of generation, even if at present it is mediated by instruction during music education periods rather than by traditional transmission in the home or during work on the farm. The impulse for teaching the local folk songs unquestionably stems from the noticeably self-confident cast of the Blata people, nurtured by a proud local history. Besides that, there has been a growing interest in folk music since the last war both in the Blata and elsewhere. At the same time, opportunities for singing at work have largely disappeared as a result of increasing mechanization and individualization of farming activities, and the efforts of several young people to establish a dance music group were never accorded much acceptance and therefore did not last. The ability to play musical instruments is found today in only about 10 percent to 20 percent of the village population, with chief interest centering on the guitar and the accordion.

At present, the Komárov villagers are brought into contact with various forms of artistic expression primarily through radio and television. Radio receivers became relatively common in the area during the late thirties and today are owned by every family. Television was introduced into Komárov toward the end of the 1950s and has become standard equipment in nine out of ten households. A local motion-picture theater, which gives performances one to three times each week, was established during the 1950s. Before that time, to see films the villagers had to visit the nearby towns, where showings had begun in the 1920s. As might be expected, only a small portion of the programs in any of these media are of real artistic merit. In theory the listeners or viewers are offered a choice of a considerable variety of programs: music of all genres and periods, domestic and foreign films, television and radio plays, prose and poetry readings, discussions of representative art, as well as live transmissions of concerts or theatrical performances. In practice, of course, most individuals select particular kinds of programs; only the old and retired, to help pass the time, tend to listen to or view almost everything. In most homes radios are turned on throughout the day and provide a background of sound, regardless of program. When it comes to actual listening or viewing, the people of Komárov give their preferences accordingly:

1. radio or television plays of realistic content or in a light and cheerful vein;
2. films of a similar nature;
3. television reports featuring natural or historical sights of interest, preferably from foreign locations;
4. brass music or popular band music, preferably of central European orchestration;
5. among young people, jazz music of classical New Orleans vintage or its later European adaptation (the appeal of rock music is limited to some among the young and is rejected by members of the middle and older generations).

The remaining programs of an artistic nature are not followed with any regularity, and their impact on the villagers is negligible.

To a lesser extent people take the time to read works of fiction. Their interest centers on realistic novels and short stories of recent or historical setting, with the works of Jindřich Šimon Baar (1869–1925), Václav Beneš Třebízský (1849–

1884), Alois Jirásek (1851–1930), and Karel Václav Rais (1859–1926) leading in popularity, along with some of the lesser authors of the interwar period, especially Josef Hais-Týnecký (1885–1964), Josef Jahoda (1872–1946), and Jan Morávek (1888–1958). Mystery stories and films have been increasingly popular among young people, but tend to be rejected as objectionable and worthless by most older individuals.

Exposure to and appreciation of representative art are promoted by group excursions to various cultural centers and historical sights: the castle at Hluboká on the Vltava near České Budějovice, which houses the Aleš South Bohemian Gallery, Karlštejn castle, and Prague are among the most popular. Visits to serious theater performances and concerts, on the other hand, are infrequent. While among older people they are viewed as examples of snobbery, increasing interest in serious music and theater has been in evidence among younger people.

In the past—roughly between 1850 and World War II—the ratio between consumption and performance of art was balanced, and to the extent that one may speak of the "cultural life" of a village the size of Komárov, it was doubtless relatively richer than it is now. In the absence of the current contribution of the mass media, it was up to the villagers to make the effort to provide for their own entertainment and enlightenment. They came into contact with relatively good music on Sundays and holidays in church, where most of them actively participated in the singing. Every villager knew at least a score of folk songs and joined in group singing whenever the opportunity presented itself. In addition, much singing was done on an individual basis, both at work and during leisure time. Storytelling was likewise quite popular during the long winter evenings whenever a group of villagers engaged in some indoor activity such as feather stripping. While outstanding raconteurs were few—old-timers put their number at about five to ten for each generation, or about 3 percent to 6 percent of Komárov's adult population—everyone tried to contribute a story, even if only a short one, whenever a suitable occasion offered itself.

Every household contained items pleasant to the eye to a greater extent than is the case now, even if the standards of living and of hygiene were substantially lower. Living quarters were furnished with ornamentally painted furniture, a cupboard with decorated ceramic dishes, paintings under glass on the wall, and elaborately embroidered textiles. Beginning in the 1880s, reproductions of Czech master painters began to be widely used for decorative purposes. Historical and patriotic themes predominated, among them especially Václav Brožík's (1851–1901) "Huss before the Council of Constance" and "Election of George of Poděbrady as Bohemian King," Mikoláš Aleš's (1852–1913) "The Meeting of George of Poděbrady with Matthias Corvinus"; to a lesser extent, landscapes were popular by Julius Mařák (1832–1899) and Vojtěch Hynais (1854–1925), commissioned for the decoration of the National Theater in Prague. From the beginning of this century, tastes became progressively lower and color reproductions from folk calendars and later even from illustrated weekly magazines came to be used instead. Some few farmers did buy oils or watercolors done by local painters, but a great many of these were of questionable artistic quality. Reproductions of landscapes used for decoration at the present represent mediocre talent at best.

The trend of the past hundred years or so from production toward mere consumption of art and preference for only a few genres and styles (namely, realism and naturalism) appears fairly universal among the peasants of industrialized countries, and the changes in the esthetic outlook of Komárov have thus in no way been exceptional.

15/ Folk music and dances of the Blata

The people of the Blata have always liked music. Villagers sang a great deal and with obvious pleasure. On festive social occasions their singing was accompanied by various instruments and quite often led to dancing. As a result of the efforts of several generations of collectors, Blata folk songs are well documented, particularly those commonly sung during the last century.

The folk music of the Blata belongs unmistakably to the larger Czech musical folk tradition: it is characterized by melodies based on the fundamental harmonic functions, numerous suspensions, and melodic movements in major, and sometimes minor, natural scales. The melody is frequently reinforced by thirds or sixths, which occasionally form a countermovement at the end of individual phrases, thus creating the suggestion of a polyphonic second voice. The notes of the songs do not necessarily derive their values from the vowel quantities of the text, nor do syllabic accent and rhythmic accent always coincide (see, for example, the first two measures of Example IA).

Whenever the melody of a song was played by an instrumental group (bagpiper and violinist, or later bagpiper, violinist, and clarinetist), it was carried by the violinist while the bagpiper provided melodic embellishments over the ground bass of the drone, pitched most commonly in E-flat major or F major but occasionally in E major or G major. When the group included a clarinetist, he provided additional harmony and embellishments, usually playing with the violinist in thirds or sixths. In a larger ensemble, instruments of low or middle ranges accompanied the melody with obbligato bass and second voice. The harmonic aspect of the accompaniment was very simple: an alternation of the tonic with the dominant, according to the nature of the melody, or mostly the tonic alone in the case of the bagpipe.

When compared with other Czech folk songs, the Blata songs differ in several details: more frequent use of minor scales, predominant incidence of the andante tempo, and a fairly large percentage of tunes characteristic of the *ländler*, the Austrian couple dance in triple time (Examples II and IV). There occur instances of modulation from a major key into a dominant minor key (based on the fifth) or relative minor key (based on the sixth)—for example from G major to D minor, or G major to E minor—distinctly reminiscent of Moravian folk songs (Example VIII). Fluctuation between a major mode and the minor mode on the same tonic is not unusual: either the melody has an ambivalent major–minor character, or it may be sung, according to the performer's mood, in either a minor or a major key. A characteristic ornamental feature of South Bohemian songs—and hence of those sung in the Blata—is a stereotyped melodic phrase referred to as *jihočeská floskule* ("South Bohemian melodic cliché"). This phrase consists of a rapid descent through 8–7–6–5, frequently terminating with a hold (Examples IA and IC).

The formal melodic structure depends a great deal on the text of the song. The most common texts consist of stanzas of four lines, each line eight syllables in length. Even-numbered lines are frequently trochaic, sometimes with the last foot incomplete: —∪ —∪ —∪ —∪ or —∪ —∪ —∪ —. Frequently the trochaic meter changes into dactylic: —∪∪ —∪∪ —∪∪ (or —∪∪ —∪∪ —). Some folk songs alternate dactyls in the first two lines with trochees or mixed feet in the third and fourth:

$$
\begin{array}{l}
\text{—∪∪ —∪∪} \\
\text{—∪∪ —∪∪} \\
\left.\begin{array}{l} \text{—∪ —∪ —∪} \\ \text{—∪ —∪ —∪} \end{array}\right\} \; \text{or} \; \left\{\begin{array}{l} \text{—∪∪ —∪ —∪} \\ \text{—∪∪ —∪ —∪.} \end{array}\right.
\end{array}
$$

Quite common also are dactylic lines of five metrical feet, with the last foot incomplete, —∪∪ —∪∪ —∪∪ —∪∪ —, or various irregular metrical arrangements.

Besides rhymes, generally of the *a a b b* or *a b b a* types, assonances and consonant-rhymes also occur. As is common in folk poetry, approximate consonantal or vocalic rhymes and grammatical rhymes are frequent.

In the minimal song, the melody is organized within phrases four measures in length, two such phrases forming one song stanza. The first phrase commonly introduces a melodic idea in an upward inflection, the second phrase—a variant of the first—concludes it in a descending manner: *a* + *a'* (Example II). But sometimes the first phrase consists of 'a short melodic idea repeated in a parallel movement or countermovement: *a* + *b* + *a'* + *b'* (Example VII). Some folk songs have the structure of a more complex song form, frequently with a shortened conclusion: *a* + *a'* + *b* + *a'* (Example V).

Alternating rhythms are fairly common in the Blata songs. Some few songs alternate rhythm from one phrase to another, one having two beats per measure, the other three. The middle portion of the three-part song form could thus be different from both the introductory and concluding sections, or the conclusion different from the rest. A few dances were even accompanied by music in which measures in two-four time alternated with measures in three-four time within one phrase:

$$\tfrac{3}{4} \; \tfrac{3}{4} \; \tfrac{2}{4} \; \tfrac{2}{4}$$

$$\tfrac{2}{4} \; \tfrac{2}{4}$$

$$\tfrac{3}{4} \; \tfrac{3}{4} \; \tfrac{2}{4} \; \tfrac{2}{4}$$

Such dances, referred to in the Blata as *bavoráky* or *baboráky* (*bavorák* or *baborák*, sing., with the meaning "Bavarian [dance]"), were sung and danced when the mood of a social gathering had considerably loosened up. The audience particularly enjoyed watching these dances, and there was great amusement when those not thoroughly acquainted with the changing rhythms and dance steps fell repeatedly into difficulties.

Thematically, the Blata songs comprise the full range of genres. The simplest songs were *halekačky* (*halekačka*, sing., a generic rather than a regional term), which were shouted by herdsmen over some distance, and short tunes with humorous texts fitting special occasions. Among the more complex were epic songs containing a considerable number of stanzas.

A number of dances were widely performed during the second half of the nineteenth century, whenever musical accompaniment was available at village social gatherings. Particularly popular was the polka, in two-four time, with the same steps as today but reportedly slower in tempo. The waltz and the mazurka both gained popularity in the 1860s and have remained unchanged in steps and rhythm to the present. According to informants, the "neighborly dance" (*sousedská*), a slow dance in three-four time (♫♫♫♫ | ♫♩♩ or ♫♩) with steps as in the waltz, was no longer danced by the end of the past century.

The so-called *tajč* (from German *deutsch* meaning "German") and *štajryš* (from German *steirisch* [cp. Steiermark], meaning "Styria[n]") were variants of the old Czech "neighborly dance," but the tunes had the character of the *ländler*. Accordingly, their dancing was sometimes accompanied by the clapping of hands.

The round dance *dokolečka* ("[dance] in a circle"), usually in three-four but more recently also in two-four time of moderate to rapid tempo, was generally danced only by girls; reportedly it disappeared completely at the end of the century.

One of the more popular dances was *obkročák* (*vobročák*, dial.), a dance in two-four time, in which partners turned by stepping around each other, making a full turn in two steps. In the fast variety of this dance, a step matched half a measure, in the regular variety a full measure (Example V).

The line dance *utíkej Káčo* ("Run, Kate"), in three-four time of fairly rapid tempo, was introduced and concluded with fanfares. The dancers stood in two rows facing each other, boys on one side, girls on the other. After the couple at the end of the row made a turn, the boy and girl separated and began to run between the rows, the boy trying to catch the girl. When "Kate" was "captured," the fanfares were sounded, and the procedure was repeated. When all the couples had taken their turn, the girls chased the boys.

In the dance called *křižalka*, the partners held hands crosswise while dancing to a fairly slow tune in two-four time. And in the dance referred to as *vrták* ("borer"), the partners stood with the tips of their toes touching, leaned outward holding hands at arm's length, and turned around rapidly in one place in rhythm with the two-four time of the music. The last three folk dances disappeared during the second half of the past century.

Before the end of the century, two other dances were brought to the Blata by sons of local farmers who studied in Soběslav to become teachers. These were the quadrille and the Czech *beseda*, a suite of dances performed to a fixed medley of Czech folk tunes by one or more groups of four couples each. Since the 1920s, some few villagers who studied in the larger cities brought back the tango, the shimmy, and the slow waltz, but members of the older generations had little liking for these forms and did not accept them. Today, the dance repertory includes the waltz, polka, tango, slow waltz, fox-trot, and to a lesser extent the mazurka, quadrille, and of course the contemporary dance fads. While most of the young boys and girls now attend lessons in social dancing, until the thirties it was customary to learn how to dance by watching others, who were eager to teach their younger friends.

Example IA. Based on No. 4a in Čeněk Holas, České národní písně a tance (Praha, 1908–1910), Vol. 3, p. 7.

Note the South Bohemian melodic cliché occurring in the third measure.

Czech	Translation
Stojí město při dolině,	There is a town standing near the lowland,
stojí město při dolině,	There is a town standing near the lowland,
nedaleko od Dunaje,	Not too far from the Danube,
nedaleko od Dunaje.	Not too far from the Danube.

The same tune as in Example IA is transcribed below in a variation as it might be played on a bagpipe in E flat to accompany dancing. (Transcriptions of Examples IB to ID were provided by Dr. Karel Krasnický.) Only the notation for the bagpipe chanter is given; the drone sounds continuously on

Example IB.

The same tune as in Example IA is transcribed below in a variation for violin (notation untransposed) and bagpipe in E flat to accompany dancing. To adapt to the bagpipe, the neck of the violin was bound with a piece of string to raise the pitch of all four open strings by a half step (from G, D, A, and E to A flat, E flat, B flat, and F, respectively). The South Bohemian melodic cliché occurs in the third measure of the violin part.

Example IC.

The same tune as in Example IA is transcribed below in a variation for the customary ensemble of clarinet in B flat (notation untransposed), violin, and bagpipe in E flat. The South Bohemian melodic cliché occurs in the third measure of the clarinet part.

Example ID.

Example II. Sung by Scheufler's mother, who had learned it from her Komárov nurse.

Czech	Translation
Náš táta mě pořád nutí:	My dad keeps urging me:
Franto, žeň se;	Frank, get married;
a já nemám žádné chuti,	But I don't feel like it,
mně se nechce.	I don't want to.
Tátovi to bylo lehký,	For dad, it was easy,
vzal si mámu;	He married mom;
já si musím vzíti	I have to marry
jinou cizí pannu.	Another, a strange girl.

Example III. Based on No. 19 in Karel Weis, Český jih a Šumava v (lidové) písni (Praha, 1928–1941), Vols. 14–15, pp. 37–38. Translation is on next page.

Czech	Translation
Já sem dobrej, dobrej,	I'm good, I'm good,
žena je zlá;	My wife is bad;
dyž přídu z hospody,	When I return from the inn,
sednu si na schody,	I sit down on the steps,
vona bublá, bublá,	And she mumbles, mumbles,
vona bublá.	She mumbles.
Nebublej, nebublej,	Don't mumble, don't mumble,
koupím ti mlejn.	I'll buy you a mill.
Budeš-li bublati,	If you keep mumbling,
proti mně reptati,	And grumbling against me,
dám ho jinej, jinej,	I'll give it to another one, another one,
dám ho jinej.	I'll give it to another one.

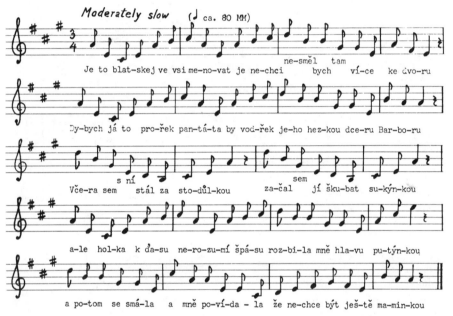

Example IV. Based on No. 11 in Karel Weis, Český jih a Šumava v (lidové) písni (Praha, 1928–1941), Vols. 14–15, pp. 22–23. Translation is on next page.

Czech	*Translation*
Je to blatskej ve vsi,	It's a Blata village,
menovat je nechci,	I don't want to name them,
nesměl bych tam více ke dvoru.	I could never visit in their yard.
Dybych já to prořek,	If I blurted it out,
pantáta by vodřek	The farmer would refuse me
jeho hezkou dceru Barboru.	The hand of his pretty daughter Barbara.
Včera sem s ní stál za stodůlkou,	Yesterday the two of us stood behind the little barn,
začal sem jí škubat sukýnkou.	And I began pulling at her skirt.
Ale holka k d'asu,	But the doggone girl
nerozumí špásu,	Didn't like my teasing,
rozbila mně hlavu putýnkou.	And hit my head with a pail.
A potom se smála	And then she laughed
a mně povídala,	And told me
že nechce být ještě maminkou.	That she doesn't quite yet wish to become a mother.

Example V. Based on No. 209/2 (778) in Karel Jaromír Erben, Prostonárodní české písně a řikadla (Praha, 1886), pp. 399–400 (196–197).

Czech	*Translation*
Za tou naší stodoličkou	Behind our little barn
moc ječmena,	There is much barley;
uvázala žena muže	A wife tied her husband
na řemena.	By a strap.
Ouvej, ženo!	Ouch, wife!
pust' mě z něho,	Let me loose,
nebudu ti nadávati	I will no longer call you
psí plemeno (slova zlého).	The bitchy kind (a bad name).
Co mě, ženo moje milá,	Why do you, my dear wife,
co mě vážeš?	Why do you tie me?
vždyt' já tobě všecko dělám,	Don't I do for you everything
co mně kážeš:	That you order me:
kážeš-li mně	If you order me
pro kvasnice,	To get some yeast,
já ti pro ně honem běžím—	I run to get some for you without even
bez čepice.	Putting my cap on.

Example VI. *Wedding song, recorded by Jaroslava Sardová in 1946 in Komárov; manuscript in the archives of the Institute for Ethnography and Folklore of the Czechoslovak Academy of Sciences in Prague.*

Czech	Translation
Andulko, sundej věnec,	Annie, take off your garland,
už je svobodě konec.	Freedom is over.
Za zelený věnec	For the green garland
dáme tobě čepec,	We'll give you a bonnet,
za zelený věneček	For the little green garland
dáme ti čepeček.	We'll give you a little bonnet.
Ona ho sundat nechce,	She refuses to take it off,
že už nebude děvče.	For she would no longer be a single girl.
Za zelený věnec	For the green garland
dáme tobě čepec,	We'll give you a bonnet,
za zelený věneček	For the little green garland
dáme ti čepeček.	We'll give you a little bonnet.

Example VII. *From Scheufler's childhood memories. Reportedly a Komárov folk song (information from Scheufler's grandmother).*

Czech	Translation
Ty a já, my sme dvá,	You and I, that makes two,
my sme z jedný vesnice,	We're from the same village,
kradem husy slepice;	We steal geese and hens;
ty a já, my sme dvá,	You and I, that makes two,
my sme z jedný vesnice,	We're from the same village,
kradem husy slepice.	We steal geese and hens.
Ty a já, zloději vobá,	You and I, both of us thieves,
my sme vobá zloději,	We're both thieves,
už nás lidi honěji;	And the people are already chasing us;
ty a já, zloději vobá,	You and I, both of us thieves,
my sme vobá zloději,	We're both thieves,
už nás lidi honěji.	And the people are already chasing us.

Sa - mi dva Mar-ján-ko sa - mi dva lí - há-me jest-li se

co sta - ne ko - mu vi - nu dá - me ko - mu vi - nu dá-me

Example VIII. Based on No. 143 in Čeněk Holas, České národní písně a tance (Praha, 1908–1910), Vol. 3, pp. 100–101.

Czech	*Translation*
Sami dva, Marjánko,	Just the two of us, Marianne,
sami dva líháme;	Just the two of us are lying down together;
jestli se co stane,	If something should happen,
komu vinu dáme,	Whom shall we blame,
komu vinu dáme?	Whom shall we blame?
Komupak jinému	Whom else
než naší mateři,	But Mother
že nezavírala	For not locking
u komůrky dveří,	The door to the chamber,
u komůrky dveří.	The door to the chamber.

16/ Epilog: from local cooperative to regional consolidation

In the mid-1950s, when agricultural production of the Blata region began to be organized on a socialist cooperative basis, virtually every village had its own unified agricultural cooperative. By the end of the 1950s, the original arrangement of separate village-based unified agricultural cooperatives came to be judged economically inefficient, and commencing in 1960 a partial consolidation of the smallest or least productive cooperaratives into larger units began to take place. For example, the nearby cooperatives of Svinky and Záluží were joined with the larger cooperative of Vlastiboř in the Vlastiboř Unified Agricultural Cooperative of the Third Five-Year Plan. The extent of this first wave of nationwide consolidation may best be appreciated from the following figures: the peak of setting up unified agricultural cooperatives was reached in 1959, when 12,560 of them existed in the Czechoslovak Socialist Republic; by 1963, the total number fell to 7,620. Beginning in 1965 the pace of consolidation slowed down considerably, only to resume its brisk pace in 1971. This time, all of the remaining Blata villages were affected: on February 18, 1972, a far-reaching reorganization was put into effect, joining the economies of a dozen villages — Vlastiboř (together with Svinky and Záluží), Vesce (together with Čeraz, Mokrá, and Nedvědice), Skalice (together with Radimov, Rybova Lhota, and Třebiště), Debrník, and Komárov (the last two operating independently up to that time).[1] The name given to this consolidated unified agricultural cooperative was "Victorious February" (Vítězný únor).

The reorganization did not stop there. As of January 1, 1975, Hlavatce (together with Vyhnanice, joined with it in 1974) was also incorporated; and a still further restructuring took place on January 1, 1978, when State Farm Dráchov was abolished and brought in. At the same time Skalice (together with Radimov, Rybova Lhota, and Třebiště) was released from the cooperative and subordinated to the branch of the state breeding enterprise located in Veselí on the Lužnice. The incorporation of Dráchov into "Victorious February" was consonant with the wholesale dismantling of unprofitable state farms in the interior of the country in order to put them on the economically self-supporting basis expected of the cooperatives. (State farms are now operated primarily in the country's border districts; those that still exist in the interior have assumed breeding, experimental, and other functions not directly productive.)

"Victorious February," which at present joins together the economies of twelve farming villages, encompasses roughly the area of an ellipse, with Vlastiboř at its center and its two most distant points about thirteen kilometers (ca. 8 miles) apart. The economic consolidation of the Blata communities was followed by a somewhat less far-reaching consolidation of the organs of government on the local level. As a result Komárov, which until the end of 1975 had its own local national committee, has been joined with Vlastiboř, which is also the seat of political administration for Svinky and Záluží. For the purposes of mail delivery, however, Komárov belongs administratively to Hlavatce, Vlastiboř to Soběslav.

Whereas the first Unified Agricultural Cooperative Act of 1949 was an instrument designed to implement socialist cooperative agriculture in Czechoslovakia, the second Unified Agricultural Cooperative Act, which became effective on October 1, 1959, reaffirmed the transformations in agricultural economy that had occurred during the intervening decade and ushered in the first wave of the consolidation of agricultural production. Since the beginning of 1976, the country's cooperative agriculture has been regulated by still another Agricultural Cooperative System Act, the third, passed on November 13, 1975. In preparing this latest act, the legislators took into consideration the changes in cooperative agriculture resulting from the large-scale consolidation of local enterprises and the increasing mechanization of their operation. The intent of the act was to promote conditions favorable to the further modernization of socialized agriculture and its integration into the national economy as a whole. An important piece of companion legislation has been the Model Statutes of Unified Agricultural Cooperatives Decree (*Vzorové stanovy jednotných zemědělských družstev*) promulgated by the government later during the year (December 4, 1975). Individual cooperatives have been instructed to derive their statutes from this model, departing from it only if local conditions made changes advisable or imperative. Among other things the decree acknowledges that as a result of the growing incomes of both the cooperatives and their members, private plots in effect have lost their former function.

On the Komárov farm (*farma Komárov*) and the other village farms of "Victorious February," the individual private plots of cooperators were abolished in fact as early as the end of 1972 and have been replaced by joint private plots (*společné záhumenky*), which can conveniently be cultivated and harvested by mechanical means. However, a "garden" adjacent to the cooperator's family dwelling may be retained, without the payment of a fee, if it is no more than 10 ares (1,196 square yards) in area, or even if it is larger — up to a maximum of 50 ares, or half a hectare (1.24 acres) — as long as it lacks utility for the cooperative and cannot be mechanically cultivated or joined with other such gardens. The loss of individual private plots has caused little if any resentment. Because the cooperators no longer have their own plowing, harvesting, and other machinery, they would have to pay the cooperative for the services rendered and, considering the small extent of the plots, cultivating them would hardly be worthwhile.

Regarding the benefit of being able to purchase some of the commodities produced by the cooperative at wholesale prices set by the state, as of January 1979 cooperators have the right to purchase a basic share consisting of 2 quintals (441 pounds) of grain and 4 quintals (882 pounds) of potatoes per year, regardless of the amount of their annual earnings, at approximately 140 Kčs and 40 Kčs per quintal, respectively. This basic share is received at no cost by those who are retired provided their monthly pensions do not exceed 700 Kčs. Actively working members may purchase at the wholesale price additional quantities of these commodities at the rate of 5 kilograms (11 pounds) of grain or 20 kilograms (44 pounds) of potatoes for each 100 Kčs earned up to a ceiling of 18,000 Kčs. For example, for a cooperator who is earning 18,000 Kčs or more per year, the entitlement, in addition to his basic share, is 9 quintals (1984 pounds) of grain (18,000/100 × 0.05), or four times the amount in potatoes. The customary assignment of commodities in such a case is 6 quintals of wheat and 12 quintals (3 × 4) of potatoes, or a total of 8 quintals of wheat and 16 quintals of potatoes, with the basic share included. Cooperators further have the option of purchasing a pig up to 110 kilograms at 15 Kčs per kilogram of liveweight in lieu of 6 quintals of wheat.

Not infrequently, there is more than one cooperator in a family. In such cases, the allotment of the basic share is multiplied by the number of cooperators in the family. Where two or more family members actively work and each reaches or exceeds the yearly income ceiling of 18,000 Kčs, the maximum additional allotments are set at 16 quintals (3528 pounds) of grain for 2 cooperators, 21 quintals for 3, and a ceiling of 25 quintals for 4. The grain, commonly wheat, is mixed with maize and barley groats purchased at retail prices and used to feed poultry and other family-held livestock. Everyone in the village now buys commercially made bread and uses commercial flour for baking.

In addition, each member of the cooperative is entitled, for the needs of his or her family, to the possession of one head of cattle, two pigs for fattening, and sheep, goats, domestic fowl, and bee colonies in quantities not exceeding the cooperative's bylaws (the number of sheep, goats, fowl, and bee colonies is set at 2, 2, 20, and 10, respectively, but these limits are not strictly enforced). In setting the limits for animals, the general criterion is that under no circumstances should the private holding of animals interfere with the operation and growth of the cooperative or be disproportionate to the cooperative's productivity and acreage assigned to joint private plots.

The butchering of beef animals at home for family consumption is against the law; they must be taken to the state slaughterhouse and sold at the wholesale price. Cooperators who do not keep beeves may wish to sell the hay from their share of the joint private plots to the cooperative. At some 40 to 60 Kčs per quintal (220 pounds), and with an average yield of about 6 quintals of hay from 10 ares (1,196 square yards), they are able to realize a supplemental yearly income of several hundred crowns. However, because of the effort involved, interest in harvesting the "gardens" or joint private plots is quite limited. To raise a pig or two is more advantageous: when a pig is slaughtered, the meat belongs to the cooperator, and only a small fee must be paid to the state veterinarian. At the present time about one sixth of Komárov's cooperator families keep an animal, whether it be a young bull for fattening, a milk cow, or a pig. Young cooperators do so only rarely: they do not wish to be tied to an animal that requires daily care, and in some cases they may even lack the requisite skills.

Belatedly, as of January 1, 1977, "Victorious February" began compensating its Komárov members for the livestock and machinery which each brought into the Komárov cooperative in 1960. Initially, the payments were made only to retired members and, of the active members, only to former smallholders (up to 10 hectares [24.7 acres]). Quite recently all members have become eligible for these payments, issued to them in 500 Kčs installments four times a year. Reportedly the delay was caused by the inability of the former Komárov cooperative to agree on the method and timing of compensation, apparently the result of eagerness to show a hefty balance sheet as evidence of successful economic management. By contrast, nearby Hlavatce paid off all of its members in full before it was consolidated in 1975.

The administrative headquarters of the Unified Agricultural Cooperative "Victorious February" is Vlastiboř, which also functions as the subcenter of one of the two economic branches (*závod,* sg.) of the entire enterprise (*podnik*). Vesce, to which the easterly villages – Čeraz, Dráchov, Mokrá, Nedvědice, and Záluží – are assigned, serves as the other subcenter. Each branch raises cattle and crops, especially wheat, in the area under its management, while the production of pigs is handled jointly. One service center provides the necessary technical support for the growing pool of agricultural machinery owned by the cooperative as a whole.

The administrative structure of "Victorious February" follows the model statutes, but in comparison with the structure of the former Komárov cooperative it is much more complex. The membership meeting – that is, all members of the cooperative in good standing – assembles once each year. The board of deputies, made up of 30 percent of all members, meets four to six times a year. The management committee, consisting of twelve cooperators, holds meetings on a monthly basis, or more frequently if necessary. The remaining committees consist of eight members each. Members of all except the management committee and the committee for safety and health protection at work serve without pay. Members of the safety committee, whose meetings are scheduled twelve times a year, are compensated on a per diem basis for meeting days. As a rule, all committee members are chosen from slates of candidates presented to the membership at its annual meeting.

The sizable accounting staff employed by the cooperative in its various departments and sectors is to a large extent made necessary by the very complex and detailed system of norms applicable to the numerous specialized activities in which the cooperative's personnel engage. In addition to Czechoslovak state norms governing primarily quality control of agricultural products and the specialized norms and terminological pamphlets prepared by various research institutes of the ministries of agriculture and food (Czech, Slovak, or federal), there are a number of norm manuals published by the Institute of Labor in the Agriculture and Food Industry of the Ministry of Agriculture and Food of the Czech Socialist Republic (in the case of "Victorious February"). Each of these, titled *Collection of Time Norms for Jobs in Agricultural Production,* covers in the most painstaking detail a particular class of agricultural activities (sowing, tillage, harvesting, livestock production, and the like). To take two very simple examples, the transfer of fodder or similar materials (Job No. 1,210) is classified according to the type of containers or conveyances used (pail, can, basket, handcart, wheelbarrow, rail cart, and many others), their carrying capacity in kilograms, and specific distances covered in meters. Norms pertaining to the tillage of one hectare are classified according to the type of activity, kind of machinery used, slope of terrain in degrees, nature of soil (light, medium, heavy), and so on. Calculating and posting payments for individual cooperators and checking their performance according to the published norms clearly require a fairly large staff of specialized personnel.

Because of the changing makeup of "Victorious February" prior to 1978, membership figures are not fully comparable on a year-to-year basis. Even since 1978 the figures have varied somewhat from one quarter to the next. On the average, some 25 to 30 new cooperators join "Victorious February" each year, while attrition generally runs somewhat higher — around 35, or sometimes as high as 45 members. Of these, 25 to 30 are lost to the cooperative by death and 10 to 15 through change of employment (another cooperative or occupation).

As of the end of 1973, the cooperative had 598 members, of whom 302 were actively working and 296 retired. During 1976 the number of "permanently active"[2] members rose to 510, of whom 274 were women. In addition to members, the cooperative employs seasonal workers and a limited number of specialists from other sectors of the national economy and provides practical training for apprentices enrolled in one- to three-year agricultural schools.

The major job categories of the cooperative and the numbers (in parentheses) of permanently active members who filled them as of the end of 1976 included crop production personnel (75 women, 28 men), milk cow attendants (86 women, 7 men), technical-economic personnel (46 men, 19 women), combine and tractor operators (61, all males), other cattle attendants (44 women, 11 men), and machine shop mechanics (30, all males).

As regards age, the highest concentration of cooperators in 1976 was in the age bracket of 60 years and above — 43 men and 60 women; by contrast, there were only 19 men and 15 women below 25 years of age. The average age of the working cooperators in "Victorious February" has been rising for many years and is now (1986) approaching 50.

The highest paid members of "Victorious February" as of July 1, 1979, were combine and tractor operators and sow attendants, who averaged just above 2,500 Kčs per month. On the lower end of the scale were workers in crop production, who averaged only 1,180 Kčs.

While the average monthly wages paid to the members of "Victorious February" are not as high as those earned in some of the other cooperatives, they compare favorably with other production sectors in the Czech Socialist Republic if one takes into account the material benefits available to cooperators and the fact that as a rule their living quarters are rent-free. The following selected figures (in Kčs) for 1979 provide a comparison: average monthly wage (net) of permanently active cooperators: 2,313; forestry: 2,700; industry: 2,683; construction: 2,858; communications: 2,270; and internal commerce: 2,120. The comparison with nonproductive sectors of the Czech national economy is even more favorable for the cooperators.

As of the end of 1973, agricultural land held by "Victorious February" amounted to 3,373 hectares (8,331 acres) of which 2,536 hectares were arable. As of 1976 the overall area had risen to 4,990 hectares, with 4,132 hectares of agricultural land (3,071 hectares arable, 1,061 hectares in meadowland). The separation of Skalice at the end of 1977 meant a loss of about 700 hectares of agricultural land, but Dráchov brought in about 500 hectares, resulting in a net loss of some 200 hectares of agricultural land. The present cooperative owns 3,850 hectares of agricultural land made up of 2,878 hectares of arable land, 819 hectares of meadowland, 143 hectares of pastureland, and 10 hectares of gardens. Some additional hectarage is forested (about 220 hectares) or included in village grounds or unusable land.

Along with several main crops, the cooperative concentrates on the production of cattle and pigs. The extent of recent animal production is evident from Table 6.

TABLE 6.   COMMERCIAL LIVESTOCK HELD BY "VICTORIOUS FEBRUARY,"
THIRD QUARTER OF 1977

Category	Plan	Actual	Percentage Achieved
total beef cattle	3,429	3,410	99.45
cows	1,400	1,359	97.07
total pigs	3,496	3,842	109.9
sows	399	397	99.5

No horses, sheep, goats, or poultry are raised for commercial purposes.

Among grains, wheat currently heads the list with about 800 hectares, followed by oats (ca. 490 hectares), barley (ca. 370 hectares), maize for silage (ca. 200 hectares), and rye (ca. 140 hectares). About 700 hectares are under cultivation with fodder plants (mixtures of legumes and grasses), and ca. 200 hectares (about 7 percent of the agricultural land) with rape (*Brassica napus oleifera*) for oil. The yields in quintals (one quintal = 100 kilograms = about 220.5 pounds) per hectare (2.47 acres) of main crop plants for 1976 and 1977 are given in Table 7.

TABLE 7.   YIELDS IN QUINTALS PER HECTARE OF MAIN CROP PLANTS IN
"VICTORIOUS FEBRUARY," 1976-1977, AS OF SEPTEMBER 30, 1977

Crop	Actual 1976	Plan 1977	Actual 1977	Actual 1977/1976	Average for cooperative sector during 1977
wheat	26.2	35.7	35.5	143.1	40.9
rye	31	36	30.8	99	33.1
barley	26.5	36.1	34.2	129	40.3
oats	24.6	36.5	23.1	93.9	not avail.
rape	23	21	30.4	132.1	24.9
potatoes	190	150	159.9	84.1	189.6

Except for rape, the yields lagged somewhat behind the averages for the Czech Socialist Republic as a whole. Among the reasons why some of the goals were not met were a severe hailstorm during the summer and unfavorable weather during the entire 1977 harvest period.

For such a small area as that of "Victorious February," plant production necessarily fluctuates from year to year, depending on the weather. Although the crop production goals set by the cooperative for 1978 were not completely reached, deliveries under state contract were met and some of the results were particularly satisfactory: the average grain yield of 38.14 quintals per hectare was the best in the cooperative's history, and particular yields on certain tracts reached as much as 47 and 52 quintals per hectare (sown by airplane) in the case of wheat and 58 quintals per hectare for barley. In livestock production, the situation in 1978 was similar: the production goals were not met, but deliveries under state contract were exceeded in the case of beef and pork, milk (by 105,000 liters, i.e., 111,285 quarts), and suckling pigs (by 402 head).

As regards animal production, the emphasis on the Komárov farm is on cows, heifers, sows, and pigs for fattening. Plant crops differ somewhat from year to year. In 1979, Komárov specialized in rape, rye, oats, and fodder crops. While potatoes are grown only for resale to cooperators, all grains are sold to the state purchasing agency. Even seed for the next season's fodder mixtures is bought by the cooperative.

On the average, the cooperative plans to increase its production by about 5 percent each year and raise wages by about 3 percent. Gross agricultural production per worker (in Kčs × 1,000) rose from an average of 60 for the former Komárov cooperative in 1970 to 80 for "Victorious February" in 1975, and for the most part has been slowly but steadily climbing since then.

The increases in crop production despite the constantly diminishing labor force are due to the continuing mechanization of the cooperative's machine pool. During 1975 alone, almost 4,000,000 Kčs were spent for new machinery, ranging from relatively inexpensive compressors to such an item as the mammoth Soviet-made tractor known as *kirovec* at 357,022 Kčs. At the same time, repairs are not always completed on time, their quality occasionally leaves something to be desired, and spare parts are frequently unavailable. The use of chemical fertilizers has been increasing from year to year, amounting to 222 kilograms (488 pounds) per hectare (2.47 acres) in Vlastiboř during 1975. Sowing and crop-dusting have been done increasingly by airplanes.

When Komárov had its own cooperative, most of the livestock was stabled in the utility buildings of the village farmsteads because construction of large cow sheds would have been expensive and there was ample space in the existing facilities. More recently, the growing emphasis on mechanization of feeding and centralization of livestock production has led to the establishment of several large stables where cattle can conveniently be taken care of by specialized personnel. Komárov has one such facility housing about 100 cows, staffed by 8 women attendants working in shifts. As a result, only five Komárov families are called upon to lend their utility buildings to shelter two to three dozen each of calves, heifers, and mature cows — in four cases throughout the year and in one for the summer only. Most of the spacious farm-yards and stables are thus unoccupied and unused.

Just as did the Komárov cooperative in earlier years, the consolidated enterprise makes every effort to provide employment for its members when crop production activities are slack. During the winter, women — particularly those who are already retired — peel potatoes for freezing in the recently constructed food-freezing plant in Hlavatce. Male drivers or tractorists transfer fodder and fertilizers or are subcontracted to nearby nonagricultural enterprises that can make use of them. Many workers also plan to take their vacations during the winter. In the spring several Komárov women plant seedlings in tree nurseries, and then care for them during the summer; in the fall additional forest grounds may be cleared for the next year's planting. On the Jitra peat banks, where the mining of peat is being discontinued, an amelioration and recultivation project is under way to make the ground suitable for raising vegetables and ornamental flowers. About five Komárov women work on this project during the growing season, earning approximately 65 Kčs for an 8-hour day. Until recently, several women bagged peat for sale as fertilizer or soil loosener. These women and others are now bused by the cooperative to wherever their services are needed.

The onset of the most profound changes in the structure of Komárov's population dates back to 1955, when socialist cooperative farming replaced the system of individual private ownership of farmholds. Since then the village population has been undergoing rapid reduction, diminishing by about 40 individuals in the course of sixteen years (by December 31, 1971) and by about the same number during the six years that followed (by December 31, 1977).

As of January 1, 1978, the population of Komárov stood at 164. Of this total, 150 persons resided in their original dwellings, while the remaining 14 were located in a recently constructed four-apartment housing unit (*bytovka*) on the periphery of the village. The occupants of the housing unit, who in early 1978 were members of three families, are not permanent residents of Komárov, nor are they considered members of the village community. The villagers do not have much regard for them and refer to them as "nomads" (*kočovní*).[3]

The 150 permanent residents represent a considerable population decrease when compared with the total of 193 recorded for January 1, 1972. The negative growth during the six-year period between that date and December 31, 1977, was due to several factors. Although 14 individuals (4 male and 10 female) died during this period, 13 children (6 male and 7 female) were born, a net loss of only one. Virtually the entire decrease was therefore attributable to the out-migration of a number of families and single individuals to nearby or more distant villages and towns: thirty-one adults, together with their children, relocated. Of the thirteen males, 4 moved to Prague, 3 to Soběslav, 2 to Čertovna (a forester's lodge near Hlavatce), and 1 each to Tábor, Sviny near Veselí on the Lužnice, and Zálší, with one remaining migratory. Of the 18 females, 9 are presently residing in Soběslav, 3 are migratory, 2 have moved to Čertovna, and 1 each live in Prague, Domažlice, Vesce, and Bečice near Týn on the Vltava.[4]

The net population decrease of 43 individuals, excluding from the count those residing in the housing unit, represents a significant acceleration of a trend that has been evident in Komárov since the beginning of the century. This acceleration during the past several years is no doubt attributable at least in part to the consolidation in 1972 of the Komárov cooperative with the larger regional Unified Agricultural Cooperative "Victorious February." As a result Komárov has become both administratively and economically a satellite village, with its agricultural production undergoing still further rationalization. Meanwhile, some of the young people of Komárov have persisted in their desire to establish themselves in communities which offer a greater choice of employment and wider opportunities for self-realization.

Apart from the new housing unit, there were 52 numbered houses (mostly farmsteads) in Komárov as of January 1, 1978. Of these, 12 were no longer occupied by the former owners or their children. The new functions of these units varied considerably: one was unoccupied and unused; four had been sold to families from Prague to serve as summer recreation cottages (*chalupy*, pl.); two forester's lodges, the so-called Komárov and Benešov lodges, were sold to families from České

Budějovice, also for recreational purposes; one was inherited by a Prague family whose members use it as a summer cottage; one serves in part as meeting place for the Union of Socialist Youth (*Svaz socialistické mládeže*), while its stables house some of the cattle of the cooperative (half of this farmstead belongs to the widow of a man sentenced during the mid-1950s to a prison term as a "kulak," the other half is the state's by confiscation); one houses some of the pigs of the cooperative (half of this farmstead belongs to the wife of a former owner, also branded a kulak — the old couple now live elsewhere; the other half is, again, the state's by confiscation); one farmstead provides for another contingent of the cooperative's pigs, with its dwelling functioning as a small poultry farm for egg production (this entire unit belongs to the state, the former owner living elsewhere); and the remaining unit, which at one time housed the village herdsman and after World War II served as the office of the local national committee and cultural center (*kulturní jizba*), has functioned as the local branch of the state savings bank (formerly *kampelička*) since January 1976 when Komárov was administratively subordinated to Vlastiboř.

The remaining 40 of the 52 numbered houses were occupied by the 150 villagers, averaging 3.75 persons and a median value of 4 persons per dwelling. The distribution of the 150 permanent residents of Komárov in the occupied dwellings is detailed in Table 8.

TABLE 8.   OCCUPATION DENSITY OF KOMÁROV DWELLINGS, 1978

Number of Occupants per Dwelling	Number of Dwellings (N = 40)	
1	8	(4 widowers, 3 widows, 1 young man)
2	5	
3	4	
4	7	
5	8	
6	4	
7	4	

Among the 40 functioning dwelling units, 11 were occupied by members of the same generation, either a married couple or a single individual, unmarried or widowed; 14 by two-generation nuclear families, occasionally incomplete or enlarged by a collateral; and 15 by three-generation vertically extended families consisting of two nuclear families, frequently incomplete in the oldest generation. The last category constitutes a particularly viable household type because it typically includes at least one elderly person free to look after small children, which enables all other adults to be gainfully employed.

Out-migration and the trend toward smaller family size has been responsible for a sharp decrease of inhabitants per dwelling unit since 1900, when the average was nearly 7.3, with the intermediate figures of just below 6 during 1921-1930 and ca. 4.3 in 1972. While the average numbers of villagers per unit were decreasing, the dwellings were undergoing considerable modernization and expansion, especially during the past dozen or so years. In terms of living space per person, the Komárov villagers are today much more comfortable than the inhabitants of the capital, where the housing shortage, critical for several decades now, continues unabated despite the constant construction of numerous new high-rise apartment buildings on the ever more sprawling outskirts of Prague.

It is worth noting that the general tendency of the young people of either sex to move away from their home villages into cities is matched by the ever increasing incidence of urban dwellers acquiring summer cottages in the country to compensate for the crowded conditions of their city quarters. Komárov is no exception to these trends.

Among the 150 permanent residents of Komárov as of January 1, 1978, there were 29 schoolchildren up to fifteen years of age, 12 male and 17 female — well below the total of 48 as of the end of 1972. At that time (in 1972) a local school served about a dozen pupils in grades one through four, after which children attended classes in Hlavatce, about five kilometers (ca. 3 miles) to the north, for five additional years. Since the fall of 1974 all schoolchildren have been bused to Hlavatce, the shrinking number of Komárov's pupils no longer meriting a separate village school.

Indicating a steadily rising average age, Table 9 gives the age distribution of the resident Komárov population.

TABLE 9.   AGE DISTRIBUTION OF KOMÁROV'S PERMANENT RESIDENTS, 1978, AND COMPARATIVE DATA FOR THE CZECH SOCIALIST REPUBLIC (CSR), 1977

Age Group	Number of Individuals (N = 150)		Percentage of Total	Corresponding CSR Percentages
0-14	29	29	19.3	23.1
15-19	7			
20-29	31	48	32.0	36.4
30-39	10			
40-49	17	41	27.3	22.9
50-59	24			
60-69	18			
70-79	5	32	21.3	17.6
80-89	9			

These figures, which clearly demonstrate the comparatively high average age of the Komárov population, would be even more striking if compared with the corresponding percentages for Czechoslovakia as a whole (namely, 24.0, 37.1, 22.5, and 16.4 respectively).

Concerning sex distribution as of January 1, 1978, there were 67 males and 54 females above the age of compulsory school attendance, or a total of 79 males and 71 females for Komárov as a whole. These figures stand in sharp contrast to the ratio of 1,000 males to 1,062 females for the Czech Socialist Republic.

The explanation of the high average age of Komárov residents rests on the already mentioned tendency for young people to out-migrate. And because there are now fewer opportunities for women to be employed in the highly mechanized agricultural enterprise, more and more young women seek jobs outside the immediate region.

Forty-two of the 150 village residents were receiving a pension from the state as of January 1, 1978. These individuals comprised 22 women and 20 men, of whom one was semiretired and several had stopped working for medical reasons rather than because of age. Twenty-three of the 42 pensioners, 10 male and 13 female, had no other income; in nearly all cases their age or state of health prevented them from supplementing their pensions by partial employment. The remaining 19 retirees derived additional income from part-time employment in the unified agricultural cooperative. Among the 10 males thus employed, 3 worked as tractorists, 2 as carpenters, 2 in crop production, and 1 each as manual worker, watchman, and in livestock production. Among the 9 females, 7 were employed in crop production, 1 in combined crop and animal production, and 1 in the local forest.

Sixty-two villagers were fully employed: 36 by the Unified Agricultural Cooperative "Victorious February" and 26 elsewhere. The number of cooperative employees has slightly decreased from the 39 recorded for mid-1972. Their ratio according to sex was exactly one to one, with 18 male and 18 female cooperators. Among the men, 5 worked as tractorists, 3 as repairmen, 3 as truck drivers, 2 in livestock production, and 1 each as mason, zootechnician, accountant, electrician, and mechanization facilitator. Except for 1 woman who worked as an accountant, all the women (17) were engaged in livestock production.

The 26 individuals employed outside "Victorious February" included 22 men and 4 women. With the exception of 1 woman, who managed Komárov's cooperative store Jednota, all held jobs outside Komárov, some a considerable distance away (as far as České Budějovice, 52 kilometers, or ca. 33 miles, distant).

Soběslav was the source of employment for the largest number of villagers: 5 men worked in Elitex, a factory for knitting and weaving machines; 3 men were employed by Silnice [Highways], a national enterprise; 1 man drove a truck for a regional agricultural purchasing and supply company; and 2 women were working in the textile industry.

The others were employed as follows: 4 men by the Czechoslovak Railroads in Veselí on the Lužnice; 2 as excavator operators by Rašelina [Peat], a state enterprise (they worked on the Jitra peat banks near Mažice); and 1 each as a machinist at Jitra, automobile mechanic in České Budějovice, employee of an agricultural construction association in Tábor, confectioner in the food industry in Tábor, mason in Dolní Bukovsko, employee of the silon [synthetic fiber] factory in Sezimovo Ústí, and district road supervisor. The remaining woman worked for Rašelina at Jitra as an accountant.

Seventeen more residents of Komárov are yet to be accounted for: 5 males were discharging their compulsory military service; 1 young woman was a student in Nové Hrady in southern Bohemia studying to become a nursery teacher; 2 young women were apprenticing as saleswomen in Soběslav and 1 young man as a turner (lathe operator) in Soběslav's Elitex; and 1 eighteen-year-old male's status was not determined. Seven women were at home unemployed, though some only temporarily because of young infants or family emergencies. Most of these women had worked previously in the cooperative or had been employed in Soběslav as saleswomen and the like, and could be expected to return to their previous employment as soon as their presence at home was no longer needed. The increasing tendency to seek and accept employment outside Komárov and the area of the consolidated cooperative "Victorious February" necessitates a fair amount of communiting, detailed in Table 10.

TABLE 10.   COMMUTERS TO WORK FROM KOMÁROV, 1978

Location	Distance (in miles)	Number of Commuters (N = 29)
Soběslav	7	14
Veselí on the Lužnice	9	4
Jitra near Mažice	5	4
Tábor	18	2
Nové Hrady	53	1
České Budějovice	33	1
Sezimovo Ústí	16	1
Vlastiboř	3	1
Dolní Bukovsko	6	1

Needless to say, the two individuals from the most distant localities (Nové Hrady and České Budějovice) returned to Komárov for weekends and holidays only. Komárov is connected with Soběslav and the surrounding villages by buses which make several runs daily, and Soběslav itself is on a busy railroad line between Tábor and Prague to the north and České Budějovice to the south. Nevertheless, a number of villagers, men in particular, frequently drive their own private cars, of which there were 27 in Komárov as of January 1, 1978 (an increase of 3 over mid-1973 even though the total number of residents fell by some 30 during the same period).[5] Despite the large number of villagers employed outside Komárov, none may now be classified as worker-peasants, a category not uncommon prior to the establishment of the unified agricultural cooperative.

Only insofar as the provenience of marriage partners is concerned do Komárov's residents still follow the practices of earlier times — and this despite the greatly increased mobility of young people of both sexes. In addition to some half a dozen married couples in which both husband and wife are from local farmsteads, those who have married into Komárov come — with very few exceptions — from an area that could be inscribed within a circle about 18 miles in diameter, and almost 90 percent of them from within half that distance. Only 1 woman among the 27 outsiders is from Slovakia. Seven of the 8 men who have married into Komárov come from localities no farther than 7 miles away, the remaining one being from Jindřichův Hradec, some 19 miles distant. The relatively high number of men who have married into Komárov farmsteads no doubt reflects the diminishing size of modern families, more of which in recent times have no male heir to take over the parents' house.

As the data brought together in this chapter must have shown, today — more than thirty years after the conversion of Komárov's economy from small private holdings to a socialist cooperative farm — the sociocultural, economic, and demographic transformations appear to be for the most part not only completed but irreversible.

The purpose of the concluding paragraphs is to summarize the nature of the restructuring and underscore the degree to which features of "traditional" village life have been supplanted by conditions of modern agricultural enterprise.

The prewar farmstead was run by the head of the family until his retirement. The heir was automatically the oldest son or, if there was no male descendant in the family, the oldest daughter. Because all agricultural land is now collectivized, inheritance of real property — with the exception of the family farmhouse and its adjacent garden — has lost all of its former significance. Moreover, by virtue of official encouragement and easy access to vocational education and technical training, young men and some women, to the extent that they choose to remain in the village at all, assume specialized tasks in the cooperative as mechanics, agronomists, zootechnicians, accountants, and the like — jobs that generally carry higher financial rewards than those available to the older villagers. While the average age of cooperators has been steadily rising, the more prestigious and better paid technical and administrative assignments are being filled by those with specialized background or the required political orientation, regardless of age. Not all of these trends have necessarily worked toward the disadvantage of superannuated persons whose basic security in old age now derives from state retirement pensions, free medical services, and other welfare benefits.

As far as division of labor according to sex is concerned, some of the older patterns are still noticeable, especially the heavy concentration of female workers in animal production. However, as mechanization proceeds further, the ratio of women employed in agriculture, in contrast to almost all other branches of the economy, may be expected to continue to decline.

There has been a steady tendency to minimize socioeconomic differences, not only between men and women and between farming families within the village, but also between individual villages. The growing mechanization of agriculture has resulted in slowly climbing production while at the same time work force has been diminishing. An important consequence has been rising wages for cooperators and improving living standards in their villages. Even villages known for their high productivity prior to the recent consolidation show an upward movement of average monthly wages under the new conditions. Komárov is a good example of this trend.

Perhaps the most telling proof of the cooperators' satisfaction with their present conditions is their firm belief that a return to private control of agricultural land would be not only practically unthinkable but also undesirable on economic grounds. What feelings of attachment to the land of their fathers may still remain among the oldest members of the village community after a full generation of socialist approach to land tenure have been largely rationalized away by the compensating advantages that members of cooperatives have managed to accrue after the bleak period of the 1950s.

At the same time, some demographic trends give pause — especially the rural exodus which, despite the fact that it has been under way since the beginning of the century, has barely begun to level off. If the present trend continues, Komárov, once a thriving, albeit small, village, may in the course of the next generation become an inconsequential rural settlement housing those few retired cooperators who choose to reside in it in preference to the city and a modest number of families of specialized agricultural or industrial workers commuting to their work in the consolidated cooperative or nearby towns. The population may swell to a somewhat larger fraction of its former size only on weekends or during the summer months when urban families come to their Komárov country homes.

Once the population of a village falls below the critical size necessary for a community to maintain its viability, it loses its local sociocultural identity in favor of a regional one. Evidence is rapidly accumulating that this may have already happened in Komárov's case: the transfer of all political-administrative and economic decisions to Vlastiboř, the closing of the primary school and assignment of pupils to Hlavatce where they attend classes together with their peers from other communities, and the increasing availability of employment opportunities in nearby towns all point to such a loss. These shifts, which are true of many other Czech villages as well, are of course not peculiar to socialist countries alone.

Chapter 5 ends with the observation that the centuries-old term *sedlák*, "peasant," has become anachronistic both as a word in the Czech lexicon and as the concept it stood for. It now seems likely that the equally time-honored term *vesnice*, "village" — a rural community the majority of whose residents are engaged in agriculture — will soon meet a similar fate.[6]

Footnotes

[1]This second wave of consolidation should be viewed in the context of an overall reduction in the numbers of unified agricultural cooperatives in the Czech Socialist Republic from 4,298 to 2,834 to 1,155 to 1,053 as of January 1, 1971, 1974, 1978, and 1985, respectively.

[2]The term "permanently active" (*trvale činný*), which is commonly restricted to those employed in agriculture, roughly corresponds to the personnel of record in the nonagricultural branches of the economy. More specifically, in the unified agricultural cooperative sector it includes, besides personnel hired on a permanent basis, members of cooperatives and persons in their families whose only or main occupation is work in the cooperative and who work at least 240 days per year, or, if they engage exclusively in crop growing, at least 130 days. Also included are those who, because of temporary disability, have been unable to accumulate the required number of working days in a particular year.

[3]The occupants of the housing unit comprised six adults and eight schoolchildren. Of the adults, three men were employed as tractorists in "Victorious February" and one worked for a lumber enterprise in Soběslav, commuting daily. The two women worked in the livestock production sector of the cooperative, one in Komárov, the other in nearby Svinky.

[4]On the basis of available data, a similar pattern obtains with regard to those who had left Komárov prior to January 1, 1972: Soběslav is at the head of the list, closely followed by Prague; a large number of former Komárov residents are settled in villages or towns in the area surrounding the Blata; the two most distant locations are Ostrava and Slovakia, with one individual each.

[5]According to the economic analysis prepared by "Victorious February" for the first half of 1977, there have been some problems resulting from the extent of commuting by its members. Most of the cooperators who happened to work close to the village of their residence were in the habit of going home for lunch and taking an hour and a half or even more for their noon break. In many cases this practice interrupted the work cycle of a team and in addition forced those co-workers without the opportunity of returning home to wait in the open, frequently in harsh weather conditions. To eliminate such situations, in April 1977 the management of the cooperative introduced uniform working hours for all centers and a lunch break of only 15 minutes. Not all cooperators have been able or willing to adjust fully to this change, but significant improvement has been effected.

[6]One may quite properly wonder how typical Komárov is of agricultural villages in the Czech Socialist Republic. While the community was selected by one of the authors by reason of established local contacts, developments in other small villages of the region follow a closely similar course. As for the Czech Socialist Republic as a whole, available statistical data and other relevant sources of information appear to corroborate the tendencies observed in Komárov with respect to comparable farming communities. The concentration on one small village obviously facilitates an analysis in depth. However, many of the issues and problems faced by rural communities in general can be viewed from the perspective of a single locality, so long as the perspective is "community outward."

Chronology of major events

Fifth century A.D.	First waves of Slavs in the territory of the later Bohemian Kingdom
ca. 900	Fall of the Great Moravian Empire; foundations of a feudal system laid
Thirteenth century	Rapid growth of the Bohemian Kingdom and colonization by a German-speaking population
Fourteenth century	Documentary evidence attesting the existence of the Blata settlements
Fifteenth century	Bohemia ravaged by the Hussite Wars
1620	Czech independence lost following the battle of White Mountain; Czech Lands fall under Hapsburg rule
1618–1648	Thirty Years' War; onset of the "second serfdom," a period of intensified exploitation of the Czech peasantry
1775	Large-scale revolt of serfs in the Czech Lands
1781	Restoration of essential freedoms to peasants by Emperor Joseph II (abolition of serfdom)
1848	Compulsory labor service abolished; peasants become owners of land on the basis of compensation
1918 (October 28)	Establishment of the Czechoslovak Republic
1938 (September 30)	Munich dictate results in the occupation of the border regions of the historic Czech Lands by German troops
1939 (March 14)	Slovakia declares itself an independent state under the protection of the Third Reich
1939 (March 15)	German troops occupy remainder of the First Republic, and the so-called Protectorate of Bohemia and Moravia is established
1945 (May 9)	Liberation of Czechoslovakia completed
1948 (February 25)	Communist party assumes effective control of the government
1949	Unified Agricultural Cooperatives Act promulgated
1955	Cooperative farming established in Komárov
1960	Adoption of a new constitution and state title—Czechoslovak Socialist Republic
1968 (August 20)	Warsaw Pact armies intervene in domestic political developments
1969 (January 1)	Federalization of the republic; Czech Socialist Republic and Slovak Socialist Republic set up
1972 (February 18)	Komárov Unified Agricultural Cooperative consolidated with a dozen other cooperatives in the Unified Agricultural Cooperative "Victorious February"

159

Pronunciation guide

An effort has been made to keep the occurrence of Czech words in the text to a minimum. For those that do occur, and for the fair number of proper names referred to, the following pronunciation guide will prove helpful. The reader is reminded that the equivalents given below are only approximate; no attempt has been made to be either exhaustive or precise in detail.

Among European languages, Czech spelling is one of the most phonetic. With few exceptions, each letter of the Czech alphabet stands for one sound only.

There are five vowel sounds in Czech, spelled *a*, *e*, *i* and *y*, *o*, and *u*.

Czech Letter	Approximate Pronunciation in English
a	*u* in *cut*
e	*e* in *met*
i, y	*i* in *kit*
o	*o* in *omit*
u	*u* in *put*

Any of these vowels may be lengthened, in which case they are written as *á, é, í* and *ý, ó*, and *ú* or *ů*.

Czech Letter	Approximate Pronunciation in English
á	*a* in *father*
é	second *e* in *Camembert*
í, ý	*ea* in *meat*
ó	*au* in *caught*
ú, ů	*u* in *rude*

The common Czech diphthong *ou* is pronounced like the *oa* in the English word *boat*. The Czech letter *ě* is pronounced like the portion of the English word *yes* before the final *s*. The distinction between short and long vowels is very important in Czech: some words, for example, *vina* ("guilt") and *vína* ("wines"), differ by virtue of the vowel length alone. The main stress in Czech is always on the first syllable of a word, regardless of the quantity of the vowel.

Among Czech consonants, those written as *b, d, f, g, l, m, n, s, v*, and *z*, closely correspond to their English counterparts.

The letters *q, w*, and *x* occur in Czech only in foreign words and approximate the English sounds of *q* as in *quart, v* as in *veal*, and *x* as in *ox*.

Under certain conditions, some of the voiced consonants become voiceless— for example, in the final position; thus *led*, "ice," is pronounced as if it were the English word *let*.

The stops *p, t*, and *k* are never aspirated in Czech, approximating the corresponding sounds in the English words *spin, still*, and *skin*. The remaining consonants of the Czech alphabet are as follows:

Czech Letter	Approximate Pronunciation in English
c	*ts* in *tsetse* or *eats*
č	*ch* in *chip*
ď	*duty* (pronounced *dyooty*)
h	*h* in *unheard*
ch	*ch* in the Scottish *loch* or the German *Bach*
j	initial sound in *yes*
ň	*ny* in *canyon* or the *ñ* in the Spanish *mañana*
r	trilled, or rolled, as in Scottish
ř	a very special sound (occurring, for example, in the composer's name *Dvořák*) that has no English equivalent and may be roughly described as the simultaneous articulation of *r* plus *ž* or *š*
š	*sh* in *ship*
ť	*tune* (pronounced *tyoon*)
ž	*z* in *azure*

Glossary of Czech terms

Throughout the book, Czech terms have been used only sparingly and supplementally to avoid interrupting the flow and intelligibility of the English text. As a convenience to the reader, they are brought together in this glossary and redefined. Entries are in the singular, but the plural form is appended if it occurs in the text.

baborák (pl. *baboráky*): see *bavorák*

Baltazar: Balthasar, one of the three wise men who paid homage to the Infant Jesus

Barborka (pl. *Barborky*): According to folk custom, one of the women dressed in white who visited households on the eve of Saint Barbara's Day with gifts for children

bavorák (pl. *bavoráky*): Czech folk round dance, with alternating rhythms

beseda: Artificial social dance suite based on folk song motifs

Blata: Bogland; the name for any of several boggy regions in southern Bohemia

Blaťák (pl. *Blaťáci*): Inhabitant of the Blata

bohatá Blata: Bogland of Plenty, so named for its fecundity (also known as *pšeničná Blata, soběslavská Blata,* and *veselská Blata*)

bratřině: Blata term for a male second cousin

buchta (pl. *buchty*): Fluffy bun made from leavened dough, usually with a sweet filling

bytovka: Colloquial term for a housing unit

celolánik: see *velký sedlák*

161

čepení: "Bonneting," the ritual decoration of the bride's head with a bonnet, denoting her new status as a married woman

černý kuba: "Black Jake," a folk dish—consisting of a mixture of dried mushrooms and groats

český: "Czech," when referring to ethnic or linguistic identity; "Bohemian," when reference is historical or geographical

čtvrtlánik: see *malý sedlák*

dělat schože (tchože): "To act like a polecat"; used to refer to the pilfering of grain from the farmer by his hired help

dokolečka: Czech folk round dance

domkář: "Cottager," a villager who owned a modest cottage with very little or no adjacent land

dožínky: Harvest home, a feast held at the end of harvest

družba: Master of ceremonies at a wedding, sometimes also the go-between

družstevník: Member of a (unified agricultural) cooperative

důstojný pán (voc. *důstojný pane*): Reverend Father (see *velebný pán*)

farma: Basic administrative unit of animal production

halekačka (pl. *halekačky*): Pastoral song shouted over a distance

haléř (gen. pl. *haléřů*): Heller, the smallest unit of Czechoslovak currency; abbr. h (100 hellers [h] = 1 crown [Kčs])

hejkal (pl. *hejkalové*): Fabulous forest spirit

hradecká pout': Annual pilgrimage originating in (Jindřichův) Hradec

chalupa: Simple rural dwelling; more recently, a recreational cottage maintained by city dwellers in the country

chalupník: Farming cottager, a farmer with a small house and only a nominal amount of farmland, generally no larger than about three acres

Chod (pl. *Chodové*): Inhabitant of any of eleven villages in southwestern Bohemia that at one time enjoyed special freedoms in return for guarding the frontier

jednotné zemědělské družstvo (*JZD*): Unified agricultural cooperative, an organizational unit of the socialist form of agricultural production

jemnostpán (voc. *jemnostpane*): "Gracious lord," a term of high deference

ježek: "Hedgehog," a roller used until World War II to crush clods in the fields

jidášek (pl. *jidášky*): "Judas cake," an Easter pastry made of wheat flour and baked in the shape of two linked horseshoes

jihočeská floskule: "South Bohemian melodic cliché," a stereotyped melodic phrase consisting of a rapid descent through 8–7–6–5

kampelička: Until 1952 a small cooperative savings and loan association serving rural customers

Kašpar: Caspar, one of the three wise men who paid homage to the Infant Jesus

kirovec: Very large Soviet-made tractor

kočovný (adjective, masc. form): Nomadic

komár: Mosquito

koruna (pl. *koruny*): Crown, the highest unit of Czechoslovak currency; abbr. Kčs (earlier Kč)

kout: "Corner"; childbed

koutňák: Special pot in which chicken broth was brought as a gift to a woman in childbed

koutnice: Bed-curtain(s) hung in the corner of the room to screen a woman in childbed

křižalka: Czech folk dance in two-four time of fairly slow tempo

kulturní jizba: Small, one-room cultural center, usually in a rural community

laufr (pl. *laufři*): "Runner," a humorous masked figure who ran around the procession during carnival

lenerovky: Stove or range manufactured in the workshop of Josef Lenner of Bechyně

Lucka (pl. *Lucky*):   According to folk custom, one of the women who visited households between Saint Lucia's Day and Christmas, frightening children and inspecting spinners' work

malý sedlák (also *čtvrtláník*):   Small farmer, one who owned approximately ten acres of land

máz: Large stein for beer; the measure of approximately a quart and a half

mazanec (pl. *mazance*):   Easter cake made of wheat flour and baked in a round loaf with a cross cut into the top

Melichar: Melchior, one of the three wise men who paid homage to the Infant Jesus

místní národní výbor: Local national committee, the lowest organ of state administrative authority

mladšinka: The younger maidservant on a farm

na černo: With or in a sweet dark sauce

Naděje: · "Hope," the name of an estate on the Komárov village lands

na modro: Boiled in water with vinegar (for example, carp)

Národopisná výstava českoslovanská: Czechoslavic Ethnographic Exhibition held in Prague in 1895

obec: Community

obkročák (dial. *vobkročák*):   Czech folk dance in two-four time

obora: Game preserve

oráč: In the Blata, the senior farmhand, the so-called plowman

ouvod: see *úvod*

pacholek: In the Blata, the younger farmhand, usually a stableboy (see *pohůnek*)

pan (voc. *pane*):   Mister, sir

panímáma (voc. *panímámo*):   "Mistress mother," a term used to refer to the farmwife or an older peasant woman

pantáta (voc. *pantáto*):   "Mister father," a term used to refer to an older male peasant

pěkná hodinka: "Pleasant hour," an added celebration for the benefit of farmhands the day after the dedication feast

podnik: Economic enterprise

podruh: Farmhand

pohůnek: In the Blata, the younger farmhand, usually a stableboy (see *pacholek*)

po chalupě: (to be referred to) "according to (his, her) cottage," that is, by the house in which one lived

posvícení: Dedication feast held on the day honoring the patron saint of the local church

pout':   Religious pilgrimage; church fair

pozemková reforma: Land reform

pracovní jednotka: Work unit used to determine remuneration in unified agricultural cooperatives

pryska: Drinking flask used for special occasions

pšeničná Blata: Wheat Bogland, so named for its principal crops (also known as *bohatá Blata*, *soběslavská Blata*, and *veselská Blata*)

půllánik: see *střední sedlák*

robota: Compulsory labor service during feudal times

roráty: Hymns sung during Advent morning masses

rychtář: Originally, the noble's representative; later, the village head

řičice: Large festive cake used, for example, at weddings

sedlák: Peasant

sestřině: Blata term for a female second cousin

s housličkami (dial. *s housličkama*): "With a fiddle"; refers to ceremonial sham-
ing of a girl who was promiscuous or became pregnant before her wedding

soběslavská Blata: Bogland of Soběslav (also known as *bohatá Blata, pšeničná
Blata*, and *veselská Blata*)

Sokol: Formerly a popular national organization concerned with gymnastics

soudruh (voc. *soudruhu*): "Comrade," a term of reference and address for
members of the Communist party, labor unions, collectives, and the like

sousedská: "Neighborly dance," a Czech folk dance in three-four time and slow

společné záhumenky (pl.): Joint private plots maintained by cooperators for their
personal use

starousedlík: "Old holder," a person settled in a place for a long time

staršinka: The older maidservant on a farm

statkář: Landowner; one who owned a large tract of land

stlačky: Ceremonial arranging of the newlyweds' bed

strejček (voc. *strejčku*): Uncle; also used as a term of address for an older man,
meaning roughly "neighbor"

střední sedlák (also *půllánik*): Middle farmer, one who owned approximately
twenty acres of land

svatý Mikuláš: Saint Nicholas, the good bishop who supposedly brings gifts
to children on the eve of Saint Nicholas's Day; roughly equivalent to
Santa Claus

štajryš: Czech folk dance in three-four time

Švéd: Swede

tajč: Czech folk dance in slow tempo

teta (voc. *teto*): Aunt; also used as a term of address for an older woman, meaning roughly "neighbor"

traktorista: Male tractorist

traktoristka: Female tractorist

trvale činný: Permanently employed in agriculture on a more than part-time basis

ty: Thou, you (informal)

utíkej Káčo: Czech folk line dance in three-four time and fairly rapid tempo

úvod (dial. *ouvod*): Ceremony of churching

vánočka: Special Christmas cake in the form of a large loaf of braided leavened
dough

velebný pán (voc. *velebný pane*): Reverend Father (see *důstojný pán*)

velkostatkář: Large landowner, one whose landholdings were unusually large

velký sedlák (also *celoláník*): Large farmer, one whose land amounted to forty
acres on the average

veselská Blata: Bogland of Veselí on the Lužnice (also known as *bohatá Blata,
pšeničná Blata*, and *soběslavská Blata*)

vesnice: Rural community in which agricultural workers predominate

Vítězný únor: Victorious February; common name given to enterprises to commemorate February 1948, when the Communist party emerged from a governmental crisis in complete control of Czechoslovakia

vobkročák: see *obkročák*

vodník: Water sprite, a male being believed to inhabit and haunt water

vrták: Czech folk dance in two-four time and rapid tempo

vy: You (formal)

zadupávání: Rhythmic "stamping in" of the deceased

záhumenek: Small private plot allowed a member of the unified agricultural cooperative for his personal use

závod: Economic unit, branch of an enterprise

zelený dílek: "Green portion," a share of green fodder from the cooperative
field to which a member of the unified agricultural cooperative is entitled

zemědělec: Agricultural worker

References

Ethnographic literature in English concerning East Central Europe is relatively scarce and for Czechoslovakia it is virtually nonexistent. The desire to fill this gap has motivated the two authors of this book. For practical reasons, we have kept the list of primary sources—all of which are in Czech or Slovak—to a minimum.

The most important Czech ethnographic periodicals and the basic sources concerning the study of Czech folk culture and its historical background are listed in Part I. Selected sources dealing with southern Bohemia and the Blata in general, and Komárov in particular, are given in Part II.

I

Československá et(h)nografie, I–X, 1953–1962. Prague.
Československá vlastivěda, Vol. II: *Člověk*, 1933. Prague.
Československá vlastivěda, Series II: *Národopis*, 1936 (1937). Prague.
Československá vlastivěda, Vol. III: *Lidová kultura*, 1968. Prague.
Český lid, I–, 1892–1914, 1924–1932, 1946–. Prague.
Národopisná výstava českoslovanská v Praze, 1895. Prague.
Národopisný sborník českoslovanský, I–XI, 1897–1905. Prague.
Národopisný věstník českoslovanský, I–XXXIII, 1906–1956. Prague.
Národopisný věstník československý, I(XXIV)–, 1966–. Brno.
Stránská, Drahomíra, n.d., *Lidové kroje v Československu*, Vol. I: *Čechy*. Prague.
Žalud, Augustin, 1919, *Česká vesnice*. Prague.

II

Fryšová, Emilie, 1913, *Jihočeská Blata*. Prague.
Jubilejní sborník městského musea v Soběslavi 1897–1947, 1947. Soběslav.
Kubeš, Richard, 1957 and 1958, *Jihočeské tance*, 2 vols. Prague
Lego, František, 1897–1898, "Kroj a vyšívání lidové na Blatech," *Český lid*, 6:149–152 and 7:152–154, 244–245 (–7).
———, 1898, "Svatební pečiva z jižních Čech," *Český lid*, 7:129–132.
———, 1899, "Ornamentika na blatském vyšívání lidovém," *Český lid*, 8:17–22.
Rozbor hospodaření za [years], Jednotné zemědělské družstvo "Vítězný únor" se sídlem ve Vlastiboři. 1975–1979.
Salzmann, Zdenek, 1983, *Three contributions to the study of socialist Czechoslovakia*. Research Report No. 22, Department of Anthropology, University of Massachusetts at Amherst.
Scheufler, Vladimír, 1959, "Hrnčířství soběslavských Blat," *Český lid*, 46:162–173.
Skálová, Anna, 1949, "Blatský kroj," *Český lid*, 36:78–84.
Táborsko: Popis přírodní, historický a národopisný. Vol. III: *Národopis*, 1921. Tábor.

Vaňous, František, 1895, "Chození s králem o Letnicích v okolí Vlastiboře (v Jihočesku)," *Český lid*, 4:32–34.

———, 1914, "Děti v plenkách," *Český lid*, 23:299.

———, 1929, *in* "Vánoční obyčeje a pověry československé," *Český lid*, 29:109–117 (113–114).

Weis, Karel, 1928–1941, *Český jih a Šumava v (lidové) písni*, 15 vols. Prague.

For historical information relating to Komárov and the Blata, the following sources were consulted: materials in the State Archives of Třeboň and the District Archives of Tábor; property and tax rolls for the Prácheň Region (*berní rula, kraj Prácheňský*), dating from the middle of the seventeenth century, in the State Central Archives in Prague; and records and manuscripts in the archives of the National Museum and of the Institute for Ethnography and Folklore of the Czechoslovak Academy of Sciences in Prague.

For recent and current statistical information, standard sources dealing with the Czechoslovak Socialist Republic were consulted, in particular the volumes of *Statistická ročenka Československé socialistické republiky* (Prague), which are published on an annual basis.